DYNAMICS OF
ADMINISTRATION

*Nursing
Administration
Quarterly
Series*

Barbara J. Brown, RN, EdD, FAAN
Editor, Nursing Administration Quarterly

AN ASPEN PUBLICATION®
Aspen Publishers, Inc.
Gaithersburg, Maryland
1994

Library of Congress Cataloging-in-Publication Data

Dynamics of administration / Barbara J. Brown, editor.
p.   cm. — (Nursing administration quarterly series)
A collection of articles reprinted from Nursing administration quarterly.
Includes bibliographical references and index.
ISBN 0-8342-0507-6
1. Nursing services—Administration.   2. Nurse administrators.
3. Nurse and physician.   I. Brown, Barbara J.   II. Series.
[DNLM: 1. Nurse Administrators—psychology—collected works.
2. Nursing Service, Hospital—organization & administration-
-collected works.   3. Administrative Personnel—psychology-
-collected works.   4. Leadership—collected works.
WY 105 D997   1994]
RT89.D93   1994
362.1'73'068—dc20
DNLM/DLC
for Library of Congress
93-24273
CIP

Aspen Publishers, Inc., grants permission for photocopying for limited personal or
internal use. This consent does not extend to other kinds of copying, such as copying
for general distribution, for advertising or promotional purposes, for creating new
collective works, or for resale. For information, address Aspen Publishers, Inc.,
Permissions Department, 200 Orchard Ridge Drive, Suite 200,
Gaithersburg, Maryland 20878.

Editorial Resources: Ruth Bloom

Library of Congress Catalog Card Number: 93-24273
ISBN 0-8342-0507-6
Series ISBN: 0-8342-0386-3

Printed in the United States of America

1 2 3 4 5

Table of Contents

Series preface

*E*IGHTEEN YEARS AGO *Nursing Administration Quarterly* was launched—a journal in which each issue concentrates on a single topic in nursing administration, examined from different viewpoints by prominent practitioners. At the time, nursing administration was looked at as a less than acceptable specialty of practice. Only clinical domains were deemed to be prestigious and sufficiently imbued with a body of knowledge requiring advanced preparation. There were only a few graduate programs in the field and even some of those were only "pathways" in administration.

I was teaching the pathway in administration at Marquette University College of Nursing, Milwaukee, Wisconsin, while practicing as Administrator, Patient Care Services at Family Hospital and Nursing Home, and found insufficient literature for graduate students and practicing Directors of Nursing. I had also written and been awarded a research and development grant from the National Institutes of Health to establish The Greater Milwaukee Area Sexual Assault Treatment Center. There was no forum for nursing administrators to share their successes and accomplishments with colleagues in a way that was useful and applicable to others in like settings.

So *Nursing Administration Quarterly* was conceived as a permanent library collection, topically focused, addressing the most timely and pertinent issues for nursing administrators to use as a resource which could be referred to in order to solve problems, create new approaches, and learn how others accomplish the ever challenging endeavor of *leading* the practice of nursing.

Leadership in nursing administration is many things to many people, depending on what task is being performed at a given moment; but it is probably best described as the positive and proactive handling of professional interaction, such as between nursing and the medical staff, the hospital administration, the patient, and the nursing staff. Leadership is a learned activity based on knowledge, skill, experience, attitudes, responsibility, accountability, and autonomy. It requires creativity and innovation, courage of one's convictions, and concern for all people, whether they be the patients and families we serve, our professional colleagues, or our personal friends and families. The nurse leader must have a high level of aspiration toward goals which nurses are seeking and should demonstrate actual success or high potential for success for attaining these goals.

Nurse executives must be knowledgeable about societal forces and constraints, political processes, and the effect on the health care systems and subsequent work accomplishments. Role theories, human relations, finance and budget, business strategies, front-line management of human resources, wage and labor standards (including collective bargaining, sexual discrimination and harassment), continuous quality improvement according to agreed upon standards, the latest in innovations in clinical practice, information systems, technology and research developments, population based care systems, empowerment, and transformational leadership are but a small representation of topics from *Nursing Administration Quarterly* throughout the years. A nurse executive today needs to be encyclopedic in order to keep abreast of all the information needed to succeed in an administrative position.

The editorial board of *NAQ* decided that it was time to cull out the best or "classics" from past issues of *Nursing Administration Quarterly* and provide a series of volumes that give this encyclopedic resource to nurse executives as well as to graduate students. The editorial board has been selected with great care to ensure readers a representation from academic settings as well as expertise in all areas of administration, with geographic distribution, different care settings, and as comprehensive a coverage of subject matter as possible. These *NAQ* editorial board members therefore have diligently sorted, reviewed, and selected the most representative articles over time, some of which are truly classics. In addition, study questions were developed for each section so that the reader can develop a thorough understanding with applicability to the future. As editor of *NAQ* for all these years, it is a special privilege to bring these volumes to the present and future generations of nurse executives.

BARBARA J. BROWN
Editor
Nursing Administration Quarterly

Preface

A S MEDICAL CENTERS grow in complexity, it is doubtful that today's organizational forms and practices are adequate to enable the centers to meet tomorrow's needs. The shape and substance of the health care systems of the future are directly dependent on the organizational environment in which health care is delivered. Whether a practice environment is educational in its thrust or fully a service setting, there is a mandate to design a structure that provides efficient functioning while maintaining a climate of maximal freedom.

Future practice environments will demand collaboration. They will demand that all disciplines within the health care system work together, sharing information and knowledge. Such sharing will lead to a solid practice environment that is equipped to serve the patients. Development of a patient-focused practice environment is the essence of the dynamics of administration.

Creating excellence in health care delivery is fundamentally dependent upon building and promoting the executive team. The competitive nature of current fiscal and economic survival strategies forces executive attention to greater priorities of budget, finance, and economic stabilization. The executive team has to assume full responsi-

bility and accountability for whatever happens in relation to patient care and nursing resource allocation. If nursing as a discipline and the nurse executive's voice of patient care advocacy are diminished in the interest of executive "team fitting," nursing as a profession will have frequent eruptions. When the executive team accepts and recognizes that nurses and nursing care are the reason to admit patients to hospitals, long-term care facilities, home care and other nursing-based services, nursing will not be coopted.

Political astuteness and ever-changing communication skills are necessary ingredients for the integration of the nurse executive. Excellence in patient care requires a strength of conviction about patient care and caring for employees that extends beyond the executive boardroom. The stakes are high—patient care and nursing practice are the losers if the game is not played successfully.

The nurse executive must be able to integrate the skills and demands of nursing, administration, medicine, and allied health disciplines, and overall organizational operations. The nurse executive walks a fine line in attempting to be a nurse advocate, patient care advocate, and collaborator with physicians and health care administrators. A thorough knowledge of nursing and advances in nursing practice is essential to developing the nurse executive. Without the ability to understand the caretaker's role, and required clinical practices, the nurse executive will lose sight of current conditions and move too far away from practicing nurses.

The major conversion of American health care systems to business entrepreneurial enterprises may diminish the importance of patient care and cause a reversion to a patriarchal leadership value system. A nurse executive may find himself or herself continually compromising to fit into the new culture of business advocacy. I, for one, have found that compromise too great and have continued to seek the interactive environment wherein the commitment to patient care is the highest priority. This *Nursing Administration Quarterly Classics: Dynamics of Administration* represents the best and most timely references in relevancy to tomorrow's administrative needs and demands. Nurse executives, educators, and students of nursing administration should find thought provoking and stimulating ideas to promote excellence in all health care systems.

BARBARA J. BROWN

Part I
Leadership

Julian S.A. Cicatiello, R.N., M.A.,
M.Ed., CNAA
Division Director
Ambulatory Services
University of Miami / Jackson Memorial
*   Medical Center*
Miami, Florida

*F*ROM A HISTORICAL perspective, leadership in the nursing profession and the theories about leadership qualities have not changed significantly over the past several years. *Nursing Administration Quarterly's (NAQ)* first volume was published in 1976, and focused solely on leadership in nursing administration. At that time, leadership meant having a broad range of skills, including academic preparation, intellectual maturity, articulateness both verbally and in writing, the ability to influence and motivate, as well as being visionary, creative, honest, sensitive, confident, flexible, adaptable, proactive, and managerially astute. In addition, he or she had to be a strong role model with personal insights and values that positively affected those with which one came in contact.

In this same time period, theorists such as Argyris, Katz and Kahn, McGregor, Blake, and Mouton and Likert introduced new strategies and systems for leadership, organization, and management. These leadership articles reflected on what makes a successful leader today. What has been espoused by these authors is current, viable, and applicable in today's environment, because their theories have been tested over the years and remain relevant.

Cutler's and Dunham's articles, for example, can be resources for first line managers, graduate students, and newly appointed chief nurses. Cutler, in particular, articulates the historical perspective of leadership and management from Fayol's management principles to a new world of values, imperatives, and attitudes for leaders of the future.

As potential leaders, there are issues and concerns that need to be queried, deliberated, discussed, and understood as you develop your own leadership style.

Nursing leadership and management: An historical perspective

Mary Jane Cutler, R.N., Ed.D.
Assistant Professor of Nursing
  Administration
University of Illinois
School of Nursing
Chicago, Illinois

*I*T APPEARS to have been a professional coincidence when I was asked to consider writing on this subject. I had just read the *Special Report* of *Life,* "Remarkable American Women: 1776-1976." I was most concerned that nursing was really conspicuous by its absence; granted Dix, Barton and Sanger are noted but not as nurses. This omission of such nurses as Robb, Nutting, Stewart, Palmer, Titus, Leone, Abdellah, Mullane, Lambertsen, Florentine, Kuehn, Rogers, and others must be the result of the continuing impotence of nursing power and recognition. In the midst of the great dilemma and scandal of the health delivery system, nursing continues to be in a non-leadership position as perceived by consumers.

My diagnosis of much of our dilemma is that nurses have not concerned themselves with the fact and the importance of: (1) "professional" administrative and managerial principles; (2) leadership that connotes followership.[1]

NEW WORLD—"NEW" LEADERSHIP

The nursing profession is caught up in a new world of values, imperatives, and attitudes; at the same time it is pressing forward to identify its members as practitioners and colleagues of other professions. There are diversities within the profession that have great impact on practice. Many of our current nurse educators and service personnel themselves are products of the hierarchical, bureaucratic, and autocratic "leadership" of past years. They show difficulties in adapting to new ways of the teaching-learning strategies, new ways of directing and providing nursing practice, new ways of creating an amiable, healthy environment, and new ways of being accountable for quality outcomes of their roles. They prevent creativity and/or independence

Nurs Admin Q, 1976, 1(1), 7–19
©1976 Aspen Publishers, Inc.

with an insistence on conformity. The very qualities for judgement and responsibility which nurses learn are inhibited.

Stingan writes:

> ... nursing, that helpful and most feminine of professions, should be coming into their own in a time of health needs and female assertiveness. Instead, it seems a lady bewildered by a multitude of paradoxes. Over a million at work, including students at all levels, nurses have had little to say about health care delivery. They have ended up dissatisfied in the skills on the job.[2]

In an unpublished research study, Citron identified the urgency of leadership to recognize that followers-nurses are eager for help and assistance in improving their capabilities to identify patients' covert problem to improve care. This project and program was made possible by my support, opportunity for orientation, plan and participation of all personnel on the experimental units and the faculty involved.[3]

The role of nursing service leadership or management is not of a technical nature. In an unpublished first manuscript for a text on Hyperbaric Oxygenation, Dr. Julius Jacobson II identifies the need for collaboration of nursing leadership in planning for clinical care:

> ... we were called one day by a physician at Bellevue Hospital about a sixteen year old boy who had developed gas gangrene of the leg following an automobile accident. The proper antibiotics had been administered and multiple surgical drainage and debridements performed, but the infection was spreading and an amputation of the leg had been scheduled for that afternoon. . . . our small experimental chamber was just large enough for a patient but it was in the dog laboratory and its plumbing connections made it impossible for it to be moved. Miss Mary Jane Venger, then the Director of Nursing at Mount Sinai Hospital was called and asked if she could convert the animal laboratory into an intensive care unit. Never has the power of a nursing director been so ably demonstrated. Within the next hour . . . ten . . . people descended upon the room and all the equipment necessary to an intensive care unit was moved into the laboratory . . .[4]

Nursing management and leadership must be able to respond to present and future needs of consumers of which we are a part. I might add that following this experience, a cross-disciplinary planning committee was formed to develop the program of care for the arrival of the hyperbaric chamber.

IN THE BEGINNING . . .

Development of Organization

The conjectures and theories of archaeologists furnish sketches of the first human organizations, nomadic tribes who banded together for mutual protection and economy of labor. It is also conjectured that these early cultures were a stern matriarchy, in which women tested the effects of ingested plants on their menfolk[5] (Mumford 1970).

Mumford emphasizes that the most significant, difficult, and far-reaching task that primitive cultures undertook was the development of language: **Communication.** Nurses have emerged through a non-communicating era where things were done but there was little communication with peers, patients, and others; feedback was almost nil. In these past few years, nurses are becoming more vocal, articulate and communicative, with their patients—there is more that needs to be done.

Ancient civilizations record the most puzzling awesome remains of Egyptian culture—the building of the pyramids. Ramses IV and his army of 8,368 men painted pictures of their transport teams: one sees a string of ten men and then an overseer with something in his hand that resembles a riding crop; then another string of ten men; these men, presumably slaves, are pulling huge sleds that transport the stone blocks. Such massive civic organization is not witnessed again until the invention of the computer and the sending of men to the moon. This account presents the Egyptians' concept of managerial principles of **planning** and **teamwork.**

Athens and other Greek cities relate their successful development of the polis, a democratic form of government that favors consultation to its citizens. Plato prescribed the need and usefulness of **specialization.**

The Italian Renaissance resulted in the arts as well as trade and manufacturing. There are records identifying such modern practices as **assembly-line techniques:** standardization of parts, inventory control, cost control, and personnel practices which were systematically utilized.[6]

Development of Management

Prior to the twentieth century, there were a number of managerial thinkers whose work was based on observation and a philosophy of man and his being. The works of Adam Smith, John Stuart Mill, Charles Babbage, Henry Metcalf, and Henry Halisery stirred an aspiring young man, Frederick W. Taylor. Taylor's physical abilities were limited because of childhood diseases, but his interest and intelligence were stimulated to learn about the working man. He worked as a laborer in a number of steel mills, while gathering anecdotal and observational data to provide sufficient evidence of his authentic interest in motivating workers to produce greater output. He observed workers at various levels, to the point that he identified "soldiering" as a strategy of the worker to gain more benefits. His main interest was with the worker and his assigned tasks.[7]

Frank and Lillian Gillbreth made advances in their time-and-motion studies of techniques. They were concerned with worker fatigue and the need to improve morale.[8] These two scientists complemented Taylor's work which sparked the attention of a young French student Henri Fayol (1841-1925) who studied Taylor's work among others and began what is known as the Classical School.

Fayol's principles

Fayol[9] spent 30 years reorganizing an almost bankrupt mining company to an expanded arch profitable one. During these years, he documented his experiments and observations and developed 14 principles. First of all, his claim was that:

> There is nothing rigid or absolute in management affairs; it is all a question of proportion. Seldom do we have to apply the same principle twice in identical conditions; allowance must be made for different changing circumstances; for men just as different and changing, and for many other variable elements. Therefore, principles are flexible and capable of adaptation to every need.

Fayol's managerial principles:
1. Division of work
2. Authority
3. Discipline
4. Unity of command
5. Unity of direction
6. Subordination of individual
7. Remuneration
8. Centralization
9. Scalar chain (line of authority)
10. Order
11. Equity
12. Stability of tenure of personnel
13. Initiative
14. Esprit de corps

Of these 14 principles, (8) centralization, (9) scalar chain, and (10) order have been criticized by management theorists in recent years. Another point of interest is Fayol's process to overcome red tape and provide opportunity by his "gangplank" theory through which peers may communicate and participate. There is an example in which Nurse F needs medication p.d.q. and pharmacist P is provided the authority to recognize and agree with the need:

```
                  A
          B       L
          C       M
          D       N
          E       O
Nurse    (F)     (P)    Pharmacist
          G       Q
```

Therefore, the need to collapse the scalar chain is simplified by allowing peer disciplines to make a decision on the need and order medication. If one were to analyze the formal chain of events, the patient very probably would never receive the needed medication.

Mayo and motivation

Fayol's early participative management, through the coordination of groups in an organization backed up by Follett's principles and philosophy of participative management, sparked the way for Elton Mayo (1880-1949), a psychologist, and his team from Harvard's Department of Industrial Research which in their now famous Hawthorne Studies sought to determine the effect of increased illumination on output. When it was found that output improved in both the experimental and control groups, Mayo and team found that every change was a motivation. When people are grouped in teams, they give of themselves, participating fully and without afterthought and are

happy to work without coercion. Mayo goes on to say:

> They worked in the knowledge that they were working without coercion from above or limitations from below. They were, themselves, astonished at the consequences for they felt they were working under less pressure than ever before . . . here then are two topics which deserve the closest attention of all those engaged in administrative work . . . the organization of the working teams and the free participation of such teams in the task and purpose of the organization as it directly affects them in their daily rounds.[10]

TWENTIETH CENTURY

At this point, let us look at nursing in this century. Nursing culture was based on the Florence Nightingale philosophy and ethics. She went about proselytizing, writing, articulating, and trying to find and form the seminal influence on the development of professional nursing.[11]

The first half of the twentieth century, with its two wars and severe economic depression, plagued American nursing with continual, acute shortages of qualified personnel and a long period of underemployment, a fluctuation that caused a proliferation of nursing schools of widely varying quality and longevity.

Education

Education gave way to apprenticeships. Most nursing directors held dual roles of service and education and this position was used as a power clout by administrators, among others to utilize students as labor! The organizational structure was hierarchical, bureaucratic and the environment rigid, sterile and met mostly physical needs. However, during this period, there was great concern about the conditions under or through which nursing was functioning. In 1898, there was the formation of the American Society of Superintendents of Training Schools for Nurses (now the National League for Nursing Education). They urged Isabel Hampton Robb to become the first instructor for graduate nurses at Teachers College, Columbia University. The course was "Home Economics." Adelaide Nutting joined her in 1907 and became the first full-time professor. In 1910, financial aid made it possible to expand the program for nurses who wished to go on to teaching and/or administration. Nurses were and have been continually faced with the problem of non-nursing tasks and their role perception by the medical staff.

Beginning in 1912, study upon study has been carried out focusing on the practitioners, the programs, the outcomes, and now the consumers. These early studies, including Nutting's "The Educational Status of Nursing" sponsored by the Federal Bureau of Education, made little impact on the nursing population.

In 1922, the New York Academy of Medicine did a time-and-motion study in New York hospitals. The findings focus on poor managerial controls, inequities in carrying nursing and medical orders, lack of follow-through because of low morale, and poor staffing and practice.

The Goldmark Report was sponsored by the Rockefeller Foundation to study 23 nursing schools and 49 public health agencies. What they found was similar to former studies: exploitation, apprenticeship of students, great inequities in curricula, substandard teacher qualifications and service personnel. The report made recommendations for training auxiliary workers, extending educational programs for public health and staff nurses, and providing for university-connected schools. This last recommendation re-

sulted in the development of the Yale School of Nursing.

Nurse shortage was reported by a statistician, May Agnes Burgess in *Nurses, Patients and Pocketbooks* (1928).

During these years, the public and the nursing profession were concerned for the lack of appropriate nurse distribution, quality of teaching, and practice. However, these conditions continued to prevail until intensive work resulted from the report *Nursing Schools Today and Tomorrow* (1934). Then the *A Curriculum Guide for Schools of Nursing* (1937) made some inroads in reorganization of curricula using these guidelines. In 1936, the National League for Nursing Education and the American Hospital Association published the first *Manual for Essentials of Good Hospital Service*. Again, some progress was made in the improvement of a nursing service organization. Few nurses knew how to bring about change. This was true for service as well as education, and most directors of nursing had these dual functions. One hand fed the other and because of the closed system resulting from poor communication, one hand did not know what the other hand was doing. This lack of ability to bring about change in many instances was due to lack of preparation, personality, and general know-how in dealing with a rigid structure of authoritarianism. These directors were dealing with the power of administration and physicians.

Fiscal Management

Concerns for fiscal management are shown in the report *Administrative Cost Analysis for Nursing Service and Nursing Education*. It was soon found that the hospital deficit was the cost of the school of nursing. Nursing directors fought for the mission of the school; the right and need for the student to be a learner; the need for a staffing pattern and a nursing budget. Some were more successful than others. As late as the fifties and sixties, I found large prestigious institutions without staffing patterns and/or budget. There were very few sophisticated programs or policies in the entire hospital administration, so how could nursing create change in this environment unless changes could be made at the top?

A collaborative report, *The General Staff Nurse,* was prepared by the National League for Nursing Education, the Catholic Hospital Association, and the American Nurses Association. This report strongly advocated an improvement in the general welfare of nurses. This forced nursing leaders and others to take a real look at fiscal management and increases in patients' cost for care.

Nursing Program

Another report concerned about staffing patterns, compensation, incentives, and nurse practice outcomes (quality of care) was *A Program for the Nursing Profession,* a result of the Committee on the Functions of Nursing originating at Teachers College, Columbia University, and prepared by the economist Ginzberg.

However, the 1948 Brown Report, *Nursing for the Future,* had the greatest impact in triggering health service leaders and educators into action. Appalled at conditions which existed for years and that were identified in studies, many nurses took issue with the findings. Brown, a social anthropologist funded by the National Nursing Council, through extensive surveying, random sampling in personal visitations and inspections, estimated there was a critical need to improve the quality and performance of all nursing personnel, in schools and the service settings.[12]

Some of the significant findings were: lack of managerial principles in the educational program, few inservice programs for professional and non-professional personnel, the need for differentiating the functions of nursing service, and the need for "engineering" coordinated efforts in all facilities to decrease duplication and increase effective performance and teamwork. She strongly prescribed that only those nurses who had been educated in professional degree-granting schools be considered "professional." Needless to say, the nursing community reacted strongly but action generated the formation of the National Committee for the Improvement of Nursing Service. Their first report *Nursing at the Mid-Century* (1950) did help create the strength necessary to provoke change in both service and education.

Leadership and Improved Performance

It was during these years that business and industry were looking at their own goods, services, costs and profit results. They realized that the social scientists were researching social and economic problems which were affecting their own missions. The data published could be adapted to any human organization. Lewin and his associates at the Institute of Social Sciences, University of Michigan, conducted a now-famous study in which they demonstrated the effects of different kinds of leadership. Groups of 11-year-old children were led by supervisors who used three different leadership approaches: autocratic, democratic, and laisséz-faire. They found that autocratic leadership produced dependency and egocentric competition among group members. Under democratic leadership, which used participative planning and group discussions, the same children evidenced more initiative, friendliness, and responsibility. These children continued to work even when the leader was out of the room. Their interest in their work and the quality of their product was higher. The number of aggressive acts decreased . . .[13] Lewin became known for his work on cross-disciplinary research teams for practical solutions to pressing problems. His Force Field Theory for bringing about change in societal situations continues to be valuable to all disciplines.[14]

Nursing has been lagging in the adaptation of some of the valid, quantitative data resulting from the growing work of social, behavioral, and industrial scientists. There seems to be a reluctance to taking risks for improvement of performance. There has been little research by nurses for nursing despite the growing numbers of prepared people capable of planning the generation of nursing knowledge.

Barnard's *Functions of the Executive* (1938), is a sociological analysis of organizations and managerial theories. Barnard, an executive of the New Jersey Bell Telephone Company, views organizations as cooperative systems. Interestingly and perhaps naively, he believes "the formal organization as the social process by which social action is largely accomplished . . . and . . . is a system of consciously coordinated activities or forces of two or more persons." Barnard introduced the fact that organizations are more than the sum of the efforts of its members and that there is an informal organization. However, he does not consider that the latter has the power to defeat the goals of the formal organization. He perceives leadership as effective only with followership.[15]

THE PRESENT

This decade has seen a virtual explosion of new knowledge of leadership, organization,

and management. There are schools of applied behavioral science as well as the systems schools.

Contributions have been made by Argyris,[16] Katz and Kahn,[17] McGregor,[18] Blake and Mouton,[19] and Likert.[20] Argyris has been a strategist for change in leadership and management. Katz and Kahn are cited for the origin of open systems approach, Blake and Mouton for their managerial grid. McGregor's Theory X and Theory Y work as catalysts for change.

Effective Organization

Likert has been one of the most prolific researchers and writers of this decade. He and his associates have been the initiators of sample interviews and field experiments. His research impacts all organizations composed of human social groups as he successfully measures organizational characteristics of existing systems so as to discover which type or types of systems were most successful. He has tested all types of organizations across America; thousands of managers were interviewed. Organizational effectiveness was judged reasonably enough by productivity and profits.

Likert generated a number of structural, managerial, and operating forms and techniques which were most successful and effective. These variables differed significantly from those found in less effective organizations. When the variables were compared, the variations formed a typology of less successful to more successful systems of organizations.[21]

On the least successful side, to the left, was an exploitative, authoritative system in which operating characteristics were seen to be purely downward communication, responsibility was felt only in the top levels, decisions were made only at the top, and motivation was formed by threats of punishment and financial exclusion. A strictly Weberian model is seen in prisons, the military, and the organization of pyramid builders.

The second type was labeled "benevolent authoritative" and its basic operating characteristics were seen to be patronizing of lower levels on the part of top management. There is much man-to-man and department-to-department competition, a divisive and goal shattering characteristic, as discussed by Taylor and Fayol.

The third type was labeled "consultative." Here, the structure is less hierarchical in nature: upward and lateral communication takes place occasionally. Responsibility is felt by most members of the organization. Cooperation is one of the organization's goals. Policies are made by top management but there is a sharing in decision-making. The informal organization both supports and partially resists the "formal organization" goals.

Likert's summative research of organizational patterns expresses itself in a fourth system, participatory management. This was seen to be the most productive organization. Characterized by trust and mutual support, it is united on all levels by group process. The formal and informal organizations are the same, united in common effort.

Linking-pin

Likert's basic unit is the work group, an overlapping of two groups which influence each other through the double-membership of the key linking-pin. He provides for a double-hinge: a communicator called a "linking-pin." The role of this person is simply to exert the influence of one work group within another and so keep all work groups in relative harmony with each other. The work group is conducted in a democratic manner; the leader directs but does not dictate. Goals are formulated, entered, and

recognized, problems are related, feedback is given, programs are planned and implemented. There is peer review, checking, and feedback operating within the communication system. Linking-pins (Likert's answer to Fayol's "gangplank") are found between departments. The organization is "flattened" by the linking-pin process. Faith and trust can be restored.

Flattening

This flattening of the organization is pyramidical and ladder-like graphic representations of traditional hierarchical organizations reveal a more complex, more flexible, and more interlaced model. It is a philosophy and an educational system. Both management and personnel must, by virtue of its new complexity, learn new skills. Likert stresses the need for a new structure, environment, and atmosphere. The process of moving toward this system may be a long one. Initiative is with top management. As superior-subordinate interaction grows, they work in groups. Subordinates learn the delight of decision making and take on greater responsibilities. There is more give-and-take of the formal and informal organizations. I initiated this program and process in three large hospitals' nursing services between 1950-67; in one hospital it took three plus years to flow smoothly. An account of the model appears in *Nursing Outlook,* November 1966, co-authored with the late Dr. Julius Yourman, "Modern Management Theory Applied to Nursing Service."

Developing a New System

In the early fifties, nursing leadership at Teachers College, Columbia University reacted to the descriptive and prescriptive Finer report, in with Finer strongly urges closing the gap between education and service. His research was funded by the Kellogg

Foundation, which was influenced by Mary Kelly Mullane's leadership experiment and study of 14 universities over a period of eight years. Her findings described the wide variation of programs, poorly qualified teachers, inadequate instruction, and high turnover of faculty.[22]

The experiment at Teachers College, initiated by R. Louise McManus and Eleanor C. Lambertsen, became the philosophy of team nursing. This was the first experiment to attempt to change traditional practice, education and service, and demanded a change in philosophy and objectives of nursing practice. For the first time, all levels of practice were recognized and were provided the opportunity to participate and gain status as members of a team, motivating creativity, education, evaluation, team building, and trust.[23]

George and Kuehn studied staffing patterns with the assistance of the International Society for Scientific Management. This pioneering attempt to scientifically demonstrate that non-nursing functions dilute and impede nurses' opportunities to give more direct care to patients resulted in their recommendations for decentralization or flattening the structure and a "parstock" program for material resources management.[24] More and more organizations are adopting both concepts.

Hagen and Wolff under the auspices of the Institute of Research and Service in Nursing Education, Teachers College studied the qualities that contributed to the state of effectiveness of nursing service. Using the critical incident techniques and sentence completions developed from industrial and military interviewing methods, they found managerial weakness and confusion at every level of nursing service leadership.[25]

The National Commission for the study of Nursing and Nursing Education created *An Abstract for Action* (1970) and *An Abstract*

for Action: Appendices (1971), two volumes that attempt to objectively study and delineate "how to improve the delivery of health care to the American people through an analysis and improvement of nursing practice and education."

Kramer's *Reality Shock: Why Nurses Leave Nursing* (1975) is concerned with the conflicts between theory and practice recently graduated baccalaureate nurses' experiences in their first nursing job; however, "reality shock" is also noticed in transfers, promotions, and during changes in policies and procedures of administration. Kramer's remedy is derived from Mertons' model of "anticipating socialization."[26]

The most recent Leininger article on leadership provides the nursing administration student with a much more positive, yet realistic and integrated model of the nursing administrator's role within the hospital. It is also an attempt to fill the gap with a survey of management theories which are applicable to nursing management. There are implications for graduate study of management, and for the nursing service director to expand her role of administration, personnel management, and hospital administration.[27]

THE LEADERSHIP CRISIS

Leininger has made an astute and critical analysis of the leadership crisis in nursing. Her recommendation is that nursing education and nursing service directors work together in providing a curriculum and environment appropriate for a quality care outcome.[28] This is but one of the problems facing nursing today. To quote the prolific writer Peter Drucker:

Failure to feedback from results may well tomorrow endanger the environment and our efforts to save it ... service institutions need to be subjected to performance tests ... they need people who do the management job systematically and who focus themselves and their institutions purposefully on performance and results . . . they need emphasis on the right results.[29]

We now need to focus on leadership in nursing administration for tomorrow. We must consider today's economic and social conditions in looking and planning for tomorrow. Some hard questions have to be answered. For example, why are managerial skills and principles not considered professional? In New York State, the Nursing Association does not grant Continuing Education Units for programs concerned with management: schools of nursing at all levels offer students very little experience in principles of planning, organization, controlling, coordination, and evaluation. Students come to programs with practically no understanding of how to administer or to manage: are these principles not necessary in the care of one patient as well as larger numbers? Do students work in a vacuum, that they are not able to assess priorities, human interactions, and conflicts?

A number of health care agencies are now being managed by consulting firms or have larger staffs of consultants assisting in many of the most elemental constructs of management as well as leadership. Nursing becomes a participant in this process.

Dr. Harry Levinson, psychoanalyst, consultant, an elite change agent and prolific writer, succinctly summarizes the leadership nursing must embrace:

> . . . I am advocating leadership . . . Leadership goes beyond expertise in managerial techniques to the effective exercise of power derived from followers and constituents toward organizational perpetuation, a task which always involves a sense of transcendent purpose built on the values of the leader . . .
>
> 1. The leader's first task is to insure the long-term adaptability of his organization. His primary concern goes beyond profit to the perpetuation of the organization . . .
> 2. The leader has followers. The leader gains followers by building identification with and commitment to organization purpose . . . A leader is powerless without the trust of his followers. There is no trust without commitment; there is no commitment without purpose; and there is no purpose without a primary focus on perpetuating the organization . . .
> 3. The leader stands for something and takes his work group or organization into the economic fray under that banner . . .
> 4. The leader encourages his people and demands the best of them . . .
> 5. A leader listens. The wise leader is frequently in the field, touching base, hearing comments in meetings, listening for what is not being said was well as what is being said. In return, he feeds back information to his people and compels them to confront the realities the organization faces . . .
> 6. The leader understands himself and his role in the organization . . . The leader seeks to develop the organization and create in it greater strength and capacity for meeting and solving problems . . . Every manager has the potential for becoming a leader. Few appreciate that potential. Those who do and who act on it experience a sense of achievement and exhilaration that only leaders feel.[30]

REFERENCES

1. Stodgill, R., *Handbook of Leadership* (New York: Free Press, 1974).
2. Spingham, I., *Nursing Chronicle of Higher Education,* February 4, 1974, p.1.
3. Citron, D.B., Identifying Patients' Covert Problems; A Learning Experience in Nursing Service, (Unpublished study funded by ANF).
4. Jacobson II, J.A., M.D., The Mount Sinai Hospital Hyperbaric Chamber (pre-publication manuscript, 1976, from the Department of Surgery, Division of Vascular Surgery, Mount Sinai Medical Center, New York, New York, by permission of the author.)
5. Mumford, L., *The Myth of the Machine; Technician and Civilization* (New York: Harcourt, Brace, Jovanovich, 1970) pp. 41-48, p. 26.
6. George Jr., C.S., *The History of Management Thought* (Englewood Cliffs, N.J.: Prentice Hall, 1972.)
7. Taylor, F.W., *The Principles of Scientific Management* (New York: Harper & Brothers) pp. 33+.
8. Gillbreth, F.B., Science in Management for the One Best Way To Do Work, *Classics in Management,* ed. Harwood F. Merrill (New York: American Management Association, 1960) pp. 243-291.
9. Fayol, H., *General and Industrial Management* (London: Sir Isaac Pitman and Sons, 1949.)
10. Mayo, G.E., Hawthorne and the Western Electric Company, *Classics in Management,* ed. Harwood F. Merrill (New York: American Management Association, 1960) p. 422.
11. Stewart, I.M. and A.L. Austin, *The History of Nursing* (New York: G.P. Putnam and Son, 1962.)
12. Brown, E.L., *Nursing for the Future* (New York: Russell Sage Foundation, 1948.)
13. Watson, G. and D. Johnson, *Social Psychology: Issues and Insights* (New York: J.B. Lippincott Co., 1977) p. 185.
14. Lewin, K., *Field Theory in Social Sciences* (New York: Haifer & Brothers, 1951) p. 188.
15. Barnard, C.I., *The Functions of the Executive* (Cambridge: Harvard University Press, 1954.)
16. Argyris, C., *Integrating the Individual and the Organization* (Men Prk: John Wiley and Sons, 1964.)
17. Katz, D. and R.L. Kahn, *The Social Psychology of Organizations* (New York: John Wiley & Sons, 1966.)
18. McGregor, D., *Leadership and Motivation* (Cambridge: Massachusetts Institute of Technology, 1966.)
19. Blake, R.R. and J.S. Mouton, *The Managerial Grid* (Houston, Texas: Gulf Publishing Co., 1964.)
20. Likert, R., *New Patterns of Management* (New York: McGraw-Hill Book Company, 1961.)
21. *Ibid.*
22. Finer, H., *Administration and the Nursing Service* (New York: The Macmillan Company, 1955.)
23. Lambertsen, E.C., *Nursing Team Organization and Functioning* (New York: Teachers College Press, 10th printing, 1973.)
24. George, F.L. and R.D. Kuehn, *Patterns of Patient Care: Some Studies of the Utilization of Nursing Service Personnel* (New York: The MacMillan Company, 1955.)
25. Hogan, E. and L. Wolff, *Nursing Leadership Behavior in General Hospitals* (New York: Teachers College Press, Columbia University, 1961.)
26. Kramer, M., *Reality Shock: Why Nurses Leave Nursing* (St. Louis: C. N. Mosby, 1974.)
27. Leininger, M., "The Leadership Crisis in Nursing: A Critical Problem and Challenge," *J.G.N.A.,* March-April 1974.
28. *Ibid.*
29. Drucker, P.F., *Management Tasks Responsibilities, Practice* (New York: Harper and Row Publishers, 1973) p. 116.
30. Levinson, H., *Leadership Vs. Management* (Cambridge: The Levinson Institute, 1976, by special permission of the author.)

Nurse executive profile of excellent nursing leadership

Janne Dunham, R.N., Ph.D.
Associate Professor
Assistant Dean of Continuing Education
University of Akron College of Nursing

Elaine Fisher, R.N., M.S.N.
Instructor
University of Akron College of Nursing
Akron, Ohio

*E*XCELLENT executive nursing leadership is vital to the survival of health care
agencies in the current turbulent environment. Nurse executives play a critical role in
determining the vision for hospital departments and in setting the climate for changing practice. It is thus crucial to identify and
define the leadership role of the nurse executive to facilitate the identification and development of strong leaders in nursing.

This study was part of a larger project
completed between 1986 and 1989 that examined excellent nurse executives' leadership styles. "Nurse executives were selected
as subjects because they are at the top of the
[hospital] organization and set the tone for
the department(s) under their jurisdiction.

Nurse executives are also key participants
in organizational planning in operations
management for the hospital as a
whole."[1(p.2)]

A convenience sample of 85 excellent hospital nurse executives was selected by the
following process: nurse executives (75 percent), nursing administration faculty (15
percent) and other nursing administration
personnel (10 percent) were asked to identify nursing executives whom they considered to be excellent. These individuals could
make one or more referrals. Specific names
surfaced consistently; these names were
given preference for selection. Other names,
mentioned less frequently, were included on
a convenience basis.

Taped interviews were done with 85 excellent hospital nurse executives either in person or by phone. Executives were asked to
describe the characteristics of excellent

In addition to all the nurse executives who gave their
time and support to this study, the authors thank
Karen Nelsen for her assistance with manuscript
preparation.
This study was funded by The University of Akron and
The University of Akron College of Nursing.

Nurs Admin Q, 1990, 15(1), 1–8
©1990 Aspen Publishers, Inc.

nursing leadership and identify their own strengths and weaknesses. No time restrictions were imposed, and interviews lasted fifteen minutes to three hours, with the average interview being one hour. Questions were asked by the researcher only when needed for clarification. The interviews were transcribed and analyzed for cultural themes using the ethnographic process.

DEMOGRAPHICS

Seventy-nine women and six men participated in the interviews. Respondents' ages ranged from 30 to over 60 years, with many in their 40s. Forty-six were married, 12 divorced, and 17 single, with ten not reporting marital status. All but two had advanced degrees; 13 had doctorates. The participants represented public and private hospitals, for-profit and nonprofit hospitals, and community and teaching hospitals in 30 states.

EXCELLENT NURSING LEADERSHIP

The following discussion identifies the primary themes that emerged from the interview data. These themes represent the ideas and concepts of the executives interviewed.

Nurse executives define excellent nursing *leadership* as universal leadership as universal leadership skill. Excellent leadership attributes include administrative competence with adequate educational background, business skills, and clinical expertise combined with a global understanding of leadership principles.

Nurse executives deviate from this general leadership description when they emphasize nursing's responsibility to influence the practice environment. They stress the importance of creating an environment in which the professional nurse can participate at both the organizational and the professional level. This emphasis on nursing practice exists because people come to the hospital for patient care. As one executive stated, "The primary role of any nursing administrator is to facilitate clinical practice at the bedside level."

A third aspect of excellent nursing leadership integrates nursing into the overall organizational effort. The effective nurse executive is a *team player* who receives interdisciplinary respect and cooperation. All disciplines work together more effectively when their common focus is on the patient. "Good leadership is simply constantly marketing nursing" while simultaneously considering the needs and problems of other departments. Team players contribute to the final product and together ultimately determine the success or failure of the organization.

Negotiation skills are another must for the excellent nurse leader. The leader appreciates the difference between negotiation and compromise. The idea becomes "give some to get some," because "winning a battle might mean losing the war." These executives were not afraid of losing or withdrawing from a battle. They preferred to reframe "battles" as team efforts toward a mutually agreed-upon outcome.

Excellent nurse executives serve as ambassadors for nursing with the medical staff, the board, hospital administrators, and the public. They have the ability to "translate the patient care needs into a language that the people of the power tables understand and appreciate."

Excellent leaders have *strong value systems.* The following qualities were identified: honesty, fairness, integrity, trust, and caring, accompanied by a drive for quality and excellence. These executives want patients to receive the kind of care that they (the executives) would want for their own families. Excellent leaders are willing to take a stand on issues and remain true to their convictions. Nurse executives "have to have very high professional, moral, and ethical standards. And one doesn't compromise these."

Nurse executives consistently *model* these values with the expectation that staff will emulate these values when caring for patients. "If you care for the caregiver, the caregiver will then be able to care for the patient with the same set of values." Excellent leaders are humanistic and respect people. One vice president, when asked to describe excellent nursing leadership, said simply, "Love one another."

Excellent nursing leaders are *creative,* have a *vision* of what can be accomplished, and are *risk takers.* The leader's vision is dynamic. Leaders have good ideas and are open to new ideas from others. "One idea is never enough. It takes the collective thoughts of many people to make good ideas grow." This dynamic process, in turn, reshapes the vision. Excellent leaders are flexible and *adaptable;* they are able to "mesh expectations with actuality."

Excellent nursing leaders are *charismatic.* They challenge, interest, and excite people about the vision, so that staff members also become committed to accomplishing the vision. The executive's vision surpasses that shared with staff members. The part of the vision shared with staff members stretches them, yet not so much that they

---

Excellent leaders are humanistic and respect people. One vice president, when asked to describe excellent nursing leadership, said simply, "Love one another."

---

think the vision is not possible. One executive said, "My personal style is to take a group of ideas and sprinkle them around. Then I water them, being patient enough that soon those ideas start coming back to me from staff. This lets people come up with the ideas as if they were their own." Executives' leadership involves *constant communication,* both written and verbal, combined with strong interpersonal skills. Executives commented that they do not communicate enough. Part of the effectiveness of the excellent nurse executives' communication resulted from their commitment to being direct and to not playing games, as well as from their ability to ask the right questions. They also stressed the importance of knowing when to say, or not to say, something, and of knowing when to listen.

Executives use their vision to structure *goals* and set the direction. One nurse executive described this process as follows: "I always use the analogy of the artist who sketches a scene on a piece of canvas. It doesn't have to have all the colors. A tree doesn't have to have all the leaves." As the vision is communicated and staff are empowered, it is important that "everyone can see that picture so you know where you're going and staff know where they're going. Each person looking at it has a slightly different vision. But they're still all going in the same direction. Everyone then begins to add color and the picture takes form. Everybody helps you do that."

However, nurse executives still have to monitor progress on a regular basis to ensure a quality outcome. "When the color or form doesn't turn out well, you have to be there to support, to guide, and to give them knowledge and skills to fix that and get on with it."

Empowerment occurs when the vision and direction are clear. The leaders empower staff members by motivating them to make the vision a reality. Empowerment is relinquishing control and decentralizing departments. "I think, rather than direction, nurses need facilitation and support." There was strong agreement on this point. "Nurses don't need to be guided by a lot of rules. They are professionals. So I minimize policy and procedure. I'm more interested in cognitive problem-solving abilities."

Empowerment requires recognizing staff potential and unleashing that potential to accomplish the vision. It involves turning "control over to nursing staff leaders while at the same time helping to guide the direction and create the environment." "Excellent nursing leadership is orchestrating your professional practice climate in such a way that the system moves effectively in the caring of patients and is cost-effective, yet your hand is hardly noticed."

Empowerment requires the executive to be available to staff in times of trouble to give guidance and support. Staff problems include: being overwhelmed, not recognizing problems, needing support to deal with problems, and needing to discuss possible alternatives. The leader provides what is needed.

Executives agree on the importance of recognizing excellence in others. Leadership "is not always being in front and having a whole army of followers." Although there is a place for the leader, leaders without an army of excellent people to support their efforts are not going to achieve what they are employed to achieve. There was agreement that power comes from below, not above.

Selection of *excellent staff* is a key factor. Some relevant comments were "A real star is a star maker." "By allowing others to shine, that light will end up somehow reflecting back to you." "You're a rock kicker, keeping rocks out of the road. You hire the best people that you can and then get out of their way so they can do the job you hired them to do."

Excellent leaders teach and train staff, often serving as role models, *mentors,* and facilitators. Excellent leadership is being visible with staff and establishing relationships with them. Nurse executives deal with ambiguity and grayness, frequently relying on intuition when they do not have all the facts. Excellent nurse leaders have a well-developed sense of timing in addition to the ability and confidence to make immediate decisions, wait for outcomes, and persevere when necessary. They know when to make decision, when to delay them, and when to let others make them. They maintain objectivity and are not "sorry for it somewhere along the line." Executives said, "It's knowing what decisions are and moving them—being a catalyst." "It's juggling many balls at one time." "It's being able to think quickly on your feet."

"The buck stops" with the nurse executive. Although nurse executives may not always be popular, they remain true to their convictions and values. The final test of the quality of the leadership is a positive patient outcome. Excellent nursing leadership is being action-, results-, or *outcome-oriented.*

Excellent nurse leaders *constantly grow and learn.* They learn by listening to those around them, staying current, challenging themselves continuously, and learning from their own mistakes and the mistakes of others. They emphasize being "well educated in an eclectic sense."

There was consensus that excellent nursing leaders have well-developed *business skills,* including an understanding of finance and budget (i.e., knowing the bottom line), resource management, long- and short-range planning, system analysis, and personnel management. Several executives think that the emphasis on finance has become too important, that "we don't give enough value to the bedside nurse and the patient." Nurse executives stress that they are leaders of a clinical discipline, not leaders of finance.

Excellent nurse leaders are professionally involved outside the hospital in professional organizations and/or in influencing governmental policy. This involvement is intraorganizational and broadbased.

Physical appearance and dress are also important components of excellent leadership. One executive said, "Act the part, look the part, speak the part." All agreed that the role takes total commitment and dedication, high energy, and a sense of humor to help one keep a feeling of perspective.

STRENGTHS AND WEAKNESSES

Common themes emerged on the topic of executive strengths and weaknesses. Often a specific strength identified by a nurse executive could be considered either a strength or a weakness, depending on the context and/or the extent to which it was used.

Strengths

There were strong similarities between nurse executives' descriptions of excellent nursing leadership and their own strengths. They have the vision to see what needs to be accomplished and are futuristic, conceptual, idea people. Their global picture always surpasses that of their staff. In addition, executives are risk takers with a good sense of timing and intuitive ability.

People skills are their forte. They are good communicators, have good interpersonal skills, and know how to listen as well as speak. Executives include others in their plans, and these individuals become equally committed to the vision. One executive said, "My staff would probably tell you that I'm a visionary dreamer. I get these wonderful ideas. And then I have the

audacity to convince staff that they want to participate in this and do some of the work involved." This is important since staff members are the ones who must actually implement the plans.

The nurse executives empower and develop people, and serve as mentors to their staff. Executives select excellent people for leadership positions. These people may have strengths different from those of the executives. Nurse executives develop an administrative team. Team members are encouraged to continue their own career development, even when this results in losing them to another organization. Several executives mentioned that they continue to network with such individuals. Executives stress team building, striving to create a climate of teamwork by encouraging staff to provide feedback and disagree on issues. Executives have an open door policy and are available to their staff.

The nurse executives consistently act on their beliefs. They keep their promises and their actions match their words. These consistent behaviors generate trust.

Nurse executives love to do rounds. They enjoy talking to nurses about practice issues. A few executives see patients on rounds as well. The executives reported differences in the frequency of doing rounds. Several vice presidents did daily rounds that had a regular place on their calendar. Most felt they needed to be doing rounds more often. All reported getting energized and motivated when they talked with staff and with patients.

The nurse administrators are sensitive to people and do not believe in laying off employees. They "give staff members the benefit of the doubt" and have an abundance of patience and understanding.

Nurse executives emphasize continuous self-development and self-evaluation. Some administrators reported evaluating their situation at specific intervals (i.e., every three or five years).

The nurse executives know they are not perfect and they readily admit to their mistakes. They acknowledge that they do not have all the answers. Likewise, they do not dwell on the past. They have a sense of humor and can laugh at themselves. Executives acknowledge that staff, too, will make mistakes when taking risks, but believe staff will also have some "shining glories." "It is to be hoped the winners will offset the losers."

Several administrators spotlight their staff members by giving them rewards or recognition for jobs well done. They take pride in the accomplishments of their personnel and consider this a reward of the job.

The issue of women's roles surfaced several times. Nurse executives discussed strategies to minimize differences. One strategy was to ask for the same salary as the chief of medicine and the chief of surgery. Executives say, "It's the good old boys. It's going into the surgeons' locker room, sitting down, and having a cigarette with them and talking about the ball game." "So much business gets done in an informal way. But we don't have access to that forum. I'm not speaking only about the bathroom differences but the golf course, let's go for a drink at the club, etc. I don't think we'll ever bridge that gap." "Until those decisions and the power base that happens in that informal setting dwindle, we'll never have access to that piece of the power game."

Nurse executives are confident, with a strong belief in self and a strong value system. They are committed to making a contribution to nursing, to the organization, and to life in general. Executives have a strong work ethic and expect others to work hard also. They are honest and fair. They have very high standards for themselves and for staff. However, many say "I am hardest on

myself." Executives consistently reported that their standards were higher for themselves than for their staff. One executive also indicated that the standards were higher for her staff members than for staff members in other departments.

Working hard is not difficult for the administrators because they "love what [they] do." This gives them high energy and motivates them to accomplish more in a day. High energy leads to qualities of persistence, determination, resilience, and enthusiasm. Many describe themselves as "workaholics." "I don't know when I'm working and when I'm playing because I have fun with what I do. I'm never working." Most report working long hours, although a few reported working regular hours and "making the most of [their] work time."

Executives consistently reported that their standards were higher for themselves than for their staff.

One executive said, "There's nothing I can't do if I want to except sleep." They like challenge, change, and ambiguity. Challenges are viewed as opportunities. Nurse executives are able to reframe bad situations by viewing them as windows of opportunity.

A final strength was their ability to identify both their strengths and their weaknesses. They actively worked to improve weaknesses and chose staff to compensate for those weaknesses.

Weaknesses

There are many commonalities in weaknesses. Almost everyone reported hating details and commented on delegating these tasks. This dislike of detail usually permeates all aspects of the role: a dislike of paperwork, of implementing details of plans, of "number crunching," and of providing staff with detailed directions. Executives frequently procrastinate in handling detail unless the detail concerns someone being paid or some other urgent purpose. Along these lines, some executives reported that as projects progress, they lose interest, having already gone on to the next project.

Although executives dislike detail, they see the whole gestalt and understand that details are part of the total pattern. If there is a hole in the gestalt, they would recognize and manage it. They first attend to details that relate to outcomes or to the bottom line.

Another weakness, letting staff problems go on too long before taking action, resulted in regret for their earlier inaction. Executives' rationales for waiting were influenced by their sensitivity to people. They believed that these people could change and they saw their good qualities. One executive explained, "I always think, well, maybe I'll give them another chance, and I can rehab them a little bit."

The nurse executives almost unanimously discussed being impatient—especially with peers, physicians, department heads, or administrators who appeared to be incompetent. The majority reported tactfully dealing with these situations, although a few said they worked at controlling their temper in these circumstances. Others mentioned being too direct or not being diplomatic with these people. Several mentioned compensating for this weakness by developing better negotiating skills and timing. "I have a difficult time working with people I don't feel are competent. [Yet] I have a tremendous amount of patience with people who are not my peers." Likewise, executives commented on being impatient with themselves.

Another common weakness executives reported was the inability to say "no," leading to overextension. "One of my weaknesses is that I'm interested in everything." "I have a reminder on my inner wrist saying, 'Don't volunteer.'" Another executive had successfully dealt with this problem: "I'm in charge of my schedule. That was not what I could say five years ago. I was literally a victim of the system. Just felt I had to meet everybody's needs all the time."

Some executives thought they lived a balanced life, giving equal time and energy to work and to family or self, while other executives did not feel that their lives were balanced. "I really believe you cannot eat, sleep, and breathe nursing." "I became pathologically involved with my work. The truth of the matter is that the institution needs your talent, they don't need you." "Between the role of nursing director, executive, mother, and wife, there's not a whole lot left." "I don't take care of myself like I expect other people to take care of themselves. There's two sets of rules." Executives achieving balance in their lives reported a variety of coping strategies, including family support, meditating by a creek in the backyard, and going out in a sailboat every weekend.

RECOMMENDATIONS

The study results present a profile of excellent nursing leadership as defined by 85 excellent nurse executives. In addition, these executives provide a description of their own strengths and weaknesses.

The characteristics of excellent leadership reported in this study provide a preliminary description of executive leadership that can be further studied and refined. These characteristics of excellent leadership can be used

- for further development of the executive role,

- by nurse executives to develop their own capabilities,
- as criteria for selection of executive candidates,
- for setting up educational programs or designing continuing education offerings to further develop these skills and characteristics in nursing leadership personnel,
- for people in key positions to make appropriate selections from the candidate pool, and
- for identifying and developing individuals for future leadership positions.

These descriptions are a beginning resource that can be used to define and further understand the role and the perspective of the nurse executive. Developing a cadre of excellent nurse leaders is critical to the future of nursing. These leaders have the potential to make major contributions for the betterment of nursing administration at all levels of nursing.

REFERENCE

1. Dunham, J., and Klafehn, K. "Transformational Leadership and the Nurse Executive." *Journal of Nursing Administration* 20, no. 4(1990):28-34.

Creativity

Barbara J. Brown, R.N., Ed.D.,
F.A.A.N., C.N.A.A.
Editor, Nursing Administration Quarterly

CREATIVITY is often expressed as the generation of ideas, the tool used to add to a body of knowledge in society, the growth of individuality. Creativity is freeing oneself of past barriers and can't-be-done attitudes and allowing exploration of new territories. It is taking a problem and turning it into an opportunity.

How is creativity being applied in nursing? The creative art-innovative science approach to nursing demands that we optimize our human resources. As creative professionals, we must: (1) challenge assumptions; (2) recognize similarities and differences; (3) perceive the commonplace in new ways; (4) make connections where connections were previously not considered; (5) take risks, regardless of the outcome; (6) take advantage of the unexpected; and (7) construct networks for a better exchange of ideas and knowledge. These thoughts were expressed at a recent exhibit at the Kennedy Center in Washington, D.C. The concepts portrayed in that exhibit, "Creativity: The Human Resource," deserve more detailed consideration. These concepts, as outlined below, will provide a way to open the doors to our own creative capabilities, develop new choices in our professional lives and reawaken our "spirit of adventure."

1. "Challenging assumptions is daring to question what most people think is true." We need bold thinkers in nursing who challenge ideas. We must show our appreciation for the questioning nurse, the nurse who seeks alternatives and tries to do things a new way, the nurse who wants to explore patient care and the process of nursing using a creative approach. We must not stifle individuals who challenge us. More importantly, we must strive to create an environment conducive to the challenging of assumptions. If we do, we have accomplished the first step in creativity.

2. "Recognizing patterns is perceiving significant similarities or differences in ideas, events, or physical phenomena." We must look for and recognize patterns of care that are successful in meeting patients' needs. We must explore the beginning step

Nurs Admin Q, 1976, 1(1), viii–x
©1976 Aspen Publishers, Inc.

in the research process, to try to test out new ideas and determine a way of creating an improved patient care system. We have researchers studying patterns of sleep, the phenomena of human touch, death and dying, all of which are recognizing patterns in the caring process. How do we apply this research?

3. "Seeing in new ways is seeing the commonplace with new perceptions, transforming the familiar to the strange and the strange to the familiar." When we look at nursing practice in our daily work, what do we see? We probably see the routine principles and practices that have been carried out for several years or have been taught recently in a school of nursing. We must look at nursing as creative artists, with new images and new types of health care processes, such as innovative group therapy. After all, primary nursing arose because certain nurses saw team nursing in a new way and realized it was inadequate. And the development of birthing rooms allowed the birthing process to be a normal, family-oriented experience.

The same creative approach could be applied to staffing. We should look at staffing as a complex collection of secret messages having to be deciphered. Then, we could look at it with a variety of creative and innovative approaches: 12-hour shifts, modified work weeks, self-staffing, variable and flexible work hours, and flextime for home visits by staff nurses in hospitals. Anything imaginable is possible, if we allow ourselves to be creative.

4. "Making connections is bringing together seemingly unrelated ideas, objects, or events in a way that leads to a new conception." Do we approach nursing practice as a challenge in which we might be able to establish new relationships between nurses, physicians, and patients through similarities of purpose? The most exciting part of my recent experience in nursing administration has been in exploring and expanding nurse–physician relationships through joint practice committees and conferences that provide opportunities for hospital administrators, board of trustee members, physicians, and nursing administrators to find new relationships.

Nursing practice utilizing biofeedback is making connections between biophysical responses of people and relaxation techniques and can be a new break-through in contributing to health care. An example is use of nursing biofeedback to control menopausal symptoms.

5. "Creative people take risks. Taking risks is daring to try new ways or new ideas, with no control over the outcome." Creative people are not afraid of being wrong. They are willing to take long shots. Nursing needs risk takers. Although it is most difficult to be in a position of authority, responsibility, and accountability, sometimes taking risks that might lead to the removal from that position, there is no other way for an effective nursing administrator to practice. Once we think we have all the answers, and that there is no more to learn or to develop in the nursing environment, it is time to remove ourselves from our position of leadership.

6. "Creative people use chance. Using chance is taking advantage of the unexpected." Often the unexpected opportunity provides the time and circumstance to take a new direction. Wellness promotion, being introduced in many acute care settings today, has sprung up because acute care nursing practitioners took advantage of an unexpected need for hospitals to become community oriented in order to survive in a competitive era.

7. "Creative people construct networks. Constructing networks is forming associations between people for an exchange of ideas, perceptions, questions, and encour-

agements." The networks between nursing service directors today, through the American Society for Nursing Service Administrators, are much stronger. Similar networks also exist in nursing within the American Nurses' Association. State, regional, and local networks acting on behalf of nursing administrators allow for personal meetings and exchanges of ideas, thus stimulating creativity.

We need to learn to nourish one another's work, give credit and respect to each other, and enhance ideas and perceptions. Creativity flourishes best where people get together to exchange ideas, encouraging and serving as catalysts for one another.

If the foregoing steps in the creative process were applied to the problem-solving process, more creativity and innovation would be experienced in the nursing profession than has been in the past.

Luther Christman represents creativity and genius to nursing and was justly recognized by Sigma Theta Tau this year, being awarded the Edith Moore Copen Award for Creativity. He is responsible for development of primary nursing and joint practice models at Rush-Presbyterian-St. Luke's in Chicago and has created the John L. and Helen Kellogg Center for Excellence in Nursing. I am pleased that he continues to support and contribute to *Nursing Administration Quarterly* through his regular book reviews. He is indeed a prolific writer and a creative leader in nursing.

In conclusion, I would like to share a quotation, which was displayed at the recent Kennedy Center exhibit: "The truly creative individual stands ready to abandon old classifications and to acknowledge that life, particularly his own unique life, is rich with new possibilities" (Frank Barron).

Part I
Study and Discussion Questions

1. The profession of nursing has had dynamic leaders from a historical perspective; why is it that today's nursing profession is perceived by the consumer to be a non-leadership role?

2. How do the works of Adam Smith, John Stuart Mills, Henry Metcalf, et al., compare with theories of Argyris, Katz and Kahn, McGregor, Blake and Mouton, and Likert?

3. What are Fayol's management principles and are they relevant to organizations today?

4. How did the Brown Report in 1948, *Nursing for the Future,* impact the nursing profession?

5. How can we foster more collaboration between nursing service and nursing education to ensure that leadership is promulgated at the grass roots level?

6. How can we articulate more leadership/management theory into all levels of nursing curricula?

7. What can be done to foster more mentoring programs and/or internships for undergraduates, as well as for graduate students in Nursing Administration?

8. As a profession, how can nursing facilitate and support more research on effective leadership styles?

9. Are there social and economical forces that impact nurses negatively from selecting leadership and/or executive positions?

10. In the last ten years, what Nursing Executives have made an impact on nursing practice because of their effective leadership/management styles?

11. Are there new leadership behaviors needed for the successful leader in the 21st Century?

Part II
Management concepts

Marjorie Beyers, R.N., Ph.D., F.A.A.N.
Associate Vice President
Nursing and Allied Health Services
Mercy Health Services
Farmington Hills, Michigan

In Part II, selected management concepts are presented. The selected articles deal with organizations, management roles and functions, management stress, and decision making. The content is helpful to nurses who want to use their talents at every level of management to provide quality patient care. It applies whether the nurse is planning patient care, struggling to balance the budget, or completing final interviews for filling staff positions. The fundamental concepts hold true through changes in management and organizational styles. They apply to transformational leadership and new types of learning organizations and are useful as we move from the era of scientific management toward new management approaches. In today's environment we are dramatically aware that the humanistic aspects of management must be balanced with the rational decision-making aspects. We realize that in health care services, work

is accomplished through people, for people. Priorities must be set to use the scarce resources to the best advantage for patients and their families.

One of the most interesting yet confounding issues in management science is how organizations should be structured to enable people to work effectively. Knowledge growth, technologic advances, health care reform, and public demand for more and better care result in management challenges. Nurse managers are doing more with less. They are empowering every person to achieve his or her best. Empowering people requires a humanistic management focus. Developing people, building relationships, dealing effectively with conflict, and meeting escalating demands are typical priorities. In today's nursing management environment it is easy to become over-committed and to become burned out. It is also easy to become intoxicated by the challenges and opportunities of change.

But to be effective, we must become proficient at decision making to cope with the changes. Such an investment is worthwhile because change is inevitable. Patient care is changing; patient and family expectations are changing. Community members want more wellness care. They want to keep all of the traditional health care at the same time. But resources are scarce and choices have to be made. Decision making is clearly one of the most important management functions in this time of change. Nurse managers are now shaping and managing change while also maintaining quality patient care. They are working in stressful environments. They are experimenting with new methods for care delivery and learning new techniques. Establishing an environment of balance and harmony has never been more important. It is that balance and harmony that will allow us to preserve the essence of nursing which is caring and valuing people through effective decision making and supportive organizational structures.

Nurse management today is as complex as the challenges facing all of us in nursing. We are challenged with many problems requiring us to cope with internal forces impacting the health care delivery systems in which we work and external forces with which we must establish balance and harmony. Effective nurse managers are members of the total management and administrative team and must participate in all areas of administration, including planning for the long range, developing policy, and establishing priorities for financial resource allocation. Nurse managers need a combination of advanced clinical nursing knowledge and managerial expertise in order to expand into the new roles required of them for the future multi-organizational health care systems.

To establish balance and harmony as managers, we must design strategies that work for us. What worked for Barbara Brown was described (*NAQ* 8:3) as **RE-LAXED.**

R-Rest and Religion are both essential to healthful living. Each person has a level of energy that can be exceeded at times, but it then must be mediated in order to stabilize a continuous autodynamic status of being. A sense of peacefulness with one's God emanates from balance and harmony. Nursing brings us close to our spiritual selves every day of our lives because commitment to people in the profession imbues valuing humanity and caring.

E-Efficiency and Economy mean having a sense of orderliness in what you do and when you do it. Planning activities, managing the work day, controlling your household, achieving a balance—all fit into the definition of economy.

L-Love and Laughter for managers is exhibited by the glow of happiness that is in you. Smiling at one's own mistakes and upsets is one example.

A-Attitude can open or close doors for communication, relationships, and ideas. A person, no matter of what age, education, or experience may profit from others in some way if the mind is kept open to thoughts, words, and ideas.

X-X-ample is for staff members, who, like children, learn by following what they do, how they deal with conflict, and how they perceive their world. Managers set the examples from which people perceive and learn from us about what we are doing, how we are doing it, and why.

E-Effort and Effectiveness grows from working together with your staff and managers for the goals that nursing has set out to achieve. Effective effort stops the forest fires instead of stomping out the brush fires of crises.

D-Daily duties can include accepting, planning, organizing, and managing the budget, staffing, planning daily patient care situations, dealing with nurse-physician challenges, and all of the rest. Keep time for strategic long-range goals that we set out to accomplish.

Decision making is one of the threads that is woven in the tapestry of balance and harmony. Nurse managers are now supported by a growing decision science to achieve goals. Decision science helps successful executives to select and use occasions for decision making. Nurse managers must now apply information to make decisions to continuously improve patient care quality. Decision making is necessary to develop flexible responses to changing demands.

Today, occasions for decisions are blatantly obvious and too numerous for comfort. One must choose which of the occasions to act on and how to act. Decisions and actions are influenced by the nature and type of decisions, the authors of the decisions, and the impact the decisions have on clinical outcomes of nursing care and the organizational performance as a health care delivery system. Nurse executive decisions typically deal with nursing practice, modes of nursing care delivery, staffing, recruitment and retention, business planning for patient care service development, quality assurance, risk management, and cost analysis. Community interactions, policy formation, program development, and strategic planning are types of decisions nurses make. The integrated person, who is able to establish balance and harmony in the environment, is most likely to be the effective nurse manager.

NAQ forum: The anatomy of an organization

Juanita R. Theile, M.S.N., M.Ed.
Consultant
Corning, Iowa

How do you assess your patient,when your patient is the organization? Nurses in administrative roles often do not see the relevance of their nursing knowledge base in the administrative position. *Organization* is often viewed as an esoteric concept, but if it is viewed in an anthropomorphic way, the nurse manager may find it more understandable and easier to assess, intervene in, and evaluate.

Defining an "organization"

Everyone talks about "the organization." Sometimes it is called "the hospital," "the college," "the company," or "the unit." It is also referred to as "they" or as "we." There are organizations and various suborganizations in everyone's life. An organization is formed whenever there is more than one person involved in an activity to achieve some purpose.

Knowles recognized the importance of the organization when he stated that the organization creates the milieu in which the purposes of that organization can be achieved.[1] Mintzberg recognized that in every human activity, from pot making to the placing of a man on the moon, there are two basic and opposing aspects, namely, the divisions of labor into various tasks and the coordination of these tasks to accomplish the purpose of the organization.[2] Simply, then, an organization is the sum total of the ways in which it divides its labor into distinct tasks and then achieves coordination among them.

Price defined an organization as a social system with a specific purpose.[3] Thompson stated that organizations can be represented as a system of interrelated variables.[4] Perrow, on the other hand, saw an organization as an open system.[5] These various definitions are very important when one attempts to gain a fuller understanding of organizational behavior. Nurse administra-

Nurs Admin Q, 1983, 7(2), 42–46
©1983 Aspen Publishers, Inc.

tors need to understand their organization to be able to assess its progress.

When looking at any organization, one needs to determine what makes it distinctive. Why is it a hospital, a critical care unit, or a rehabilitation unit? What are the necessary parts to achieve the stated purpose? An organization should be viewed as an entity to achieve some desired purpose and not as an end in itself. Often this is confused, as expressed in such statements as "That is not done here" or "The organization doesn't like that."

Structural parts of an organization

In viewing an organization as a tool to achieve some stated purpose, it is useful to closely examine and describe its parts. Price identified 22 different parts or variables that describe the different aspects of an organization. He stated that there is little standardization of tools to measure organizations, and that there is a need for researchers to come to some agreement so that findings can be compared and theories developed.[6]

The literature discusses many different structural forms for organizations and provides various terms to describe the various structural parts.[7] Galbraith and Nathanson believed that any organization has a variety of structural forms and organizational processes from which to choose. These authors contend that organizational members should allocate the time and effort necessary to plan their organizational form just as time and effort are allocated for the formulation of other plans.[8] For example, an educator will spend long hours developing objectives and course content and identifying learning experiences but will probably give little thought to the suborganization he or she is creating. The nurse manager will write objec-

tives or plan the budget and may not consider the needs of the different parts of the organization.

Price's variables

Among the variables identified by Price, 15 are relevant to this discussion:

- Administration staff—members who contribute indirectly to primary output.
- Autonomy—amount of independent power the organization has.
- Centralization—degree of power concentrated in a social system.
- Communication—degree to which information is transmitted among members.
- Coordination—the degree to which each of the various interdependent parts of a social system operates according to the requirements of the other parts and of the total system.
- Dispersion—membership is spatially distributed.
- Effectiveness—organization achieves its goals.
- Formalization—norms of the organization are explicit.
- Mechanization—use of inanimate sources of energy.
- Motivation—the degree to which members are willing to work.
- Bases of power—individual capacity to obtain performance from other individuals. Social power: reward, coercive, legitimate, referent, and expert.
- Routinization—the degree that the performance of a role is repetitive.
- Satisfaction—members have positive affective orientation toward membership in system.
- Size—scope of operation (budget, number of professional personnel).
- Span of control—number of members managed by administration.[9]

In Figure 1, the variables identified by Price have been grouped and identified as key human anatomical parts: the nerves, muscle, structure, heart, and blood. This conceptualization could be called the anatomy of an organization.

Parts of the organization according to an anatomical model

The "muscle" of the organization includes the budget, professional staff, size, mechanization or technology, and secretarial staff. Many times an administrator of an organization thinks that the organization is not successful because it does not have enough muscle.

The "nerves" of the organization include the communication system, both formal and informal. Communication in the organization is as critically important as it is in the human organism. Without appropriate

The study showed that size, power, and structure were not as important factors in effective organizations as the job satisfaction and the motivation of their members.

messages going between systems, the body cannot function. Similarly, the organization cannot function without a vital communication system. The nerves also include the coordination of the various tasks of the organization.

The "bones," or structure, of the organization consist of all of its policies, procedures, and formalized statements, including its philosophy and its mission statement. The structure also includes the routine tasks that are done repeatedly but possibly not written down. The organization chart shows the structure, the span of control and the dispersion of the organization. These documents have a similar function within the organization as the bones do in the human body. These documents give form and shape to the organization.

The "heart," or power, of the organization includes the amount of autonomy and centralization the organization has. Power can be delegated and can be assessed by how much decision making is allowed by the central organization or the administration of the larger organization.

The most important part of the organization, as determined in a research study,[10] is the "blood," or "hemoglobin" of the organization. This part of the organization consists of the motivation and job satisfaction of the members of the organization. The study showed that size, power, and structure were not as important factors in effective organizations as the job satisfaction and the motivation of their members.

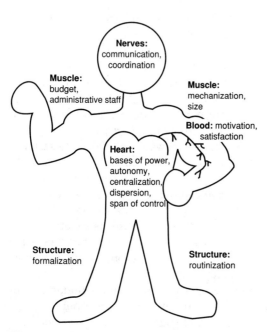

Figure 1. The anatomy of an organization.

Using the anatomical model

The nurse administrator using the anatomical model can more easily assess, intervene in and evaluate the organization. Price, in his *Handbook of Organizational Measures,* lists tools that can be used to assess these various organization components.

There are various types of organizations in our lives. Each organization is formed to help achieve some purpose or goal. The organization is the means to an end and not an end in itself. The organization should be assessed periodically to see that its different parts are functioning and helping to achieve its overall purpose. In the human body, one part cannot be ill without affecting the whole; similarly, any change or breakdown of any part of the organization affects the total organization.

The nurse administrator can indeed assess the patient, even when the patient is an organization.

REFERENCES

1. Knowles, M. *The Modern Practice of Adult Education* (Chicago, Ill.: Associated Press, Follett Publishing Co. 1970) p. 59.
2. Mintzberg, H. *The Structuring of Organizations* (Englewood Cliffs, N.J.: Prentice-Hall 1979) p. 2.
3. Price, J.L. *Handbook of Organizational Measures* (Lexington, Mass.: D.C. Health 1972) p. 2.
4. Thompson, J., ed. *Approaches to Organizational Design* (Pittsburgh, Pa.: University of Pittsburgh Press 1966) p. 5.
5. Perrow, C. *Organizational Analysis: A Sociological View* (Belmont, Calif.: Brooks/Cole 1979) p. 2.
6. Price. *Handbook of Organizational Measures,* p. 1.
7. Hall, R. *Organizational Structure and Process* (Englewood Cliffs, N.J.: Prentice-Hall 1972).
8. Galbraith, J.R. and Nathanson, D.A. *Strategy Implementation: The Role of Structure and Process* (St. Paul, Minn.: West Publishing 1978) p. 1.
9. Price. *Handbook of Organizational Measures,* p. 19-180.
10. Theile, J.R. " A Structural Analysis of Nursing Continuing Education Organizations and Programs." Ed.D. dissertation, Drake University 1981.

Helping nurses through the management threshold

Susan Gleeson, R.N., M.S.N.
Director of Patient Services
Visiting Nurse Association of Boston
Boston, Massachusetts

Oscar W. Nestor, Ph.D.
Chairman
Industrial Relations Department
Pace University
New York, New York

Andrew J. Riddell, B.S., M.B.A.
Executive Director
Administration
Visiting Nurse Association of Boston
Boston, Massachusetts

MANAGEMENT CAN BE called the ability to establish an environment conducive to group effort that encourages and enables individuals to contribute to group objectives with the least amount of input (money, time, efforts, discomfort, and materials). As recognized by business, management is critical to achieving objectives. This is not to say that management principles are always practiced properly, but

such principles do exist, and serious attempts are being made to strengthen management skills at all levels. A recent article in the *Wall Street Journal* demonstrates the business industry's commitment to management development, presenting the following facts: (1) nearly 500,000 managers take some form of management education at least once every year; (2) the number of applicants to University of Pennsylvania Wharton School minicourses for executives has soared to 7,800 a year (six times the number in 1974); and (3) American Telephone and Telegraph annually enrolls 14,000 of its managers in in-house management seminars.[1]

It appears that no philosophy of management has been established in voluntary, nonprofit agencies to the extent that it has in the for-profit sector. Drucker notes that businessmen and civil servants "tend to underrate the difficulty of managing service institutions." The businessman thinks management is "a matter of being efficient"; the civil servant thinks it is "a matter of having the right procedures and controls." Neither idea is correct, says Drucker, since "service institutions are

Nurs Admin Q, 1983, 7(2), 11–16
©1983 Aspen Publishers, Inc.

more complex than either businesses or government agencies."[2]

The management of home health agencies is becoming an increasingly important and complex issue. These agencies have grown in size, bringing an increase in the number and variety of management situations and problems; inflation has driven costs up, requiring greater emphasis on cost controls and improved productivity; and, in some cases, unions or the threat of unions has forced managerial changes. Clearly, more professional and sophisticated methods of management are needed to deal with these challenges. The development of such methods, however, seems to lag behind that in other segments of society.

One significant reason for this lag is that historically (for about 100 years) the home health care industry has been managed by nurses. Considering the content of basic nursing education, it is obvious that nurses are not prepared to be managers. As expressed by Stevens, basic nursing education prepares nurses to cope with the environment, not manage it. "Managers, head nurses, or subordinates need some formal education preparation to implement management principles. Management is a job in itself, requiring knowledge in a new discipline, management science. The nurse manager then, must . . . synthesize 2 disciplines—nursing and management."[3]

Lack of adequate management preparation can be devastating. Knollmueller described some of the potential dangers to an organization: "Promoting individuals from within the ranks, although thought to be one of the best ways to fill supervisory positions, . . . has its pitfalls. *Being a good staff nurse does not always mean becoming a good supervisor! Indeed, being an effective supervisor does not ensure that one can be an effective director, either!*"[4] Knollmueller also states that when administrators appoint a nurse to a supervisory position, they are often less concerned with the nurse's supervisory philosophy and capacity for working with staff than with the nurse's ability to function as a technical assistant. The nurse selected may not be the best supervisor.

According to Knollmueller, nurse managers inadequately prepared may overreact to the need for documentation and accurate recordkeeping. Meeting patient and employee needs becomes secondary, which can be dangerous.

To avoid these and other pitfalls, nurse managers must be adequately prepared. This will be possible only when home health agency leaders do the following:

- accept the fact that they may not possess all the skills required to effectively manage;
- view the working relationship with business and management experts as complementary and not advisory;
- become aware of and sensitive to the adjustments an employee must go through when moving to a management position; and
- actively commit themselves to preparing potential managers for a management position.

MANAGEMENT PROGRESSION

The entry levels

Figure 1 illustrates how a technical trained person, in this case a nurse, moves through increasing levels of responsibility and the changes that occur as this happens. The point at which the individual crosses into management, the "threshold," is critical since it requires a major shift of expertise, philosophy, and skills. It is a threshold step for which many people are ill prepared. As the individual moves higher in management, there is a subtle but significant shift in

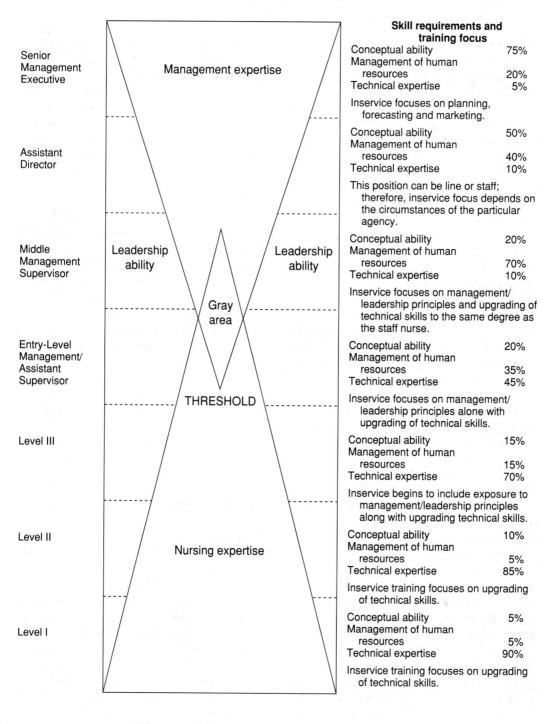

Figure 1. Management progression for nursing.

the kinds of skills required. The manager must be willing to acquire new skills as he or she progresses up the ladder.

Levels I and II of management progression are the entry levels of employment in the agency. The skill requirements at these levels focus on the ability to handle the technical aspects of the position. Continuing education and inservice at these levels would concentrate heavily on improving technical skills and would perhaps provide casual exposure to some supervisory techniques. Leadership ability is not particularly important at these levels.

Some nursing professionals would disagree with the previous statement, saying that nurses manage their patients. *Leadership* here refers to managing employees in such a way that they perform the way they are expected to. Often employee goals differ from manager goals, and it takes good leadership skills to get employees to meet goals other than their own.

When a nurse reaches Level III, he or she is beginning to approach the threshold of management. Level III is a difficult one, since it is at this point that the nurse begins to experience the transition from staff nurse to management. The expertise required now begins to take a different course. The ability to conceptualize, lead people, and manage human resources is a skill that is required. This is the time when it can be determined whether the nurse will be able to cross the threshold of management. More than a casual exposure to management principles should be offered at this level.

Crossing the threshold

The management threshold is crossed when the nurse becomes an assistant supervisor or supervisor. What does this mean? Fulmer defines a supervisor as "someone who is responsible for directing the perfor-

mance of one or more workers so that organizational goals are accomplished."[5] The supervisor is responsible for the performance of others as well as him- or herself.

As shown in Figure 1, the nurse enters a gray area at this point. He or she must have the technical skill to demonstrate techniques and assist other nurses, and the managerial skills to lead other nurses appropriately. In a sense, the nurse is neither a clinical nurse nor a manager. Sasser and Leonard note that being a first-level supervisor is a difficult and challenging job. This supervisor must be able to administer a unit and determine which daily tasks are the most important to accomplish. Even at the first level, the supervisor must be able to think and act in terms of the total system of operation. This includes defining and assigning priorities, planning and organizing, programming and coordinating the operating tasks of a department so that the objectives of both the department and the company as a whole are achieved. The first-level supervisor must also excel in interpersonal skills. Employees tend to be a heterogenous mix of individuals, "many of whom are not especially dedicated to their jobs, their departments, or their companies. Handling the variety of attitudes and values in the multiple generation worker base has become extremely difficult."[6]

PREPARING THE NURSE FOR MANAGERIAL RESPONSIBILITY

Supervisors can be the strongest or the weakest link in the management chain. It is from this level of management that future leaders are developed. It is to the organization's benefit to train and prepare nurses entering management.

As the nurse moves up the ladder, there is less emphasis on technical skills and more emphasis on human resource management skills and conceptual ability. The administrator is a catalyst for the organization. He or she should be able to see the overall goals of the organization, surround him- or herself with the people best able to realize these goals, and give them the incentive, guidance, and support needed to fulfill the goals.

The transition and adjustment to management can be eased by the way in which the nurse has been prepared to assume managerial responsibility. There are many methods of training available, including appointing the nurse as a team leader on special projects, assigning the nurse to help resolve special conceptual problems or to act in a temporary managerial capacity in the absence of the supervisor, and appointing the nurse to serve on special committees and trouble shoot for the supervisor.

The lower levels of employment are a time for the individual and the agency to look to the future. During performance evaluation sessions the individual's personal goals

> *The transition and adjustment to management can be eased by the way in which the nurse has been prepared to assume managerial responsibility.*

should be discussed. If he or she indicates a desire to move into management, special assignments such as those mentioned above can be valuable. Such assignments can be allotted to a variety of persons who show interests in and aptitude for management. Even if some of these persons do not become supervisors, their point of view will be broadened, which will be a benefit to the organization.

The first move into management is often the most challenging, but there will be new challenges as the manager moves higher. Careful planning should help the manager prepare for each new step.

REFERENCES

1. Riclefts, R. Back to School, More Executives Take Work Related Courses To Keep Up Advance. *Wall Street Journal,* March 3, 1980.
2. Drucker, P.F. Managing the Third Sector. *Wall Street Journal,* October 3, 1978 p. 26.
3. Stevens, B. Improving Nurses' Managerial Skills. *Nursing Outlook* 27 (December 1979).
4. Knollmueller, R. What Happened to the PHN Supervisor? *Nursing Outlook* 27 (October 1979).
5. Fulmer, R.M. Supervision: *Principles of Professional Management* (New York: Glencoe Press 1976).
6. Sasser, W.E., Jr. and Lenonard, F.S. Let First-Level Supervisors Do Their Job. *Harvard Business Review* 58 (March 1980).

Burnout in nursing administration

Patricia L. Harris, R.N., M.S.
Pulmonary Clinical Nurse Specialist
Department of Nursing Administration
St. Luke's Hospital
Phoenix, Arizona

*I*N THE LITERATURE focusing on the widespread problem of burnout among professionals today, nursing has been cited as one of the professions especially susceptible to the burnout syndrome. Burnout is described as a state of disillusionment, fatigue, and exhaustion relating to one's profession. This phenomenon has been cited as a strong factor in the exodus of nurses from the profession.

In past studies, researchers have focused on burnout in the staff nurse. Research has shown that burned-out staff nurses often seek administrative positions as a solution to their problems,[1] and it is common knowledge that entrance into administration is most often through middle-management positions, usually a head nurse or supervisory role.

A study was recently conducted to determine whether differences existed between levels of burnout expressed by middle managers of general care areas and critical care areas or between levels of middle management (head nurses and supervisors).

REVIEW OF THE LITERATURE

Burnout

Burnout, as defined by Veninga,[2] is a "debilitating psychological condition brought about by work frustrations that results in lowered productivity and morale." The individual suffering from burnout, according to Freudenberger[3] is "someone in a state of fatigue or frustration brought about by devotion to a cause, way of life, or relationship that failed to produce the expected rewards."

The signs and symptoms of burnout are many. Numerous authors describe physical

The study presented in this article was partially funded by grant monies from Sigma Theta Tau, Beta Upsilon Chapter of Arizona State University.

Nurs Admin Q, 1984, 8(3), 61–70
©1984 Aspen Publishers, Inc.

symptomatology: feelings of exhaustion and fatigue, frequent headaches, gastrointestinal upset, sleeplessness, and others.[4-6] The same researchers identified the feelings common to burnout: detachment of self from clients, dehumanization of clients, boredom, denial, depression, negative self-concept, and negative job attitudes. Those identified as burnout victims seem to be easily angered, suspicious, inflexible, and overconfident and seem to block progress and constructive change. The usually active contributor at meetings becomes silent. Administrators stop taking risks and begin to structure activities to promote their own job security.

Veninga[7] and Pines and Maslach[8] have correlated burnout with poor performance, absenteeism and high job turnover. They also found it associated with alcoholism, substance abuse, mental illness, marital conflict, and suicide.

The process of burnout has been summarized by many, including Maslach and Mendel. Maslach[9] reported that professionals lose positive feelings, sympathy, and respect for their clients. They become cynical and hold dehumanizing perceptions of clients and label them in derogatory ways. As Maslach notes, "A common response to burnout is to quit and get out, either by changing jobs, moving into administration, or even leaving the profession."[10]

Mendel[11] described a cycle of burnout affecting an organization. Burnout among staff elicits decreased effectiveness, decreased therapeutic interactions, and increased antitherapeutic behaviors. Consequently, the patients respond less and the personnel become increasingly frustrated. Staff members express frustration toward their peers and supervisors, thereby losing each others' support. This cycle continues, decreasing patient wellness and increasing organizational burnout.

In summary, burnout, as represented in the literature, is a syndrome of emotional exhaustion affecting a number of occupations and professions. It has specific characteristics and patterns of progression—enthusiasm, stagnation, frustration, and apathy. Because the profession of nursing has been identified as a target for burnout, nurses need to examine the syndrome of its implications for the quality of service received by their clients.

Middle management

The literature indicates that middle management can be defined as a position held within an administrative network placing the worker subordinate to the director level of the hierarchy and as supervisor to the workers of the organization.

Vash described middle managers as "go-betweens."[12] The go-betweens sometimes take a request to high management, lose and lose again when the denial is taken back to the subordinates, who understand why the request was refused and are angry at the middle manager for not getting approval. Forbes stated that middle managers are caught in the middle between two sets of people who can demand different kinds of behavior from the middle manager.[13] She estimated that approximately 15 percent of the middle manager's work time is engaged in resolving these conflicting demands.

The dilemma of the middle manager is apparent in health care settings. Vash stated that most middle managers in health care did not start out to be administrators.[14] She categorized most as "people-helper administrators" who often need acceptance from subordinates but who must make unpopular decisions. She described these middle managers as being especially vulnerable to criticism and, at times, to becoming approval driven.

> *"People-helper administrators" often need acceptance from subordinates but must make unpopular decisions. She described these middle managers as being especially vulnerable to criticism and, at times, to becoming approval driven.*

The literature on burnout in middle management identifies several influential factors. Patrick stated that employees in positions of leadership feel isolated due to the necessity of making unpopular decisions.[15] She also stated that administrators are susceptible to burnout due to the pressure to maintain an adequate support system for personnel who deliver health care services. Veninga reported that responsibility without authority is associated with middle-management positions.[16] He noticed that middle managers are often charged with responsibilities but have not been given the appropriate authority or resources to carry out these responsibilities successfully. Emener noted that the disillusionment these administrators experience gradually extinguishes the hopes and dreams they brought with them to the position.[17]

Burnout specific to middle management in nursing services differs little from the above description. Clark[18] noted that a major factor is the "reluctance of nurse administrators to legitimize their own right to health and well-being." She thought this might conflict with the emotional demands of the staff. She reported that frequently the administrators' personal identity and work identity may fuse and work may substitute for a satisfying personal life. To aggravate the situation, the manager feels that she is not fully accepted by either side.

Holloman stated that nurses are often not happy once they are promoted.[19] He reported that often nurses find administrative work more difficult than they had originally perceived. He noted that research has shown a strong inverse relationship between the desire of nurses to serve others and their feelings about supervising others. An example of burnout is provided by Dooley and Hauben's description of transition from staff nurse to head nurse.[20] They reported working longer hours in an attempt to rid themselves of imperfections and offering apologies for not completing promises, only to find themselves facing an angry staff.

The literature clearly indicates the problems of middle management in nursing in that it recognizes the stressors resulting from an individual's effort to combine two stressful occupations: administration and nursing. Such a combination suggests a susceptibility of the middle manager in nursing to burnout.

There seems to be a specific problem with the administration of critical care units. Cassem and Hackett reported that the nurses felt that administrators were unfamiliar with complexities of care and that supervision was lacking in the evening and night shifts.[21] They later found a competitive aggressiveness between the staff nurse and the head nurse.[22] Bilodeau believed that staff does not always see administration as competent and may not ask for advice or may ignore any advice given.[23] Staff members sometimes resent limits placed on their decision making. Bilodeau advocated weekly meetings between the head nurse and staff to discuss staff problems. She also recommended the selection of a head nurse who not only possesses clinical expertise and leadership capabilities, but also is able to exercise authority and tolerate her staff's reactions. Mann agreed with Bilodeau; furthermore, she specified that abilities in delegation, communication and problem identification were necessary managerial qualities in critical care areas.[24]

The literature indicates that stress can lead to burnout, that middle managers are in stressful situations and that burnout exists in middle management. The literature reports different characteristics and stressors of workers in areas of general nursing care and critical nursing care. Although the literature supports the occurrence of burnout in critical care nurses, no research has focused on burnout in general care nurses.

METHOD

Sample

The convenience sample for the study comprised hospital nurse managers in a southwestern state. Of the 84 nurses who received initial packets in the mail, 71 completed and returned the surveys, a return rate of 85 percent.

Instrument

The Maslach Burnout Inventory (MBI) was used with permission from Dr. Christina Maslach of University of California, Berkeley. The MBI holds respectable reliability and validity values. It consists of 25 statements of job-related feelings to which the subject is asked to respond on a six-point frequency scale and a seven-point intensity scale. The scores for each of these statements were categorized into four mutually exclusive subscales: Emotional Exhaustion, Personal Accomplishment, Depersonalization and Personal Involvement. The scores for each subscale were averaged, leaving one mean score for each subscale, per subject, for each dimension: frequency and intensity. Higher scores for Emotional Exhaustion, Depersonalization and Personal Involve-

ment correspond to higher degrees of burnout, and lower scores on Personal Accomplishment correspond to higher degrees of burnout.

The four subscales measure different feelings associated with burnout. The Emotional Exhaustion subscale contains statements about fatigue, stress and exhaustion. The Personal Accomplishment subscale examines feelings of self-confidence, energy and exhilaration. The Depersonalization subscale concerns callous behavior toward recipients, emotional detachment and noncaring attitudes. The last subscale, Personal Involvement, measures the degree to which the respondent feels similar to or relates to the recipient's problems.

Data analysis

The data obtained using the MBI were treated as interval data. As some subjects reported supervising areas of both critical and general care, three independent groups—critical, general, and mixed care— were statistically examined using one-way analysis of variance for independent samples. The subjects were then reclassified into two categories: head nurses and supervisors, regardless of area type. A t test for independent samples was used for analysis. The demographic data were selectively examined using Pearson product-moment correlations.

Since the sample was not randomly drawn, the results cannot be generalized to all middle managers in nursing.

RESULTS AND DISCUSSION

Sample characteristics

The demographic questionnaire provided the following data. The basic nursing educational preparation for the sample of

71 nurses was associate degree (ADN), 15; diploma, 34, and baccalaureate degree (BS), 22. The distribution for the highest degrees held was ADN, 9; diploma, 21; BS, 34 and master's degree, 7. The sex distribution was 70 females, 1 male. The mean age was 38.7 years. There were 55 head nurses and 16 supervisors (department heads and associate directors of nursing were included in this category); 32 general care unit managers, 23 critical care managers, and 16 managers of mixed areas. The mean number of years the total group of managers occupied their present positions was 3.2, and the mean years in nursing was 13.5. Of the sample, 72 percent maintained 24-hour responsibility for their areas. The mean number of subordinates was 37.3. The average number of hours worked per week was 44.9. The distribution of these hours was mean hours spent with patients, 15.4; with subordinates, 15.6; with superiors, 5.2; in the office, 9.0; in meetings, 8.0; in education, 5.7. Previous work experience was 22.5 percent, general care staff nurses for more than 3 years; 16.9 percent, critical care staff nurses for more than 3 years; 33.8 percent, managers of general care areas for more than 3 years; 11.2 percent, managers of critical care areas for more than 3 years; 1.4 percent, general care staff nurses for less than 3 years; and 14 percent, backgrounds containing various experiences, not amendable to categorization.

Burnout in sample

Mean scores were computed for frequency and intensity dimensions on the MBI using the Emotional Exhaustion, Personal Accomplishment, Depersonalization and Personal Involvement subscales. These mean scores were compared with the means of the total sample reported by Maslach and Jackson.[25] (See Table 1.) All means revealed a level of burnout comparable to Maslach's norms.

Correlation with demographic variables

Pearson product-moment correlations were performed on demographic variables. These variables were found to correlate significantly with burnout at the .05 level. These variables were the subjects' job titles which had been arranged in a hierarchy, the number of hours per week spent with subordinates and the total number of hours worked per week.

The significant, negative correlation between the job title and the frequency dimension of the Personal Involvement subscale means that the higher the level of management, the less frequently the individual was personally overinvolved with subordinates. These data support Maslach's contention that advancement into administration can be effective as an escape from burnout.[26] Forbes also discussed the idea that first-line supervisors, such as head nurses, experience more stress than do administrators at higher levels.[27] She suggested that the decreased amounts of power and autonomy, along with the need to juggle peers, subordinates and supervisors, is central to the difficulties these first-line managers face daily.

The two remaining significant findings can be interpreted as complementing each

She suggested that the decreased amounts of power and autonomy, along with the need to juggle peers, subordinates and supervisors, is central to the difficulties these first-line managers face daily.

Table 1. Mean sample scores compared with Maslach's normative data[1]

	Sample (n = 71)		Maslach and Jackson (n = 925)	
	M	*SD*	*M*	*SD*
Subscale scores				
Emotional Exhaustion				
Frequency	2.50	.09	2.71	1.31
Intensity	3.32	.35	3.33	1.51
Depersonalization				
Frequency	1.30	.96	1.57	1.17
Intensity	1.39	.33	2.13	1.52
Personal Involvement				
Frequency	2.43	1.14	2.29	1.28
Intensity	3.32	1.34	None reported	
Personal Accomplishment				
Frequency	4.80	.78	4.23	1.04
Intensity	5.48	.71	5.02	1.12

[1]Maslach, C. Personal communication, 2 November 1980.

other: First, the negative correlation between the number of hours spent with subordinates and the frequency dimension of the Personal Involvement subscale can be interpreted to mean that the lower the number of hours spent with subordinates, the more frequently guilt feelings associated with such interactions emerged. Second, the positive correlation between the number of hours spent with subordinates and the scores in the Personal Accomplishment subscale means that the lower the number of hours spent with subordinates, the lower the sense of personal effectiveness as a manger and vice versa.

These findings are congruent with Stevens's discussion of the difficulties that head nurses frequently face.[28] She described a nurse-manager who is frustrated with the administration component of her role, and wishes to continue her commitment to expert clinical skills by interacting and working side by side with staff more hours than allowed her by her job responsibilities. As the head nurse's office is usually geographically close to the patient care area, she is acutely aware of unit activity, and the limited amount of time available to spend out in the area with her subordinates can be a constant frustration for her as she performs her administrative duties.

The positive correlation between the number of hours worked per week and the intensity dimension of the Personal Accomplishment subscale is difficult to interpret in light of the controversy in the burnout literature on this point. This correlation implies that a higher number of hours worked per week leads to more intense feelings of effectiveness as a manager. Freudenberger describes the burned-out individual as one who works more hours and accomplishes less.[29] However, Pines and Maslach reported that long work hours correlated with stress and negative staff attitudes only when these long hours involved continuous, direct care with clients.[30]

The data from the study do not reflect continuous direct care as they are associated with managers. As Freudenberger has not reported any studies about the effects of long working hours on the degree of burnout and Pines and Maslach have not used middle managers as subjects for their extensive investigation of burnout, the inferences made from the study's data concerning long hours cannot be supported by the literature. Some ideas concerning the finding that longer work hours contribute to feelings of personal effectiveness have been derived by looking at what tasks act as job satisfiers for managers. Perhaps a manager works longer hours than expected by administration in order to accomplish tasks that are personal satisfiers, such as professional reading, staff-manager interactions that are not mandated, patient-oriented interactions, educational programs, and other job-related, self-enrichment activities.

Differences in unit type

The differences between the mean MBI scores of the critical care, general care, and mixed area managers were analyzed using one-way analysis of variance. None of the F values reached significance at the .05 level, indicating no significant differences between these groups.

Differences between head nurses and supervisors

For further analysis, the sample was reclassified into two groups irrespective of unit type: those employed as head nurses or assistant head nurses, and those who are supervisors of areas or associate/assistant directors of nursing.

In two of the four subscales of the MBI (Depersonalization and Personal Involvement), a t test for independent samples revealed a significant difference between the mean scores. (See Table 2.) The difference between the mean scores of feelings of depersonalization (frequency) was significant at the .01 level, and the differences between personal involvement (frequency) with recipients was significant at the .001 level. None of the mean intensity scores was significantly different.

The Depersonalization subscale reflects feelings about treating recipients as objects and becoming less emotionally involved with people in the work area. It has been previously stated that entry into management in nursing is usually accomplished by progressing through the ranks, that is, staff nurse to assistant head nurse to head nurse. According to Edelwich and Brodsky, feelings of alienation between the former peers and the managers who "rise from the ranks" are common.[31] As these feelings of alienation progress, head nurses respond with feelings of isolation, in a process described by Patrick.[32] After feeling isolated, the head nurse begins to depersonalize staff, and feelings associated with burnout emerge.

The group of head nurses also had high mean scores in the frequency dimension of the Personal Involvement subscale. This finding can be explained by the geographic location of the head nurse, as opposed to that of the higher level supervisor. Because the head nurse is usually situated on the unit,

Table 2. Comparison of mean MBI scores of head nurses and supervisors

	Head nurse (n = 55)		Supervisor (n = 16)			
	M	*SD*	*M*	*SD*	*t*	*P*
Subscale scores						
Emotional Exhaustion						
Frequency	2.56	1.11	2.31	1.02	0.83	0.42
Intensity	3.78	1.38	−3.99	1.25	−0.60	0.55
Depersonalization						
Frequency	1.40	1.05	0.95	0.42	2.55	0.01*
Intensity	1.96	1.41	1.65	1.00	1.00	0.33
Personal Involvement						
Frequency	2.59	1.21	1.85	0.60	3.35	0.002*
Intensity	3.38	1.45	3.15	0.83	0.81	0.42
Personal Accomplishment						
Frequency	4.80	0.79	4.80	0.77	−0.006	0.99
Intensity	5.40	0.67	5.75	0.80	−1.59	0.13

*Significant finding.

she is more aware than the supervisor of patient and staff problems. She has increased accessibility to that information. The supervisor is generally located in an office within the nursing administration department and spends a substantial amount of time in meetings and fulfilling office tasks. The supervisor only occasionally makes rounds and is exposed to patient and staff problems, usually when the head nurse brings such issues to the attention of the supervisor. In contrast, continuous geographic exposure to unit operations may enhance the head nurses' feelings of personal involvement with staff and patients on the unit.

Conclusions

The study results support the presence of the phenomenon of burnout in management roles. The data show that although higher level management in nursing is less burned-out than the staff level, management is, nevertheless, suffering from burnout. Furthermore, the type of units that one manages does not affect the level of burnout.

• • •

The phenomenon of burnout has been described as a state of disillusionment, fatigue, and exhaustion relating to one's profession. Burnout has been cited as a strong factor in the exodus of nurses from the profession. The study revealed some factors in burnout in nurse middle managers, but it may be important to examine the effect that a burned-out manager can have on a group of staff nurses.

The results of the study illustrate the levels of burnout in a small sample of nurse middle managers. The concept of decreasing levels of burnout as the distance from patient care increases is one proposed by Maslach, and is supported by the study. The susceptibility to burnout among those who hold positions of authority needs more investigation. If aspects of management contribute to the phenomenon of burnout in staff, then thorough investigation and data-based interventions are necessary in order to combat the present exodus of nurses from employment.

REFERENCES

1. Maslach, C. The Burnout Syndrome and Patient Care. In *Stress and Survival: The Emotional Realities of Life-Threatening Illness,* ed. by C.A. Garfield. (St. Louis: Mosby, 1979.)
2. Veninga, R. Administrator Burnout—Causes and Cures. *Hospital Progress* 60, no. 2 (1979):45
3. Freudenberger, H.J. *Burnout* (Garden City, N.Y.: Anchor Press, 1980) p. 1.
4. Freudenberger, H.J. Burnout: The Organizational Menace. *Training and Development Journal* 31, no. 7 (1977): 26-27.
5. Pines, A., and C. Maslach. Characteristics of Staff Burnout in Mental Health Settings. *Hospital and Community Psychiatry* 29, no. 4 (1978): 233-37.
6. Veningna, Administrator Burnout—Causes and Cures, 45-52.
7. Ibid.
8. Pines and Maslach, Characteristics of Staff Burnout, 233-37.
9. Maslach, C. Job Burnout: How People Cope. *Public Welfare* 36, no. 2 (1978): 56-58.
10. Maslach, The Burnout Syndrome and Patient Care, p. 113.
11. Mendel, W.M. Staff Burnout: Diagnosis, Treatment, and Prevention. In *New Directions for Mental Health Services,* vol. 2, ed. B.F. Riess. (New York: Grune & Stratton, 1979.)
12. Vash, C.L. *The Burnt-out Administrator.* (New York: Springer, 1980) p. 38.
13. Forbes, R. *Corporate Stress.* (Garden City, N.Y.: Doubleday) 1979.
14. Vash, *The Burnt-out Administrator,* p. 48.
15. Patrick, P.K. Burnout: Job Hazard for Health Workers. *Hospital* 53, no. 22 (1979):87-90.
16. Veninga, Administrator Burnout—Causes and Cures, 45-52.
17. Emener, W.G., Jr. Professional Burnout: Rehabilitation's Hidden Handicap. *Journal of Rehabilitation* 45, no. 1 (1979): 55-58.
18. Clark, C.C. Burnout: Assessment & Intervention. *Journal of Nursing Administration* 10, no. 9 (1980):39.
19. Holloman, C. The Nurse Enters Management. *Supervisor Nurse* 2, no. 4 (1971): 54-67.
20. Dooley, S.L., and J. Hauben, From Staff Nurse to Head Nurse: A Trying Transition. *Journal of Nursing Administration* 9, no. 4 (1979): 4-7.
21. Cassem, N.H., and T. Hackett, Sources of Tension for the CCU Nurse. *American Journal of Nursing* 72, no. 8 (1972): 1426-30.
22. Cassem, N.H. and T. Hackett, Stress on the Nurse in the Intensive Care Unit and the Coronary Care Unit. *Heart and Lung* 4 (March-April 1975): 252-59.
23. Bilodeau, C.B. The Nurse and Her Reactions to Critical Care Nursing. *Heart and Lung* 2 (May-June 1973): 358-63.
24. Mann, J.K. Nursing Leadership in the Critical Care Setting. *Nursing Clinics of North America* 13, no. 1 (1978): 131-38.
25. Maslach, C., and S.E. Jackson, The Measurement of Experienced Burnout. *Journal of Occupational Behavior* 2, no. 2 (1981): 99-113.
26. Maslach, C. Burned-out. *Human Behavior* 5, no. 9 (1976): 18-22.
27. Forbes, *Corporate Stress.*
28. Stevens, B.J. *Firstline Patient Care Management* (Wakefield, Mass.: Contemporary Publishing, 1976.)
29. Freudenberger, Burnout: The Organizational Menace, 26-27.
30. Pines and Maslach, Characteristics of Staff Burnout, 233-37.
31. Edelwich, J., and A. Brodsky, *Burn-out* (New York: Human Sciences Press, 1980) p. 105.
32. Patrick, Burnout: Job Hazard for Health Workers, 87-90.

Is it lonely at the top?

E. Ann Hillestad, R.N., Ph.D.
Assistant Professor
School of Nursing
University of Texas Health Science Center
San Antonio, Texas

ARE NURSING service administrators professionally lonely? If they are, what difference does it make? Furthermore, what can be done about it?

Questions such as these prompted an investigation of professional loneliness and supportive relationships among nursing service administrators. The findings warrant consideration not only by nursing service administrators themselves but by other persons interested in and committed to the development of professional nursing leadership in health care institutions.

Are nursing service administrators professionally lonely? In Texas, 135 nursing administrators were asked whether they were professionally lonely. In addition, each administrator was asked to complete a professional-loneliness questionnaire and an instrument assessing professionally supportive relationships. Of the 89 nursing service administrators responding to the question, 42 (47 percent) reported that they were professionally lonely. Table 1 shows the average professional-loneliness scores taken from the loneliness questionnaires of those administrators who responded yes and those administrators who responded no. To determine whether these means were significantly different, a two-sample t test was conducted. It yielded a t ratio of 7.238 ($p < .001$).

Table 2 shows the average supportive-relationship scores by reported professional loneliness. Statistical analysis yielded a t ratio of 3.899 ($p < .001$). Hence, those administrators who reported being lonely had higher average loneliness scores and lower average supportive-relationship scores than those administrators who did not report professional loneliness.

To understand the significance of these findings, the concept of loneliness must be understood. This understanding will clarify why professional loneliness among nursing service administrators warrants attention.

Nurs Admin Q, 1984, 8(3), 1–13
©1984 Aspen Publishers, Inc.

Table 1. Professional loneliness by reported professional loneliness

Professionally lonely?	Mean	Standard error	Sample size
Yes	2.258	.070	42
No	1.645	.050	47

PROFESSIONAL LONELINESS

Loneliness as a phenomenon is receiving increased emphasis. Two major books have been published on loneliness since 1980: *The Anatomy of Loneliness*[1] and *Loneliness: A Sourcebook of Current Research, Theory, and Therapy.*[2] In spite of this increased emphasis, a definitive theoretical model of loneliness has yet to be developed.

Authors through the years have commented on the dearth of theory related to loneliness. In 1959 Fromm-Reichmann stated that loneliness is one of the "least satisfactorily conceptualized phenomena, not even mentioned in most psychiatric textbooks."[3] Leiderman attributed his lack of success in researching loneliness in the literature to the "absence of an adequate theoretical model."[4] Russell concludes his chapter in the sourcebook on loneliness, mentioned above, by saying that "for our understanding to progress, we need to develop theoretical models of loneliness."[5]

Table 2. Average supportive-relationship scores by reported professional loneliness

Professionally lonely?	Mean	Standard error	Sample size
Yes	2.395	.081	42
No	3.007	.070	47

In spite of the lack of theory, a number of authors have explored the concept. One of the earliest was Sullivan. He discusses loneliness as an outcome of childhood situations in which a child experiences rejection. In response, the child builds defenses whose patterns become automatic and continue into adulthood. These responses include doing whatever is effective in gaining the attention of and contact with others regardless of its appropriateness. An adult responding similarly cannot be expected to become involved in activities whose pursuit brings criticism or whose outcomes are uncertain, for fear of bringing about loneliness again.[6]

Peplau describes loneliness in the following terms:

> Often loneliness is not felt; instead the person has a feeling of unexplained dread, of desperation, or of extreme restlessness. These feelings are so intense, so unbearable, that automatic actions are precipitated. Although he is not aware that loneliness is one of the feelings which govern him, his automatic responses recur and become patterns of living. . . .[7]

Peplau regards the opposite of loneliness, closeness and relatedness to people, as so intense a need that the lonely person has an inclination toward hero worship, the selection of one person on whom to be dependent. She sees the need to feel and to know the active interest of mature persons and the attentive participation of these persons in the activities of the lonely person as vitally important.

In her later years, as a result of her experiences with people, Fromm-Reichmann became increasingly interested in loneliness. She understood loneliness as an especially unpopular phenomenon in a group-conscious culture, something experienced as so frightening and so uncanny that people are unwilling to discuss it. She observed that "in this culture, people can come to a valid self-orientation, or even awareness of themselves, only in terms of their actual overt relationships with each other."[8] She believed that the lonely individual takes whatever action is necessary to escape from his or her lonely state.

Moustakas characterized loneliness as the separation of self from others. He described the lonely person as deeply suspicious, perceiving even tangential remarks as criticism. Lonely persons fear failure in everything that is undertaken and strive constantly to win the praise and approval of others. When devices and strategies do not work, they respond with aggression or give up.[9]

Weigert saw loneliness and trust as being in dialectic opposition to each other. When a trusting relationship is available, a person can risk failure and invest energy in decision making and fulfilling individual potential.[10]

According to Mannin, the most acute kind of loneliness is "the lack of contact with one's own kind, or the feeling of being isolated in one's ideas."[11] This kind of loneliness is imposed by force of circumstance and has nothing to do with physical isolation but rather with mental and emotional isolation.

Two types of loneliness were described by Weiss: (1) the loneliness of emotional isolation secondary to the loss of a close emotional attachment and (2) the loneliness of social isolation secondary to the loss of engagement with peers.[12] Lynch also viewed loneliness as a social isolation whose critical factor is the way one responds to and interacts with one's fellow humans. In order to prevent or overcome loneliness, he recommends dialogue—reciprocal communication involving the sharing of thoughts, ideas, ideals, hopes and feelings, and characterized by reciprocity, spontaneity and aliveness. A major precondition for dialogue is trust, which involves both commitment and predictability.[13]

In order to prevent or overcome loneliness, he recommends dialogue—reciprocal communication involving the sharing of thoughts, ideas, ideals, hopes and feelings, and characterized by reciprocity, spontaneity and aliveness.

Hartog details certain imperatives (i.e., basic needs and drives) responsible for different kinds of loneliness. He speaks of a biological drive for gregariousness; a neurological imperative requiring an optimal range of sensory input satisfied only by human interaction; a social imperative that implies that social isolation leads to problems of adaptation, safety, achievement, and the fulfillment of physical needs; and a cognitive imperative to be understood and to understand. He says that loneliness is counteracted by reliance on the support provided by the census of others. Loneliness is described as tolerable for a defined period of time but intolerable to the individual who sees no end in sight.[14]

Audy regards loneliness as being with people who "live in a different world,"[15] with whom no interests are shared. Mijuskovic recognizes "an opposite to loneliness and that is togetherness with an interest; or pursuing a 'cause'; or enjoying the proximity of intimate friends."[16]

Russell, the principal developer of the UCLA Loneliness Scale (used in the study reported here to assess loneliness), believes that loneliness is a disturbance in social relationships that is severely distressing. He views all types of loneliness as the same phenomenon, which varies only in degree of intensity.[17]

In summary, in the literature loneliness is generally viewed as an affective experience that results from a disturbance in an individual's relationships with others. It is universally discerned as unpleasant. In the study discussed here, loneliness was conceptualized as a continuum with isolation at one extreme (greater loneliness) and intimacy at the other (lesser loneliness) and as varying in degree as isolation and intimacy vary. The experience of loneliness is also viewed as negative and undesirable; therefore, lonely individuals will seek to alleviate it either consciously or unconsciously. Their efforts will be directed toward not engaging in activities they believe will result in loneliness (e.g., innovation, risk taking and conflict) or toward escape from the circumstances they believe responsible for their loneliness. These are the activities that make loneliness significant to nursing service administrators.

SUPPORTIVE RELATIONSHIPS

Nursing service administrators were also asked to respond to a number of incidents developed and tested by the investigator that assessed the supportive relationships available to the administrators in their work settings. The incidents consisted of common problems or decisions that nursing service administrators face; they were asked to indicate how supportive their superior, peers, subordinates or others in their hospital settings would be in regard to the specific incidents. Supportive relationships were defined as associations or connections with persons working for the same hospital in which there is a mutual upholding, aiding or sustaining. Upholding, aiding or sustaining were characterized as sharing values, goals, concerns, problems and feelings.

A number of authors have spoken of supportive relationships. Most of them, however, have not been concerned specifically with the work place but have dealt with social support available to persons from any number of sources, including work. Kaplan, Cassel, and Gore observed that most of the studies dealing with social support either implicitly or explicitly define it as (1) the meeting or gratification of a person's basic social needs (i.e., approval, esteem, succor) through social interaction with others; or (2) the relative presence or absence of support supplies (i.e., significant others and opportunities for interaction).[18] They suggested that social support could be strengthened by the development of supportive interpersonal relationships on the job.

Cobb conceived social support to be information belonging to one or more of the following three classes: (1) information leading one to believe one is cared for and loved; (2) information leading one to believe one is esteemed and valued; (3) information leading one to believe one belongs to a network of communication and mutual obligation.[19] Cobb postulated that social support facilitates coping with crisis and adaptation to change as life progresses. Support emanates from the mother, then from other members of the family and, finally, from peers at work and in the community.

Norbeck proposed that the need for social support is a function of the properties of the person and of the situation. Influential properties in the person include individual needs, abilities and orientations, as well as demographic variables such as age, sex, marital status, religion and culture. She sees the sources of support expanding with age while the gross amount available decreases. Specifically, peer support reaches a peak in adolescence and continues to a lesser degree in adulthood, when "role-related support is sought from work associates, other parents, etc."[20] The properties of the situation that Norbeck identifies include role demands, resources and stressors. She points out that support is needed on a day-to-day basis and not spasmodically if it is to promote individual well-being and adequate role performance.

Barnett recognized the significance of work roles to the individual. He observed that a person derives assumptions about self from a number of sources, including work. Data provided by these sources influence the sense of self and the operations that stem from it.[21]

Cohen discusses the importance of work in peoples' lives. He states that individuals tend to see themselves as others see them and gauge whether they are measuring up; work is one arena in which this occurs.[22]

Sadler and Johnson also point out that it is through the social environment, which provides organized relationships such as those occurring at work, that the terms of memberships, roles and destiny are established. If the perception is one of not belonging, self-awareness tells one that one is "an outcast, an outsider, a loner, an oddball, or a disconnected individual."[23]

Bowlby pointed out that research indicates that people of all ages are able to function most effectively when they are confident that someone will come to their aid should problems occur. He perceives the healthy person as one who can recognize the suitable persons willing and capable of providing support and then can collaborate with them in reciprocal relationships.[24]

Sheldon linked social involvement with commitment to the organization and its goals.[25] Hill concurred when he linked the relationship between an employee and the social reality of the work place. He believes it influences whether the employee stays, leaves, is absent, offends company policy or is injured.[26] Gosling surmises that part of the astronauts' self-confidence comes from their interaction with fellow crew members and ground control, all of whom are judged to be effective, winning and

behaving appropriately to the task at hand.[27]

In summary, social support is viewed as positive. It is seen as promoting coping, adaptation and effectiveness and as involving interactions characterized by trust and reciprocity. The abilities to cope, adapt and interact effectively are necessary attributes of nursing service administrators; without these abilities, role performance is negatively affected.

THE ROLE OF THE ADMINISTRATOR

The role of the nursing service administrator has always been large. Erickson reviewed the role from the late 1800s to the present and observed that the administrator was initially expected to be clinician, teacher and supervisor. In the 1920s the role continued to be a dual one involving responsibility for service and education. Erickson describes the role in the following terms: "The superintendent of nurses was a busy, worried person, carrying an enormous responsibility. If anything went wrong in nursing service, the penalty was severe and might even include the death of a patient."[28] This pattern did not change through the 1930s and the 1940s, and not until the 1950s was a distinction made between education and service and the importance of skilled administration to the provision of nursing care identified.

In the 1960s the focus became leadership as it relates to the role of the nursing service administrator. The literature pointed out the need for and lack of leadership skills on the part of nursing service administrators and the discrepancy in expectations regarding the role among hospital administrators, physicians and nursing administrators themselves.

Arndt and Laeger published a study of nursing service administrators in California. The study showed that nursing administrators experienced a high level of stress. They are expected to assume a variety of roles that are often antagonistic and whose demands are unpredictable and hard to control. Many administrators reported a lack of clarity about what is expected of them and confusion about what their roles are.[29]

Among the responsibilities of nursing administrators is the meeting of patients' needs for nursing service. It is often difficult to fulfill this responsibility, however, while supporting and meeting the needs of the nursing staff at the same time.[30] The nature of the work—24-hour responsibility, physical aspects and unpredictability—and the nature of the workers—professional and nonprofessional and primarily women—are often in conflict. Attempting to fulfill responsibilities to patients often results in conflict with and isolation from the nursing staff.

Managers both in nursing and elsewhere can be characterized as being the "persons in the middle." Greenwood justifies his use of this phrase by pointing out that managers are expected to interface with, and mediate, the demands of their superiors and their subordinates, each group and each individual having their own personal goals and desires.[31] Myrtle and Glowgow apply the phrase specifically to nursing service administrators. They observe that, as roles change and become less traditional and functional lines blur because of expansion of the team concept and shared responsibility and authority, the nursing service administrator is forced to be the "person in the middle."[32]

Beyers, in discussing future leadership in nursing, writes that "isolation occurs when people fail to develop supportive relationships in their jobs"[33] and offers as a solution the development of constructive support systems. Shores states that one of the reasons many administrators and many supervisors are demanding leadership development is to have an opportunity to explore problems and situations within their areas of responsibility.[34]

Power and loneliness are related. Power isolates an individual from other people and reduces opportunities for intimacy: Loneliness results. The problem was summed up by Darby after she studied the role of a regional nursing officer in England. Darby writes: "But where does an R.N.O. turn to when the going gets really tough, and there seems no way out of a problem? Life at the top can be lonely."[35]

> *Power and loneliness are related. Power isolates an individual from other people and reduces opportunities for intimacy: Loneliness results.*

Nursing service administrators are, therefore, executives with many, often conflicting, responsibilities. The nature of the role is such that they cannot be totally responsive to the needs of their subordinates, nor can they be primarily business oriented as are their peers and superiors. The result is isolation from both of these groups, as well as the isolation that is a byproduct of all roles involving the power to make consequential decisions. Isolation is a hallmark of the role.

THE STUDY

Theoretical framework

Based on the review of the literature, the following theoretical framework underpinned this study:

1. Loneliness is an affective state that results when individuals lack intimate relationships and are isolated

from others with whom to share important aspects of their lives.

2. Supportive relationships involve interaction with others, which is characterized by trust and mutual sharing of goals, values, concerns, problems, and feelings.

3. Loneliness and the presence of supportive relationships are inversely related (i.e., an increase in one is associated with a decrease in the other).

4. The nature of the role of the nursing service administrator is such that supportive relationships associated with it may be lacking. In those instances where there is this lack, nursing service administrators can be expected to be professionally lonely.

Study design

The study design was ex post facto/correlational in nature; that is, the research was conducted after the variations in the presence of supportive relationships had occurred. The variables were not manipulated by the investigator. The report is also a descriptive correlational study intending to describe an existing relationship rather than to infer a cause-and-effect relationship.

The population for the study consisted of administrators of nursing service in the 474 hospitals having more than 25 beds and licensed by the Texas State Department of Health. The sample consisted of 94 nursing service administrators, or 20 percent of the population. Sampling procedures considered both geographic location and hospital size and were random within these specifications.

Instrument packets consisting of a demographic questionnaire, two versions of the UCLA Loneliness Scale, and the supportive-relationship instrument were mailed to each nursing administrator who agreed by telephone to participate in the study. Samples of questions from the Loneliness Scales and one of the eight incidents in the supportive-relationship instrument are shown in Figure 1. Of the packets sent out, 80 were completed and returned.

Professional loneliness was assessed by a modified version of the UCLA Loneliness Scale. The scale was modified by adding phrases that directed the respondents' attention to the work setting. An unmodified version of the work scale was used to assess personal loneliness. Reliability and validity had been established by the developers of the scale and were supported by data obtained in this study.

Supportive relationships were assessed by an instrument in which the nursing administrator was asked to indicate how supportive each of four possible support sources would be relative to eight incidents. The instrument was developed by the investigator; reliability and validity studies were done prior to its use. These studies were inconclusive but evidential that reliability and validity were present. Additional supportive evidence was gained in this investigation.

Hypothesis and questions

A hypothesis and ten questions or sets of questions were used as the basis for data analysis:

Hypothesis: Nursing service administrators who indicate a greater presence of supportive relationships within the institutions in which they are employed will experience less professional loneliness in fulfilling their roles than nursing service administrators who indicate a lesser presence of supportive relationships.

1. Among nursing service administrators, is there a relationship between professional and personal loneliness?

Professional Loneliness

Indicate how often each of the statements below is *descriptive of you as a nursing administrator*. Circle one letter for each statement:

O indicates "I *often* feel this way."
S indicates "I *sometimes* feel this way."
R indicates "I *rarely* feel this way."
N indicates "I *never* feel this way."

1. I am in tune with the people around me in this hospital.	O	S	R	N
2. I lack professional companionship at work.	O	S	R	N
3. There is no one I can turn to on the job.	O	S	R	N
4. I do not feel alone in my job.	O	S	R	N

Personal Loneliness

Indicate how often each of the statements below is *descriptive of you as a person*. (Instructions were repeated as above.)

1. I am in tune with people around me.	O	S	R	N
2. I lack companionship.	O	S	R	N
3. There is no one I can turn to.	O	S	R	N
4. I do not feel alone.	O	S	R	N

Supportive Relationships

The director of the laboratory has decided that one way he can stay within his budget is to discontinue the drawing of blood by lab personnel after 7:00 p.m. It is true that there are not many requests for blood drawing from 7:00 p.m. until 7:00 a.m. and the burden on the nursing staff would not be great. You, however, do not think it is appropriate for nurses to draw blood; you think they ought to be devoting their time to direct patient care, care planning or staff development activities. In your efforts to make nursing in your hospital more patient oriented and less task oriented, this seems a step backward. To what extent will the following persons be *sympathetic to the nature of your concern?*

	Minimum	*Moderate*	*Considerable*	*Maximum*
Your superior	_____	_____	_____	_____
A peer	_____	_____	_____	_____
A subordinate	_____	_____	_____	_____
Someone else who works for the hospital	_____	_____	_____	_____

Figure 1. Sample questions from the instrument packet. Reprinted from Dan Russell, Letitia A. Peplau, and Carolyn E. Cutrona, "The Revised UCLA Loneliness Scale: Concurrent and Discriminant Validity Evidence," *Journal of Personality and Social Psychology,* no. 39, pp. 472–480, with permission from the American Psychological Association, © 1980.

2. Does having an associate or assistant affect the presence of supportive relationships or professional loneliness?

3. If the associate or assistant has the same educational background as that of the nursing service administrator, is the presence of supportive relationships greater or professional loneliness less?

4. Does hospital size affect the presence of supportive relationships or professional loneliness?

5. Does the age of the nursing administrator influence the presence of supportive relationships or professional loneliness?

6. Does the educational background of the nursing administrator influence the pres-

ence of supportive relationships or professional loneliness?

7. Does the length of time employed as a nursing service administrator affect the presence of supportive relationships or professional loneliness?

8. Does the sex of the nursing administrator influence the presence of supportive relationships or professional loneliness?

9. Do nursing administrators report that they are professionally lonely?

10. Do nursing service administrators indicate that there are sources of support in the hospital in which they work?

Findings

The hypothesis and each question were examined separately. Significant relationships were found between professional loneliness and supportive relationships and between professional and personal loneliness. The average supportive-relationships scores differed significantly between nursing administrators whose associates or assistants had attained the same or different educational levels than the administrator. Those whose associates had attained different educational levels had a higher average supportive-relationships score.

The average supportive-relationship scores differed significantly (<.05) between nursing administrators less than 50 years of age and those 50 years of age and older and between those administrators with 8 or less years of service and those with more than 8 years. Older administrators with greater lengths of service had higher average supportive-relationship scores. The average professional-loneliness scores differed significantly (<.05) between the two age groups of nursing administrators. The younger group had higher average professional-loneliness scores. Significant differ-

ences were not found in relationship to the other variables.

From among all nursing service administrators, 47 percent reported that they were professionally lonely. The average scores between the groups reporting and not reporting loneliness differed significantly (<.001).

Average supportive-relationship scores by amount of support reported are shown in Table 3. An analysis of variance was used to test whether or not there was a significant difference in the average scores by response; it yielded an F ratio of 9.858 (<.001). Hence, in these data, there is a significant difference in average supportive-relationships scores by reported adequacy of support.

Discussion

Since loneliness is defined as a negative affective state experienced by an individual as being apart from other people, as mental and emotional isolation, and as the feeling of being isolated in one's ideas, persons who are professionally lonely experience these same feelings in relationship to their work life. These negative

Table 3. Supportive-relationship score by reported supportive relationships

Reported supportive relationships	Mean	Standard error	Sample size
All wanted	3.306	.137	9
Mostly adequate	2.926	.064	54
Less than would like	2.444	.097	26
Inadequate	2.712	.121	4

feelings result in a reduced ability to fulfill role expectations and, hence, have a direct impact on the profession and on health care.

The flavor of what it means to be professionally lonely may perhaps be best illustrated by noting a few of the comments made by the nursing administrators who participated in the study:

> Administration . . . is more interested in the hospital political arena and is prone to say "That, my dear, is your problem. Take care of it the best way you can."

> The higher one "rises" in the organization, the lonelier the position. There are feelings that one cannot discuss even with close friends.

> Not being able to discuss administrative problems with a peer is very frustrating.

> It always seems as though "superiors" . . . can't be used as "sounding boards" or "think times" [sic] because it always comes back to haunt, either in evaluations or in conversations—(comes back negative!!).

> Some days I win, some I lose. Again shifts, depending on the issues. I always try and be ready to answer both sides of the question and be prepared. Every nursing director feels the good and the bad. The good is coming more often I believe.

> Thanks for asking!

These nursing administrators lack supportive relationships and experience professional loneliness. Their comments illustrate this. The lack of supportive relationships stems from the differences in focus between nursing administrators and other hospital administrators. According to Arndt and Huckabay, the latter are business oriented while the nursing administrators are concerned primarily with patient care needs.[36] When the nursing administrators attempt to gain autonomy in order to promote pa-

tient care, a power struggle and peer conflict often result.[37]

In this study, professional and personal loneliness were closely related. The data did not indicate the nature of the relationship. However, the role of the nursing administrator may be sufficiently stressful to carry over into the administrator's personal life. One participant in the study seemed to indicate this possibility when she said:

> Being in a rural hospital with quite a fluctuating census causes tremendous nursing service pressure that affects work-time and home-time. I am on call 7 days/24h/day. This is the first truly lonely job that I have ever had, and it is the first one that, by its very nature, isolates me personally as well . . . Insofar as professional loneliness—if only the administrator and I could understand each other, I could probably handle the rest—It is, however, presently very bleak.

These conclusions apply more specifically to the nursing service administrators included in the sample. The sample represents the population from which it is drawn. To the extent that nursing service administrators in the United States as a whole are similar to these administrators in Texas, the results are generalizable to that population also.

Recommendations

Recommendations for both practice and research can be made. Research in a practice discipline such as nursing has as a major objective the improvement of the service it renders. Both hospital and nursing service administrators need to be aware of professional loneliness and its potential impact on performance. Theirs is a joint responsibility to take steps to alleviate the problem. Nursing administrators should actively seek to build supportive relationships within their institutions and with their colleagues in other institutions. They should also be aware of the advantages of networking within the profession, and actively work to become part of a network of nursing administrators. Participation in professional organizations and national meetings and workshops could be used as a means of establishing and maintaining a network. Nursing educators and nursing service administrators should work together as colleagues to structure the environment in which the major portion of professional nursing takes place. Through a sharing of goals, values, and problems, reciprocal supportive relationships could be built. Joint appointments could be used to strengthen the ties between the two groups.

Recommendations for research include replication of this study to lend support to or refute these findings. Replication should include other variables as well as those in this study (e.g., marital status, social network, and professional network). The nature of the relationship between professional and personal loneliness needs to be clarified so that efforts to decrease loneliness could be directed appropriately. More data are needed about the role of education, sex, and size of hospital. Finally, the preparation (nonacademic) that administrators have prior to assuming their roles should be investigated. These investigators might focus on mentors or preceptors during the formative years in nursing administration.

REFERENCES

1. Hartog, J., J.R. Audy, and Y.A. Cohen, eds. *The Anatomy of Loneliness* (New York: International Universities Press, 1980.)
2. Peplau, L.A., and D. Perlman, eds. *Loneliness: A Sourcebook of Current Research, Theory, and Therapy* (New York: Wiley, 1983.)
3. Fromm-Reichmann, F. Loneliness. *Psychiatry* 22 (August 1959): 1.
4. Leiderman, P.H. Loneliness: A Psychodynamic Interpretation. In *Aspects of Depression*, eds. E.S. Schneidman and M.J. Ortega (Boston: Little, Brown, 1969) p. 155.
5. Russell, D.W. In Peplau and Perlman, *Loneliness: A Sourcebook*, p. 39.
6. Sullivan, H.S. *The Interpersonal Theory of Psychiatry* (New York: Norton, 1953.)
7. Peplau, H.E. Loneliness. *American Journal of Nursing* 55 (December 1955): 1476.
8. Fromm-Reichmann, Loneliness, 7.
9. Moustakas, C.E. *Loneliness* (Englewood Cliffs, N.J.: Prentice-Hall, 1961.)
10. Weigert, E. Loneliness and Trust—Basic Factors of Human Existence. *Psychiatry* 23 (May 1960): 121–31.
11. Mannin, E. *Loneliness* (London: Hutchinson, 1966, p. 9.)
12. Weiss, R.S. *Loneliness: The Experience of Emotional and Social Isolation* (Cambridge: MIT Press, 1973.)
13. Lynch, J.J. *The Broken Heart* (New York: Basic Books, 1977.)
14. Hartog, J. Introduction: The Anatomization. In Hartog et al., *The Anatomy of Loneliness.*
15. Audy, J.R. Man the Lonely Animal: Biological Roots of Loneliness. In Hartog et al., *The Anatomy of Loneliness*, p. 112.
16. Mijuskovic, B. Loneliness: An Interdisciplinary Approach. In Hartog et al., *The Anatomy of Loneliness*, p. 68.
17. Russell, D.W. The Measurement of Loneliness. In Peplau and Perlman, *Loneliness: A Sourcebook.*
18. Kaplan, B.H., J.C. Cassel, and S. Gore, Social Support and Health. *Medical Care* 15 (May 1977): 47–58. Supplement.
19. Cobb, S. Social Support as a Moderator of Life Stress. *Psychosomatic Medicine* 38 (September–October 1976): 300–314.
20. Norbeck, J.S. Social Support: A Model for Clinical Research and Application. *Advances in Nursing Science* 3 (July 1981): 48.
21. Barnett, J. On the Dynamics of Interpersonal Isolation. *Journal of the American Academy of Psychoanalysis* 6 (January 1978): 59–70.
22. Cohen, Y.A. You're O.K., How Am I? In Hartog et al., *The Anatomy of Loneliness.*
23. Sadler, W.A., Jr. and T.B. Johnson, Jr. From Loneliness to Anomie. In Hartog et al, *The*

Anatomy of Loneliness, 50.

24. Bowlby, J. Self-Reliance and Some Conditions that Promote It. In *Support, Innovation, and Autonomy,* ed. R. Gosling (London: Tavistock, 1973) pp. 22–43.

25. Sheldon, M.E. Investments and Involvements as Mechanisms Providing Commitment to the Organization. *Administrative Science Quarterly* 16 (June 1971): 143–50.

26. Hill, J. Aspects of Employment: The Role of Stayer, Leaver, Absentee, Offender, and Casualty. In *Support, Innovation, and Autonomy,* ed. R. Gosling (London: Tavistock, 1973.)

27. Gosling, R. Introduction: The Roots of Autonomy. In *Support, Innovation and Autonomy,* ed. R. Gosling (London: Tavistock, 1973.)

28. Erickson, E.H. The Nursing Service Director, 1880–1980. *The Journal of Nursing Administration* 10 (April 1980): 8.

29. Arndt, C., and E. Laeger, Role Strain in a Diversified Role Set. *Nursing Research* 19 (May–June 1970): 253–59; (November–December 1970): 495–502.

30. McClure, M.L. The Administrative Component of the Nurse Administrator's Role. *Nursing Administration Quarterly* 3 (Summer 1979): 1–12.

31. Greenwood, J.W. Management Stressors. In *Reducing Occupational Stress,* ed. A. McLean. Washington, D.C.: Government Printing Office, 1978, pp. 41–61.

32. Myrtle, R.C., and E. Glowgow, How Nursing Administrators View Conflict. *Nursing Research* 27 (March–April): 103–106.

33. Beyers, M. Leadership for the Future. In *Leadership in Nursing,* ed. M.G. Mayers, Wakefield, Mass.: Nursing Resources, 1979, p. 160.

34. Shores, L. Staff Development for Leadership. *Nursing Clinics of North America* 13 (March 1978): 103–109.

35. Darby, C. A Lonely Life at the Top. *Nursing Mirror* 148 (26 April 1979): 23.

36. Arndt, C. and L. Huckabay, *Nursing Administration: Theory for Practice with a Systems Approach* (St. Louis: Mosby, 1975.

37. Stevens, B.J. *The Nurse as Executive* (Wakefield, Mass.: Contemporary Publishing, 1975.)

Decision making in today's complex environment

Kathleen Kerrigan, R.N., M.S.
Per Diem Pool
Hahnemann University Hospital
Philadelphia, Pennsylvania

*T*HE ENVIRONMENT for providing health care services has changed dramatically over the past few years in response to drastic cutbacks in reimbursement from state and federal government and third party payors. Nursing, a major and vital health care provider within the health care system, is feeling the pinch. In order to survive in this era of rapid change, the health care system has placed great burdens upon the nurse manager. As a change agent, the nurse manager must be able to make timely and efficient decisions. Such a manager is faced with many complex challenges and choices. The challenges to continue to provide high-quality patient care in the light of decreased revenues compel the decision maker to develop innovative and creative ways of delivering this care at a lower cost. The choices to meet these challenges require one who is knowledgeable and astute in the

basics of the decision-making process. Using decision-making skills in the face of these complex challenges and choices can be a contributing variable to improving patient care, enriching job satisfaction, maximizing retention among nurses, decreasing liability, and promoting cost containment.

DEFINITION

Decision making is choosing options that are directed toward the resolution of organizational problems and the achievement of organizational goals. King, a noted nursing theorist, clearly defines decision making within an organization when she states "Decision making in organizations is a dynamic and systematic process by which goal-directed choice of perceived alternatives is made and acted upon by individuals or groups to answer a question and attain a goal."[1(p.132)]

The purpose of decision making within the health care organization is the coordination of goals and objectives of its members to deliver optimal patient care while controlling cost. The nurse manager, as a decision maker, has a vital role to play in bringing to

Nurs Admin Q, 1991, 15(4), 1–5

fruition the achievement of these organizational goals and objectives.

CHARACTERISTICS, INFLUENCES, AND BARRIERS

Schaefer[2] outlines certain characteristics essential for the decision maker to make effective and efficient decisions. First, the nurse manager must have the freedom to make the decision in question. This requires the necessary power and knowledge to select the decision. Second, the manager must have the capacity and ability to make a wise decision. This requires sound judgment, deliberation, objectivity, and experience. Finally, the manager must have the will, motivation, and commitment to choose. This requires volition, a conscious activity of the will to make a decision. These qualifications are essential for the nurse manager, since decisions impact upon others and may encompass life-and-death situations.

There are numerous factors that influence the decision maker. These include past experience, personal and social values, counsel from others, and experimentation. Some subtle obstacles to rational and objective decision making include biases or prejudices, ignorance, time and financial constraints, resistance to change, unclear goals and objectives, and the fear of risk taking. If the nurse manager is unable to surmount these obstacles, decisions made can have a negative impact on health care. The nurse manager must make a conscious effort to be constantly attuned to these human influences in order to make intelligent and objective decisions. There are a series of steps to guide the decision-making process.

DEVELOPMENTAL STEPS

Before a decision is made, a substantial amount of intellectual activity must be gen-erated. A decision is the end product of a process. Levey points out that

> [a] decision is the conclusion of a process through which we choose among available alternatives for the purpose of achieving a set of desired objectives. Decision making in-volves a great deal of thought and activity, and it is of primary importance to all human beings.[3(p.193)]

It is the duty and responsibility of the nurse manager to understand the developmental steps of the decision-making process to achieve an optimal outcome.

It is the duty and responsibility of the nurse manager to understand the developmental steps of the decision-making process to achieve an optimal outcome. The steps in the decision-making process are delineated differently by administrative authorities. However, essential agreement in the intent and content of the process would include

- establishing goals and objectives,
- searching for alternatives,
- evaluating and comparing alternatives,
- choosing an alternative,
- implementing the decision, and
- evaluating the implemented decision.

Establishing goals and objectives

The entire process is influenced by the goals and objectives clearly defined in the early part of the decision-making process. That is, when goals and objectives are ini-tially dealt with thoroughly and comprehensively, better decisions are made.

Searching for alternatives

This step involves the gathering of innovative, relevant, and valid alternatives worth pursuing in light of the goals and objectives to be achieved. It is here that creativity comes into action. Brainstorming is a helpful approach, because it produces the greatest possible number of options in the shortest possible time through the use of imaginative and uncritical thought processes.

Evaluating and comparing alternatives

Objectivity is essential when evaluating and comparing the alternatives. The decision maker should think of all the pros and cons for each alternative and try to imagine the consequence of each. Alternatives should be considered according to their importance.

Choosing an alternative

After analyzing the various alternatives in an orderly fashion, the decision maker must select the best possible option. Selecting the most desirable alternative requires critical thinking and judgment.

Implementing the decision

Making the decision is only half the job; executing it is the other half. The nurse manager must inform all who are involved in the plan of the goals and objectives and make every effort to consider their opinions. By doing this, the manager reaps the benefit of many alternatives and suggestions and creates a spirit of commitment and acceptance that is necessary for the successful and enthusiastic implementation of the decision. The nurse manager

must be able to persuade and excite those involved. As a catalyst, the manager must be able to sell the decision by demonstrating a spirit of excitement and conviction. Hopefully, this contagious spirit will have a positive impact on the successful implementation of the decision.

Evaluating the implemented decision

This evaluation involves the feedback mechanism, the assessment of output. The nurse manager must continuously assess the implemented decision. Is it accomplishing the anticipated goal or objective? If the decision is proved to be ineffective after a fair amount of trial, it must be reevaluated and possibly changed. Each of the steps described is not an isolated activity. Rather, the process involves a series of interrelated steps.

TOOLS AND TECHNIQUES FOR EFFECTIVE DECISION MAKING

There are several techniques or aids the nurse manager can utilize in making more competent and effective decisions. These are known as quantitative decision tools. They force the manager to think about the stages of the decision-making process. The tools "uncover things they had not thought of and they use probabilities in a manner that is much more systematic."[4(p.266)]

Two cognitive tools that the nurse manager can use are the Payoff Table and the Decision Tree. These tools assist the manager in overcoming personal preferences or biases in order to arrive at an impartial and objective decision. The Payoff Table aims at a statistical decision by establishing a methodical approach for choosing an action. Probabilities are assigned to various possible outcomes. The payoff is the

	Results	
	180 (.6)	200 (.4)
180	1 $9	2 $24
200	3 $10	4 $10

(row label: Alternatives)

Expected costs if 180 are ordered:
$9 (.6) + $24 (.4) =
$5.40 + $9.60 = $15.00

Expected costs if 200 are ordered:
$10 (.6) + $10 (.4) =
$6.00 + $4.00 = $10.00

Figure 1. The payoff table. Alternative 4 appears to be the least costly option while providing a sufficient number of gowns.

key component in selecting an option (see Fig 1). Figure 1 depicts data from an outpatient department of a large hospital where paper gowns are used. It is determined that on a weekly basis, there is a 60 percent probability that 180 gowns will be used and a 40 percent probability that 200 gowns will used. Costs are assigned to each of these alternatives. the cost of 180 gowns is $9.00. The cost of 200 gowns is $10.00. If there were a shortage of gowns, a special order would entail an extra cost of $15.00. Thus, if 180 gowns are available and the amount used during the week is 180 the cost is $9. If 180 gowns are available but 200 gowns are needed, the cost will be $24 ($9 for available ones plus $15 special order). If 200 gowns are available and 180 are used the cost is $10. If 200 gowns are available and used the cost is $10.

The Decision Tree (Table 1) represents a graphic visualization of goals, available alternatives, and outcome probabilities. Table

Table 1. The decision tree

Objective of decision	Alternative/action	Probability	Expected outcome
Adequate staffing with wisest expenditure of money	1. Hire FT R.N. $16/hr	a. Increased patient load (.7) (will have to pay) $16 × .7 = $11.20 b. same patient load (.3) $16 × .3 = $4.80	$16.00 adequate staffing
	2. Pay OT $24/hr	a. Increased patient load (.7) (will have to pay) $24 × .7 = $16.80 b. same patient load (.3) (will not have to pay)	$16.80 adequate staffing
	3. Hire per diem R.N. $20/hr	a. Increased patient load (.7) (will have to pay) $20 × .7 = $14.00 b. same patient load (.3) (will not have to pay)	$14.00 adequate staffing, least cost

Decision: Alternative 3 appears to be the least costly option while providing adequate staffing.

1 shows data from an intensive care nursery in which it is predicted that during the fiscal year 1991, patient census will increase. There is a 70 percent probability that the patient load will grow and a 30 percent probability that it will remain the same. The goal of the unit is to provide adequate staffing of nurses while controlling cost. Salary for a full-time (FT) registered nurse (R.N.) is $33,280 or $16 per hour. Overtime (OT) cost is $24 per hour, while per diem R.N. cost is $20 per hour.

Decision-making tools should be tailored to the kind of decision needed. Although these tools are not accurate descriptions of what the situation is, they nevertheless can assist the nurse manager.

•   •   •

In this era of turbulence within the health care industry, decision making is not simple. Yet it is an essential task within the scope of nursing practice. Appropriate skills are needed by the nurse manager when making a sound decision.

Although decision making is an important facet in nursing practice, the principles used can also be applied in one's personal life, such as budgeting, financing, or selecting a school for continuing education. These principles aid in setting priorities and controlling one's life. They assist one in dealing most effectively with today's and tomorrow's challenges.

REFERENCES

1. King, I. *A Theory for Nursing-System, Concepts, Process* (New York, N.Y.: Wiley, 1981.)
2. Schaefer, J. The Interrelatedness of Decision Making and the Nursing Process. *American Journal of Nursing* 74, no. 10 (1974): 1862–65.
3. Levey, S., and N. Loomba, *Health Care Administration: A Management Perspective* (Philadelphia, Penn.: Lippincott, 1984.)
4. Mitchell, T. *People in Organization—Understanding Their Behavior* (New York, N.Y.: McGraw-Hill, 1978.)

Improving clinical care through project management

Mary Lou Wesley, R.N., M.S.N.
Associate Vice President of Nursing

Alice Easterling, R.N., M.S.N.
*Project Manager, Nursing Care
   Management*
St. Joseph Mercy Hospital
Pontiac, Michigan

MANY CHANGES ARE occurring in health care delivery systems today. Notable changes include the development of managed care, the expansion of alternatives to traditional acute care hospital delivery of patient care, and the increased demand for nursing services complicated by a national nursing shortage. The major challenge to nursing is how to provide safe, effective, quality patient care amidst these forces for change. Both nursing and hospital management literature address this challenge extensively; as a result, a broad spectrum of solutions is offered. Restructuring the patient care delivery model is the identified solution that offers the most promise.[1]

In 1988 an in-depth assessment of the Department of Medical-Surgical Nursing was completed at St. Joseph Mercy Hospital in Pontiac, Michigan. St. Joseph Mercy Hospital, a division of Mercy Health Services, is a 531-bed, full-service, community teaching hospital. The assessment of the Medical-Surgical Nursing Department served to identify internal issues and external forces for change. The results of that assessment led to the decision to redesign the nursing care delivery system to support a nursing case management model. This article describes how project management techniques were used to implement the redesign.

There are several advantages of using a project management approach to implement a major change process. This approach was designed to obtain maximum input from everyone affected by the project, while also successfully meeting objectives in a timely manner. The project management

The authors acknowledge Lorraine Berlin, R.N., Ph.D., who provided support and encouragement during the implementation process of this report.

Nurs Admin Q, 1991, 15(4), 22–28
©1991 Aspen Publishers, Inc.

approach flattens the organization and promotes communication through all levels of personnel.

Various project management techniques were studied, and the most useful was the process outlined by House.[2] In this process, project management research and human relations research are combined to achieve project success. The approach used for implementation of nursing case management was an adaptation of this process.

Five guiding principles were used during the planning, implementation, and stabilization of the project:

1. plan strategies to communicate with people and groups affected by the project,
2. examine how project success is affected by the communication styles of the project manager and team members,
3. view conflict as an expected part of the change process and plan how to manage it,
4. provide support to the project team during implementation, and
5. provide support for the maintenance of the change.

In the following sections, each principle is explained, and the implementation experience is described.

COMMUNICATION STRATEGIES

Planning strategies to communicate with people and groups affected by the project is an essential step in project management. Since a project has the inherent tendency to get out of control, strategies must define in detail the relationships needed within the project and between the project system and the outside. This process is called integration and is an important aspect of project management, since it promotes support for the project.

To accomplish external and internal integration, the project manager must identify the key people and their positions across boundaries in the organization. The project manager must determine who the decision-makers, clients, and team members are in relation to the project. For example, it was determined that the clients in this project were the patients, staff, physicians, hospital administrators, and board members.

In addition to identifying the key people, it is necessary to organize what is known about the key people. It is helpful to make notes on each individual's personal style, relationships with other team members, and pressures to accept or reject project goals.

The project manager must determine what each of the key people identified will gain from the project and what each will lose. This information is valuable when presenting a new idea to a group. For example, it was identified that the physicians would gain better communication, continuity, and collaboration from nursing case management. The physicians would lose absolute control of a patient's progress through the hospital stay.

It is very important for the project manager to develop a win-win negotiation style. This step has proved invaluable when presenting the idea of nursing case management to various groups. The project manager should begin the presentation by incorporating the person's (or group's) strongest job-related reason to resist into an empathy statement. Next, a connecting word must be used to let the listener know that the direction of the discussion is changing. A good connecting word is "however." The project manager then incorporates the person's strongest job-related reason to accept the idea in a statement of the problem. The following example may be used when presenting the idea to physicians: "We understand that you might perceive that we are suggesting a 'cookbook approach' to medicine; however, we feel this approach to patient care will improve nurse-physician communication and collaboration and improve the continuity of care for patients." Finally, the project manager selects a connecting word to tell the listener that there is more to come. An example is: "therefore, we would appreciate your support for this project."

Because the implementation of nursing case management was considered a development project, both external and internal integration were applied. External integration refers to the establishment of formal communication links with key people outside of the project. Internal integration refers to the establishment of an effective project team.

External integration was accomplished by several methods. The director of Medical-Surgical Nursing met individually with all of the hospital administrators, the directors of departments such as pharmacy, laboratory, and social work, as well as the directors of the other nursing departments to inform them of the project. A formal presentation was given to the hospital board to outline the project and expected outcomes.

External integration was also achieved through the establishment of a Nursing Case Management Steering Committee. The members of the committee include the vice-president for nursing, the associate vice-president for nursing operations, the associate vice-president for professional training and development, the assistant to the chief financial officer, two associate vice-presidents for professional services, and nursing department directors. The project manager for nursing case management chairs the committee. Additional members of this committee are ad hoc, since the supervisors and clinical nurse specialists rotate

through the committee during the active implementation stage of nursing case management in their area. This committee meets on a monthly basis, and additional meetings are called as necessary.

The steering committee serves as a forum to address issues that have a key impact on the strategic planning, implementation, and evaluation of the collaborative practice model. Functions of the steering committee include reviewing and approving Gantt charts for unit implementation of the collaborative practice model and facilitating communication among all disciplines regarding the collaborative practice model.

Another mechanism by which external integration was planned was through the Nurse Case Manager Meetings. This group meets on a monthly basis and often invites hospital personnel from other areas such as Human Resources and Utilization Review to speak to certain concerns.

External integration refers to the establishment of formal communication links with key people outside of the project.

Ongoing systematic communication with key people in the organization was also planned and achieved by several mechanisms. Formal evaluation results and progress of the project are reported on an ongoing basis at the Hospital Administrative Council. Progress of the project and outcomes are also reported at several interdisciplinary committee meetings including the Utilization Review Committee, the Department of Medicine Quality Assurance Committee, the Medical Records Committee, and the General Patient Care Committee, and also throughout the Mercy Health Services Corporation through presentations, newsletters, and other publications.

Hospital and physician office staff and other members of the health care team are updated about the project in an ongoing manner. Physician office staff are informed and updated about the nursing case management project through newsletters, presentations, and personal contact by the nurse case managers. Staff meetings are held with pharmacy, laboratory, dietary, utilization review, and social work staffs to discuss the concept of the collaborative practice model and the role of the nurse case manager. A discussion was also held concerning how staff members can be involved in this new model for patient care.

The consumers in the hospital market area also receive information about the collaborative practice model. One way patients are informed about the project is by receiving the nurse case manager's business card. On the back of the business card, there is a brief description of the role of the nurse case manager. Patients have been observed arriving on nursing units and asking, "Do you have nurse case managers?" The project manager for nursing case management works closely with the public relations staff to publicize the project.

Internal integration was achieved by first appointing a project team for every nursing unit to involve nurses and other staff in plans to implement nursing case management. This team's charge was to determine how case management would be operationalized on the unit. The membership of this team includes a representative from all job classifications on the unit. Other members include physicians, social workers, physical therapists, clinical nurse specialists, occupational therapists, and others. It is important to have experienced personnel who have worked together before on the project team. Equally important is the need to include personnel who are negative about

the impending change. These people are able to get direct information about the project instead of hearing rumors.

The project team meetings follow a predictable course. At the first meeting, the project manager assigns a secretary to keep minutes and outlines the goals of the project team. At the ongoing weekly meetings, the team discusses issues and concerns raised by the unit staff. Decision are made by consensus, and the project team is expected to communicate progress to the rest of the unit's staff on a regular basis. The project team also completes an anonymous culture assessment of its work group. This exercise can identify areas of greatest strength and the areas for potential growth within the work group. For example, the group may perceive that communication is a problem on the unit. The team defines communication mechanisms to keep the unit staff informed about the project.

PROJECT SUCCESS

The project manager's major responsibilities are to develop team members, set priorities, and track progress. In this project it was also important to think through the relationship between the project manager and the nurse manager on the pilot unit. Potential areas of conflict to be resolved were differences in role expectations, a lack of clarity in purpose or process, and other issues on which work needed to be done.

The project manager is expected to keep the project moving and on target and to coordinate the activities of implementation. Successful project managers view conflict as useful and promote open discussion of disagreement, so that passage through the conflict can occur. The selection process for the project manager should include assessing how much control the project manager expects. Project managers who have an external locus of control tend to be more successful, because they are able to delegate work to team members and deal with decisions that are beyond their control. Project managers with internal orientation need to control every aspect of a project and that can lead to dissatisfied team members and a frustrated project manager, since very little is under control during project implementation. It is important for the project manager to utilize a systematic approach to interpersonal relationships.

Another issue related to the selection of a project manager is that of power. The project managers must be able to empower themselves and others on the project team. The project manager's authority is based on power that stems more from personal abilities and less from position. Personal power is a set of skills and abilities and involves the way one works with and responds to others. Successful project managers know how to use this personal power to get the job done. Expert power refers to one's special knowledge or information relevant to the task or problem on hand.[3] Successful project managers earn the respect of the team and use their expert power in such a way to promote the team. It is important for the project managers to share the information they posses to help the team grow and evolve.

In addition to the above skills, the project manager should have a wide range of conflict-management skills and be able to choose the best course of action depending upon the situation. The project managers should study their behavior in specific relationships.

The project manager builds four key elements into negotiations with team members and others by:

- collaborating with team members in setting goals,
- consulting with key people before a critical event to set parameters,
- enlisting moral support for team members to accomplish project tasks, and
- securing autonomy for team members to do what needs to be done.

CONFLICT

The project manager should expect conflict and be prepared to manage it. A list should be prepared that outlines the possible areas of conflict. The data should be analyzed according to the information the project manager has collected under the first two guiding principles with regard to conflicting pressures, relationships, and personalities. Then plans are made to deal with the conflict when (not if) it occurs. It is important to view the conflict nonjudgmentally as a normal reaction to any change, and part of the project manager's role is to help others understand this. Lewin's theory for change and also a change agent tool were used to help the project team and staff through the change process. It is also helpful for the project manager to establish a win-win presentation negotiation style. The project manager may find it helpful actually to write a script in order to approach a conflict situation.

The project manager must be able to recognize a stressful situation in time to do something about it. It is important to have a stress management plan in place before the project begins. It is helpful to find humor if possible and to identify a support person outside of the project.

The project manager must encourage project team members to ventilate their feelings and at the same time not to take this personally. The natural reaction is to fight back, but successful project managers must put their own agendas aside and give full attention to the person ventilating.

In addition to encouraging expression of feelings, the project manager must be able to excavate the real issues. If an issue comes up two or three times after it has been dealt with, the real problem must be uncovered. For example, the staff on the pilot unit told the project team that they were not being given enough information about the new nurse case manager role. After several information sharing sessions, the staff continued to voice this issue. At this point, the project managers asked the staff what was really bothering them. They revealed the real issue, which was that the staff felt devalued due to the role changes. The project team then implemented a plan for assisting the staff to deal with this problem.

Project managers should look for win-win alternatives. Some people will never support the project, so leave them to management. Picture things going well and not catastrophize. Identify the priorities and implement a plan to accomplish these tasks. The surgical unit was chosen for the nursing case management project because the case types were more predictable, the surgeons were supportive, and the nursing staff was strong. This combination made for a win-win situation.

Sometimes the project managers must cut their losses. Watch for inconsistencies in behavior and words that might indicate a serious problem and act on them immediately. When a team member's words and behavior do not match, believe the behavior. Management may need to be asked to deal with the resistant person, or all of the time and energy will be spent on this person.

SUPPORT DURING IMPLEMENTATION

The amount of support that the project team requires during the implementation process varies. At the beginning of the project, it is necessary for the project manager to provide direction, leadership, support, and task definition to individuals and groups. Members of the project team need to know what their tasks are, how to do them, and what is expected of them. The unit implementation Gantt chart is shared with the project team to provide direction and task definition.

It is important to get people committed and excited. This can be done by inspiring a shared vision about the project's purpose and goal, increasing visibility of the project team's efforts, empowering people, and providing positive reinforcement.[4]

Members of the project team need to know what their tasks are, how to do them, and what is expected of them.

The project manager supports the project team in facing and managing conflict. Staff members require education about conflict management and role modeling of conflict management behaviors. Often it is helpful to actually role-play a conflict situation and provide a script that could be helpful to assist staff. As the project team progresses to an open exchange of ideas, the project manager assists by sharing political information and teaching the staff how to negotiate the system.

The project manager must constantly balance the energy of the team in order to complete the task and at the same time provide support to the team. Part of the role of the project manager involves assessing which interpersonal roles and skills are required within the project team. For example, someone on the project team will need to initiate activity, coordinate tasks, seek other opinions and information, and summarize. Also, someone will need to express group feelings, encourage the group, and gatekeep.

The project manager will encourage group performance of these roles and skills. It would be impossible for a project manager to perform all of the previously mentioned roles alone, and it would not be desirable. It is best if various team members perform these roles. To encourage this, the project manager should pay attention to team member behavior and give feedback that is specific, immediate, and goal-related.

Sometimes it is necessary to develop the missing roles and skills in other team members. If team members who have potential do not assume necessary roles, the project manager may need to develop them by delegating roles to capable people, rotating roles, or providing formal training. Sometimes the potential does not exist within the team. In that case, the project manager may need to supply the missing role and skills by borrowing or hiring a person to fill the role or by filling the role personally.

Project managers need to recognize signs that their group is headed for groupthink, burnout, demolition, or collapse. Groupthink results from an excess of positive energy directed toward the team without the balance of positive energy for the task. Burnout results from an excess of positive energy directed toward the task without the balance of positive energy for the team. Demolition results from an excess of negative energy directed toward the team. Collapse results from an excess of negative energy directed toward the task.

The project manager needs to supply antidotes to dysfunctional roles. Some antidotes include seeking other opinions and information to avoid groupthink and having group celebrations to prevent burnout.

MAINTENANCE OF CHANGE

Another task for the project manager is to ensure the continuation of the project. Since the activity level is higher during the active implementation part of the project, this is when the project manager is most active with the project team and work group. It is during this period that the project manager assumes the majority of the responsibility in directing the project. The responsibility of the project is also shared with the unit nurse manager.

The nurse manager and project manager meet to outline plans to transfer responsibility for the continuation, support, and maintenance of the project to the nurse manager. The project manager meets with the nurse manager and nurse case managers to discuss the future direction of the model on the unit. The nurse manager's input provides information about the unit goals and objectives.

The nurse case managers and unit manager examine the unit goals and then outline the future projects for the nurse case managers. For example, the nurse case managers wanted to develop a postdischarge follow-up program. After examining the high-volume diagnosis-related group (DRG) case-type on a unit, they determined that this patient population was problematic on the preadmission side instead of the postdischarge side.

During this period of time, the project manager should communicate with the nurse manager and nurse case managers on the unit. The role of the project managers includes providing support, information, and feedback about the nurse case manager role.

The project team is no longer necessary after the active part of the implementation process. Some unit managers have kept the group together and call this group the unit practice committee. This committee meets on a regular basis to discuss and resolve unit practice difficulties.

•   •   •

These project management techniques have proved to be invaluable in the implementation of nursing case management. By using this organized approach, the implementation goals were successfully achieved in a much shorter time frame with cooperation and understanding.

REFERENCES

1. Porter-O'Grady, T. *Reorganization of Nursing Practice: Creating the Corporate Venture* (Gaithersburg, Md.: Aspen, 1990.)
2. House, R. *The Human Side of Project Management* (Reading, Mass.: Addison-Wesley, 1988.)
3. Bothwell, L. *The Art of Leadership* (New York, N.Y.: Prentice Hall, 1983.)
4. Randolph, W.A. *Effective Project Planning and Management; Getting the Job Done* (Englewood Cliffs, N.J.: Prentice Hall, 1988.)

Study and discussion questions

1. Identify two structural types of organizations and compare similarities and differences in nurse managers' roles in them.
2. Define four strategies the nurse manager may use to integrate the domains of nursing and management at the entry, middle, and top management levels.
3. Describe what is meant by commitment to one's position. How does commitment relate to job satisfaction? to dissatisfaction? to achievement?
4. How does the nurse manager recognize burnout in: self/colleagues/staff nurses?
5. List three reasons why middle managers are particularly vulnerable to burnout.
6. Based on the understanding of the reasons for an effect of burnout on managers and the staffs they work with, develop three strategies to prevent burnout and deal with the effects of burnout.
7. List three characteristics of effective decision makers. Do you think these characteristics can be learned?
8. Explain how a manager attains project integration through communication.
9. List three strategies for dealing with conflict in organizations.

Part III
Change and organizational development

Sally A. Sample, R.N., M.N., F.A.A.N.
Director, Center for Nursing
Medical Center Hospital of Vermont
Burlington, Vermont

Leaders throughout our society are focused on the concept of change: change that is not a single isolated event, but a complex series of events occurring concurrently. They ponder the changes affecting our planet. They seek to influence the political, social, and economic changes affecting their organization. They react to science and technological advances that change the pattern of business, health, and education. They assess the changing demographics and diversity of the workforce. Contemporary leaders of today seek to understand what is happening to change their environment and how they can be masters of change in their organization.

The decade of the nineties has evolved leaders who are striving to articulate a vision for the future that will inspire and motivate the human resources in their orga-

nization. They are evolving strategies to transform the current reality toward the vision, while adapting and integrating the significant changes in their environment. Nowhere is this phenomenon more evident than in health care organizations.

Nursing leaders have been visionary and strategic in developing their nursing organizations to provide quality patient care for decades. *NAQ* has featured their stories of transformational leadership described in "On The Scenes." One case study has been selected as a classic, recognizing that many nurse leaders have contributed and shared their strategies for organizational development over the years.

This case study identifies the subtle principles of change, i.e., trust, support, and networks to accomplish its goals and attain its vision. It describes "responsive nursing management . . . that includes an awareness of changes within the profession that alter the work environment and a vision of what the future might hold." It states the threats and opportunities as together the leadership and staff shape a professional practice environment to provide exemplary patient care to its consumers.

The head nurse: A managerial definition of the activity role set

Nancy Kay Jones, R.N., B.S.N.
Director of Nursing Services
Fort Worth Children's Hospital
Fort Worth, Texas

Jack William Jones, Ph.D.
Assistant Professor of Management
M.J. Neeley School of Business
Texas Christian University
Fort Worth, Texas

WHAT DO HEAD nurses do? An unequivocal answer to this question is important for nursing administrators to recruit effectively for the head nurse position, to enhance their head nurses' professional skills, and to evaluate performance fairly and effectively. However, such an answer is not readily available.

The contemporary literature recognizes the managerial nature of the head nurse position and identifies various aspects of it, but the activities that comprise the operational role are rarely defined very specifically.[1-5]

For instance, Barrett argues that head nurses need to recognize their administrative position, responsibility, and authority; yet she says that the management of nursing care involves determining needs for care, planning, delegating, teaching, supervising, and evaluating.[6] Stevens, contending that the head nurse position is a pivotal link between nursing management and nursing care, defines three main areas of head nurse responsibility: patient care, staff management, and administration of nursing division policies.[7] Kron identifies the head nurse as a manager and as the key person within the hospital; she cites planning, organizing, directing, and controlling as the head nurse's principal functions.[8] According to Manez, nurse managers must develop well-organized plans of care; demonstrate management skills; maximize the effectiveness of human resources at their disposal; and be skilled in counseling, interviewing, problem solving, directing, and controlling.

Many other articles and studies have worked with similar role definitions. The pattern is to discuss the managerial nature of the head nurse role in (1) general nursing

Nurs Admin Q, 1979, 3(2), 45–57
©1979 Aspen Publishers, Inc.

terms and (2) such traditional management literature terms as planning, organizing, coordinating and controlling. The problem is that these words tell little about what head nurses actually *do* in their work activities. If one watches what head nurses do, it is difficult to relate what is observed to terms such as the ones above. At best the terms indicate some vague objectives head nurses pursue when they work.

A study of head nurses was conducted recently at the Fort Worth Children's Hospital (FWCH) in Fort Worth, Texas, with the specific objective of reaching a clearer, more specific, more practically useful description of what these key personnel actually do.

THE MINTZBERG MODEL: A ROLE-SET DEFINITION OF MANAGERIAL WORK

The framework of our study at FWCH was Mintzberg's ten-role set description of managerial work, the publication of which in 1973 represented a significant conceptual breakthrough concerning the nature of management.[9] The Mintzberg framework was judged to provide the best available tool to accomplish a role delineation study aimed at describing head nurse work activities in terms and concepts that could be readily used by nursing directors and their associates in the discharge of their daily managerial responsibilities. Also, our underlying assumption was that the head nurse position is basically managerial in nature.

Who the manager is

A manager is that person formally in charge of an organization or one of its subunits. This definition would include hospital administrators, nursing directors and their associates, nursing supervisors and head nurses.

> ***Managerial activities are categorized into three role groups; interpersonal, informational and decisional.***

The manager's job can be described in terms of various roles, with a role being defined as "an organized set of behaviors belonging to an identifiable position."[10] Mintzberg's description of managerial work comprises the ten roles depicted in Figure 1. Managerial activities are categorized into three role groups: *interpersonal roles—ac-*

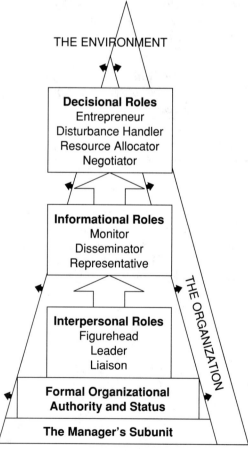

Figure 1. The manager's roles

tivities that are concerned primarily with interpersonal relationships; *informational roles*—activities that deal primarily with the transfer of information; and *decisional roles*—activities centered around decision making.

What the manager does

Interpersonal roles: Figurehead, leader, liaison

The manager's formal position provides the starting point for an explanation of the Mintzberg framework. The manager was defined as being formally in charge of an organizational unit. This formal authority leads to a special position of status in the organization. And from formal authority and status come three *interpersonal* roles: figurehead, leader and liaison.

By virtue of being head of an organizational unit, all managers must perform some duties of a ceremonial nature. These duties constitute the *figurehead* role. And because managers are in charge of a unit, they are responsible for the work for that unit's people. The manager's actions in this regard constitute the *leader* role; it is here that the influence of the manager is most clearly seen. Although formal authority vests the manager with great potential power, leadership determines to a large extent how much of it will be actualized. In the *liaison* role managers make contacts outside their vertical chain of command. They cultivate such contacts largely to get information. The liaison function builds up the managers' own external information systems—systems that are largely informal, private and verbal, but can be very effective.

Informational roles: Monitor, disseminator, representative

By virtue of interpersonal contacts, both with subordinates and with the private information network, managers emerge as the nerve center of their organizational unit and thereby assume certain *informational* roles.

As *monitors,* managers perpetually scan the environment for information, query liaison contacts and subordinates, and receive unsolicited information, much of it as a result of their network of personal contacts. A good part of the information managers collect in the *monitor* role arrives in verbal form, often as gossip, hearsay, and speculation. Much of this information must be shared and distributed.

In the *disseminator* role, managers pass some of this privileged information directly to their subordinates, who would otherwise have no access to it. When these subordinates lack easy contact with one another, managers will sometimes pass information from one to another. It is the manager's responsibility to be sure that subordinates receive the information they need to discharge their responsibilities.

The disseminator role is internal to the manager's unit; the *representative* role is external. In this capacity, managers send certain information outside their unit. An important part of the representative role is to inform and satisfy the influential people who control the manager's own organizational unit.

Decisional roles: Entrepreneur, disturbance handler, resource allocator, negotiator

The manager plays the major role in a unit's decision-making system. Information is the basic input to decision making. As the unit's nerve center, only the manager has full and current information for making decisions. And as its formal head, only the manager can commit the unit to important new courses of action. The manager's decision-making activity is performed through four *decisional* roles.

In the *entrepreneur* role, managers act as initiators and designers of much of the controlled change in their organizational unit. While the entrepreneur role is primarily one of control, the *disturbance handler* role is one in which managers respond to pressures beyond their control. Here they must act because the pressures of the situation are too severe to be ignored. All managers must spend considerable time responding to high-pressure disturbances. As the unit's formal authority, they must oversee the allocation of organizational resources to and within the unit. This is the third decisional role of *resource allocator.* The manager's final decisional role is that of negotiator. Negotiation is integral to the manager's job and cannot be shirked. Negotiation is resource trading in "real time." It requires the presence of someone with enough authority to commit the quantity of resources at stake, and to do it quickly.

THE FWCH STUDY OF HEAD NURSES

Methodology

Intensive expert observation was employed to study head nurse work activity over a period of four months. This certainly a powerful method, but extremely demanding of research resources. Both the method and the 106-bed hospital size imposed strong constraints on sample size. It was therefore decided to study both head nurses and assistant head nurses when functioning as head nurses. This gave a total sample size of eight. All significant work activities performed by each head nurse were identified and then classified in terms of one of Mintzberg's ten roles. Together these role activities constitute the job of head nurse.

Although we could not develop much quantitative data on job characteristics as a result of the small sample, we felt that gaining more powerful data on the job activity *content* justified this loss. The trade-off was for depth at the expense of breadth. We believe that these head nurses in their work were typical of head nurses of other hospitals, and that important basic similarities exist between the work activities studied at FWCH and those of head nurses elsewhere.

The Head Nurse Functions

Interpersonal roles

Head nurses are in charge of their floor. From the formal authority and status accompanying this position, all three of Mintzberg's interpersonal roles can be identified in the head nurse's activities.

Being the unit's *figurehead,* head nurses must carry out some duties of a ceremonial nature. Observed among these were: representing the floor at head nurse and other meetings, attending hospital parties and acting as "hostess" to persons of importance touring the head nurse's own unit. Some of these activities seemed unimportant to several subjects in the study; however, when the figurehead role is ignored, the smooth functioning of the unit is disrupted.

The second interpersonal role is that of *leader.* The formal authority of the head nurse position invests head nurses with potential power, but is the head nurses' individual leadership styles and abilities

---

The formal authority of the head nurse position invests head nurses with potential power, but it is the head nurses' individual leadership styles and abilities that determine whether and how that power is exercised.

that determine whether and how that power is exercised. Many leader-oriented activities beyond serving as their unit's role model were identified among head nurses during observation and interviews. These included orienting new personnel and students; teaching nursing personnel, students, patients, and/or their families; introducing new employees to *all* unit personnel; conducting employee evaluations; demonstrating clinical expertise when warranted; supervising patient care; maintaining and coordinating schedules; conducting ward conferences; and ensuring that students are supervised in medicine preparation.

In the *liaison* role, head nurses develop contacts outside their vertical chain of command to obtain information needed for the efficient operation of their units. These contacts occur both within and outside the organization, and are established by both formal and informal means. Formal meetings of head nurses and of committees for procedure, audit and patient teaching are all organizational sources of information. External sources can be established through memberships in professional associations, by attending conferences and by attending seminars for continuing education.

The three interpersonal role activities together engaged about ten percent of the time of the head nurses in the study sample.

Informational roles

By virtue of the contacts developed through the interpersonal roles, head nurses are the unit's key processors of enormous amounts of information—from all the allied health services; the patient and/or family; the physician; and the head nurse's subordinates, peers and superiors.

Head nurses as *monitors* constantly gather information from surroundings as well as receive oral and written reports. Some identified monitoring activities include: receiving a report at the beginning of the work shift; controlling narcotics; making rounds; accepting verbal laboratory reports over the telephone; gathering information from patients and/or family; checking charts for accurate documentation of nursing care as well as for information on the patient's medical progress; checking emergency carts and unit medical supplies; and checking laboratory reports for pertinent information.

The *disseminator* role is one of sharing and distributing information acquired through the monitor role to subordinates within the unit. Activities performed in the role of disseminator include: passing on information from first shift meetings to second- and third-shift personnel; implementing physicians' orders by transferring them to staff; requisitioning laboratory tests, x-ray procedures, supplies, medications, etc.; informing staff of changes in orders; calling attention of unit personnel to new memos and procedures; sharing with staff the information obtained while making rounds with physicians; holding ward conferences; and giving instructions to nurses after "spot checking" their charting.

In the third informational role, that of *representative*, head nurses send information outside the unit. Representative activities include: telephoning patient information to a physician or delivering it verbally during rounds; answering the questions of patients and/or family members as well as giving them needed support; sending requisitions to other patient service departments; responding to questions from other departments; communicating information to nursing administration; and teaching patients, families, students and staff from other units. Communicating information obtained during nursing assessment to the physician or advising physician of laboratory test results are other role activities of head nurses as representatives.

The study showed that head nurses spend about 15 to 20 percent of their work day in informational role tasks.

Decisional roles

The most crucial part of head nurses' work is that occurring in the four decisional roles. To perform them well, head nurses need clinical nursing expertise as well as management skill. The activities categorized in the decisional roles involve the making of significant decisions.

A number of frameworks have been put forward to describe the phases of decision making,[11-14] including Simon's intelligence-design-choice sequence.[15] According to this model, the intelligence phase is the initiating activity of looking for and selecting situations that require decisions. The design phase is the heart of decision making; in it, available options are identified and evaluated. In the choice phase, one of these options is chosen or accepted.

Another approach categorizes decisions along a continuum according to the stimuli that evoke them.[16] At one extreme are "opportunity decisions." These are decisions initiated at will, without any particular pressure, simply to improve a basically stable and satisfactory situation. At the other extreme are "crisis decisions" involving unstable situations and intense pressures—here the decision maker has no choice but to act, often very quickly. "Problem decisions" are those that fall between these two poles.

In terms of the Mintzberg framework, head nurses as *entrepreneurs* make voluntary, noncrisis decisions that encompass the initiation and design of systematic change in their unit. This decisional role can include formulating the unit's strategies—e.g., ways of mediating between the unit and other nursing services and hospital operations; identifying unit weaknesses and designing plans to remedy them; deciding when to notify a physician of changes in patient condition; developing nursing care plans; and assisting staff with decisions regarding patient care.

In the *disturbance handler* role, head nurses function at the other end of the decision spectrum—dealing with immediate crisis situations that cannot be ignored. Here head nurses are real-time decision makers who must react quickly and accurately. Due to the dynamic nature of the nursing environment, nonroutine or crisis situations are numerous. The head nurses in the FWCH study were observed having to respond to a "Dr. H"; coordinate external disaster drills and fire drills; start difficult intravenous therapy and restart infiltrated intravenous therapy; adjust shift assignments due to sudden staff illness; resolve intershift conflicts; respond to telephone calls at the desk; and assist in treatment for unscheduled procedures.

The third decisional role, that of *resource allocator,* encompasses what is to be done, who is to do it and what structure will be operative. It also involves authorizing decisions made by subordinates. These are basically problem decisions. Perhaps the most important resource to be allocated is *the head nurse's own time.* To achieve efficient organizational operations, head nurses must make optimal allocation of their time and expertise as well as that of staff. Typical resource allocation activities selected from numerous observed examples are: making patient care and room assignments; overseeing personnel to insure that breaks and lunch periods are staggered appropriately; and using own time—to assist physicians in the treatment room, restock intravenous therapy trays and floor supplies, perform dressing changes, start intravenous therapy, administer medications and give other direct patient care.

During the study it was observed that head nurses spent a significant amount of their time engaged in technical activities that are familiar and satisfying. For example, they frequently chose not to delegate the task of initiating intravenous therapy even though staff contained several RNs who could easily have done it instead.

The decisional role of *negotiator* is one that head nurses must accept as an integral part of their job. Here head nurses negotiate with other organizational units or individuals and make problem-oriented decisions. Negotiations include soothing physicians regarding things they are unhappy with; soothing disturbed patients and/or family; working out intershift and interdepartmental disturbances; negotiating for additional staff; and negotiating for new equipment.

One of the more interesting findings of our study is how much time head nurses spend in these four decisional roles. They account for approximately 75 to 80 percent of the head nurse's working day. In particular, we noted than an inordinate amount of time appears to be spent in the resource allocator and disturbance handler roles where the head nurse becomes involved in daily task activities. This has a negative impact on other role responsibilities of the position.

The FWCH study provides new and useful insights into the nature of the head nurse's work. The specific composition of the activities identified in the study is not nearly as important to nurse administrators as recog-

nizing and understanding the ten roles the activities express. In applying the ten-role framework, nursing administration should focus on using it to clarify communication with head nurses concerning role responsibilities and expectations.

The Importance of Balancing the Role Set: A Proposed Model

The study showed head nurses spending excessive time on resource-allocating and disturbance-handling activities at the expense of discharging their other decisional, interpersonal and informational role responsibilities. As an example of a better balanced activity role set for head nurses we propose the normative model in Table 1. This model by no means claims to present an optimal time balance and activities identification for the job, but rather to serve as a general foundation that can be adjusted or modified to meet the needs of individual nursing administrators in working with head nurses.

Delegating tasks

The proposed role model emphasizes the managerial nature of the head nurse job and stresses the value of the head nurse's own time. In this model, head nurses must relinquish considerable task responsibility in order to develop the full scope of their job.

A portion of the time gained by delegating more task activities can be effectively allocated by the head nurse to developing the important informational roles of monitor, disseminator and representative. As monitors, head nurses must establish the vital interorganizational and external channels of information necessary to fulfill the goals of their unit. As disseminators, head nurses need to be sure subordinates have the information necessary to properly discharge their responsibilities. And head nurses as

---

Head nurses spend excessive time on resource-allocating and disturbance-handling activities at the expense of discharging their other decisional, interpersonal and informational role responsibilities.

Table 1. A proposed head nurse activity role model

Role	% Time Spent	Typical Activities
Interpersonal Roles Figurehead	30%	represents unit at meetings; attends organizational parties; greets new patients and introduces self; acts as tour hostess to important visitors
Leader		assumes 24-hour responsibility; holds ward confer-ences; actively attempts to motivate; supervises patient care; conducts employee performance evaluations; coordinates schedule of daily activities; demonstrates clinical expertise when required; teaches; acts as role model
Liaison		attends patient care, procedure, audit, etc. committee meetings; attends professional conferences; holds professional memberships; attends informal peer group meetings
Informational Roles Monitor	40%	accepts report; makes rounds; accepts informational telephone calls; checks charts, lab reports, equipment, etc.; reviews new labor reports; performs information gathering from patient and/or parent, physician, staff and other allied professionals; reviews professional journals and other nursing information for new skills, techniques, technologies, etc.
Disseminator		holds ward conferences; communicates organizational and policy information to *all* nurses on all shifts; aids in implementation of new policies and procedures; passes information required to implement physicians' orders; provides staff feedback
Representative		performs coordination of patient care with other health care professionals; keeps nursing administration informed of patient information, complaints, special needs and problems; completes patient condition sheets; teaches family, patients, staff, students; acts as patient advocate by reporting information to physician; serves as unit's expert
Decisional Roles Entrepreneur	30%	engages in strategy formulation; identifies unit's weaknesses and designs remedial plans; makes routine decisions; develops nursing care plans; acts as resource nurse—includes helping staff with patient care plans as well as direct care decision making on when to notify physician of change in status of patient

Disturbance Handler	conducts drills—trains staff to handle these expected disturbances; answers "Dr. H" calls; confronts intershift and intrashift disturbances; starts intravenous therapy only when appropriate; assists in treatment room
Resource Allocator	makes patient care assignments; makes special duty assignments—includes delegation of routine tasks; coordinates lunch and break arrangements; conducts patient care for select patients
Negotiator	mitigates disturbances involving physician, staff, and/ or patients; negotiates for staff and/or equipment; handles intershift and interdepartmental conflict

representatives must present to administration any information concerning unit activities that is needed to maintain a coordinated effort in overall nursing services. This would include advising of unit needs for staff, equipment and inservice along with communication problem situations that require attention.

Developing interpersonal roles

Head nurses must also attend carefully to the interpersonal aspects of their job. They must perceive and present themselves as their units' figureheads and leaders; this will help to develop cohesiveness in the unit. Actively assuming liaison type activities is important; head nurses should attend committee meetings, interact with educational personnel associated by student contracts to the hospital, and attend social functions and professional meetings. These activities develop the required information channels needed for the full discharge of the head managerial nurse's responsibilities.

The benefits of role balancing

Our model allocates head nurse working time relatively evenly to interpersonal, informational and decisional role activities. It is recognized that the particular circum-

stances of each day will of course influence the balance of item allocation. However, an awareness of the need to balance roles will help the head nurse to achieve a better distribution of time. Learning to appropriately delegate more of the tasks not requiring their own immediate expertise or personal attention will make more time available to head nurses to pursue their total role set.

This new allocation of time and expertise will increase head nurse job satisfaction, accelerate unit staff development, improve teaching and establish better communications—both interdepartmental and intradepartmental. Improvement in these areas will certainly contribute to the goal of nursing service—quality patient care.

Using the General Role Model in Nursing Administration

The well-being of the nursing services department depends largely on the quality of its administrators; thus no administrative activity can be more important than that of selecting them. Effective recruitment for the head nurse position requires a realistic, understandable job role description in terms in which candidates' interests, experience and abilities can be considered and evaluated. For successful recruitment, head nurse candidates and their superiors must have a common understanding of what the role of head nurse comprises. During the recruitment process, the head nurse activity role model can be employed to explain to the candidate the nature of the job, with its many managerial facets, and to present administration's recommended allocation of work time to the various job roles. Ensuring that a potential head nurse understands both the breadth and the managerial nature of the job is very important in avoiding dissonance later on.

In order to accomplish a fair and productive performance evaluation, the head nurse role must be clearly delineated and both evaluator and evaluatee must understand performance expectation for the head nurse job. The general model can assist the nurse administrator in this regard. The role descriptions along with recommended time allocations can help establish the measurable criteria and objectives necessary for job evaluation.

The general model should also be made available to assist the functioning head nurse in identifying and ordering job tasks and responsibilities. By using it as a job framework, the head nurse should be able to better plan and coordinate the daily activities of her unit.

Other Implications of the FWCH Study

The study findings suggest still further implications for nursing administration.

Increasing Responsibility. The leader role in a typical managerial environment usually includes some responsibility in the area of hiring and firing of personnel. However, many head nurses have little, if any, formal input into hiring decisions and only slightly more influence concerning terminations. A measure of the organizational leverage head nurses command is their influence on hiring a replacement, adding a new staff nurse position to unit staff and determining appropriate disciplinary actions.[17] It is suggested that more direct and more consistent involvement of head nurses in the employment process will enhance organizational participation, develop the head nurses' influence and ultimately strengthen their position as leaders of their unit.

Need for Clerical Assistant. It was found that head nurses spend too much of their scarce time engaged in low-priority task activities. As already emphasized, head nurses must dissociate from many of these tasks to free themselves to develop the activities comprising their interpersonal and informational roles. The employment of secretarial help to perform all clerical work (including transferring physicians' orders, stocking supplies and handling all telephone calls that do not actually require the head nurse's attention) and to direct floor traffic is proposed as a partial solution to relieving the head nurse of routine tasks. With this kind of assistance, head nurses should be able to perform better in those roles they cannot delegate.

Staff Development. Although nursing administrators, educators and professional leaders recognize the managerial nature of the head nurse role, our findings indicate that many professional nurses do not. Stevens presents another dimension to this problem by arguing that the nurse's "education seldom prepares her for the management aspect of her role."[18] Yet the FWCH study highlights the need for the head nurse to utilize management skills.

Therefore, inservice programs and seminars as well as continuing education programs should be developed. These should focus on such basic management topics as motivation, leadership, teaching-learning concepts, small group behavior and evaluation techniques. It may be argued that RNs have been presented with much of this information in their basic educational program. Even when this is the case, it is easy under the demands of adjusting to the clinical situation for this exposure to fade and for potential management skills to remain undeveloped by the practicing nurse. Consequently, at the time the nurse is ready to assume the head nurse role, many of these concepts need to be reviewed.

No job is more vital to quality patient care than that of the head nurse. It is time to study the head nurse role realistically, to develop a clear and communicable picture of its scope and content. Only then can the difficult task of making significant improvements in its performance commence.

REFERENCES

1. Stevens, B.J. The Head Nurse as Manager. *The Journal of Nursing Administration* 4:1 (January 1974) p. 36–40.
2. Stevens, B.J. *The Nurse as Executive* (Wakefield, Mass.: Contemporary Publishing, Inc., 1975).
3. Barrett, J. *The Head Nurse* (New York: Appleton-Century-Crofts 1968).
4. Kron, T. *The Management of Patient Care* (Philadelphia: W. B. Saunders Co., 1971).
5. Manez, J. The Untraditional Nurse Manager: Agent of Change and Change Agent. *Hospitals* 52:1 (January 1978) p. 62–65.
6. Barrett. *The Head Nurse.* p. 20–22.
7. Stevens. *The Nurse as Executive.* p. 101–104.
8. Kron. *The Management of Patient Care.* p. 60.
9. Mintzberg, H. *The Nature of Managerial Work* (New York: Harper and Row, 1973).
10. Ibid. p. 54.
11. Dewey, J. *How We Think* (New York: D.C. Heath & Co., 1933).
12. Witte, E. Field Research on Complex Decision-Making Processes—a Phase Theorem. *International Studies in Management and Organization* 2:2 (Summer 1972) p. 156–182.
13. Newell, A. and Simon, H.A. *Human Problem Solving* (Englewood Cliffs, N.J.: Prentice-Hall, Inc., 1972).
14. Argyris, C. Single-Loop and Double-Loop Models in Research on Decision Making. *Administrative Science Quarterly* 21:3 (September 1976) p. 363–377.
15. Simon, H.W. *The New Science of Management Decision,* revised ed. (Englewood Cliffs, N.J.: Prentice-Hall, Inc., 1977) p. 39–81.
16. Mintzberg, H., D. Raisinghani, and A. Theoret, The Structure of Unstructured Decision Processes. *Administrative Science Quarterly* 21:2 (June 1976) p. 251.
17. Comstock, D.E. and W.R. Scott, Technology and the Structure of Subunits: Distinguishing Individual and Workgroup Effects. *Administrative Science Quarterly* 22:2 (June 1977) p. 189.
18. Stevens. *The Nurse as Executive.* p. 37.

Peer review: Change and growth

Dawn Boyar, R.N.
Primary Nurse Practitioner

Joyce Avery, R.N.
Primary Nurse Practitioner
University Hospital
Seattle, Washington

A DELIBERATELY PLANNED and carefully managed change process can be a means of alleviating many problems common to settings in which nurses work. At University Hospital in Seattle, a system of peer review was instituted to improve the nursing environment in a unit of closely monitored, dependent patients requiring complex care. Careful planning of the systems operation, combined with direct efforts to reduce initial staff resistance, produced a program that strengthened the professional roles of nurses and stimulated individual growth.

The nursing climate was clearly unsatisfactory before the program began. Evaluations and consultations were overdue because of excessive time demands on the head nurse. Individual and group morale had reached a low point. There was no pathway for consistent peer feedback. "When there is some dysfunction of an organization, expansion of the capabilities of that organization, or recognition of a missing factor, a change becomes necessary."[1]

CONCEPTUALIZING THE CHANGE PROCESS

What change would alleviate these problems? At the head nurse's suggestion, the staff decided to form a committee to investigate the feasibility of peer review. The conducive and adverse factors involved in the situation were identified. The conducive factors include: (1) the need for perspective on one's nursing practice; (2) staff interest in peer review; (3) a cohesive, trustful group, and (4) supportive nursing administration. The adverse factors are: (1) staff insecurity about receiving and giving evaluations; (2) natural resistance to change, and (3) lack of usable peer re-

The authors thank Elaine Larson, M.S., for her help in the preparation of this article.

Nurs Admin Q, 1981, 5(2), 59–62

view tool. The literature on change theory was reviewed, and it was decided that Lippitt's theory provided a useful framework for the implementation of a change to a peer review system.[2,3] (See boxed insert.)

Several basic concepts related to peer review were used to help formulate the system. According to Gold and Sachs, an effective method of peer review focuses on the nurse's role in patient care, stimulates professional growth and promotes a positive self-concept.[4] Mermet described self-concept and role performance as peer review influences.

Self-concept is the image built through interpretation of judgment by others. Self-expression helps form self-concept and identity in addition to increasing satisfaction. Job satisfaction is the result of an individual's personality interacting with the social system through performance of a role among role reciprocals. Role is defined as what society expects of an individual occupying a given position in a group.[5]

ESTABLISHING GOALS

With these basic premises and using guidelines developed by a task force at University Hospital in 1978, the nursing staff developed goals and objectives for its peer review plan. The goals were to:

- improve nurses' awareness of the effects of their actions in both giving and receiving evaluations; and
- improve the quality of care delivered to patients as a result of direct peer input.

The staff expected that once it was functioning, the peer review system would:

- identify strengths and weaknesses of individual skills in direct patient care, reliability, cooperation, leadership, clinical knowledge, self-expression, stress management, initiative, flexibility, professional growth, creativity and sensitivity;
- stimulate immediate and long-term goal setting;
- allow opportunities for nurses to develop expertise in giving and receiving constructive criticism; and
- effect positive change through open communication.

IMPLEMENTATION

The primary focus was to create a system that was fair as well as nonthreatening. Staff expressed many fears about receiving peer evaluations. The major fears concerned negative feedback, lack of relevance and inaccurate evaluation.

To decrease staff resistance, participation was made voluntary, confidentiality was required, anecdotal documentation for poor scores was encouraged, and optional inclusion of the evaluation in the permanent

---

Lippitt's Theory of Change*

1. Development of a need for change, problem awareness and desire for change.
2. Establishment of a change relationship, group assessment of validity of the change agent.
3. Diagnosis of problem, data collection.
4. Examination of alternative routes and goals, proposals formulated into a plan of action.
5. Transformation of intentions into actual change efforts, implementation of plan with system for feedback.
6. Stabilization of change, evaluation to determine effect.
7. Achieving terminal relationship with change agent.

*As adapted by Mermet, S. *Responses Resulting from Introduction of Change into a Nursing Unit.* (Seattle: University of Washington), p. 10–11.

> *To make evaluations more relevant, individuals were encouraged to complete a self-evaluation (using the same form) prior to receiving peer input.*

employment record was allowed. Also, official support for the program was given by the nursing administration, staff were involved in the planning phase, consistent group response was encouraged during the implementation period, and a mechanism was provided for feedback and critique. To make evaluations more relevant, individuals were encouraged to complete a self-evaluation (using the same form) prior to receiving peer input. Forms were provided for ongoing criticism of the peer review process. Evaluation criteria were developed, based on staff input and a system used in the Public Health Department of Portland, Oregon by Billi Odegaard, RN. Staff were to be rated on a one-to-five scale.

The reviewer was to provide documentation, comments and optional constructive criticism of performance. The reviewee could request a verbal conference with the reviewer for further discussion of the evaluation. Fixed time frames for initiating and completing the evaluation allowed easy maintenance of the peer review system. (See the appendix for reproduction of the peer review form.)

EVALUATION

Staff participation in the system was a good measure of its success. Almost three-fourth of the staff volunteered for peer review. All participants stated that their evaluation was complete, useful and accurate. Several persons commented that peers evaluated them more positively than they evaluated themselves. Many valued the written comments and anecdotal information.

Staff input into program changes increased involvement in peer review. The majority of participants stated that they were comfortable with the process. Areas of difficulty were: (1) giving constructive criticism, (2) evaluating peers who worked other shifts, and (3) receiving evaluations after the due date. With one exception, all participants were eager to continue peer review.

To test the reliability of the peer review form, voluntarily submitted peer evaluations were compared with administrative evaluations of the same individual. The t test for comparison of the main difference in scores was nonsignificant ($p = 0.3$).

Because of the positive effects of practicing peer review, participants surmise that the quality of patient care has also improved. It was decided that the peer review committee would keep the system active by initiating the process every six months, reviewing staff feedback and making necessary adjustments.

REFERENCES

1. Olson, E. Strategies and Techniques for the Nurse as a Change Agent. *Nursing Clinics of North America* 14:2 (June 1979) p. 323–336.
2. Lippitt, R., Watson, J. and Westley, B. *The Dynamics of Planned Change* (New York: Harcourt, Brace and World, 1958).
3. Welch, L.B. Planned Change in Nursing: The Theory. *Nursing Clinics of North America* 14:2 (June 1979) p. 307–321.
4. Gold, J. and V. Sachs, Peer Review—A Working Experiment, *Nursing Outlook* 21:10 (October 1973) p. 634–636.
5. Mermet, S. *Responses Resulting from the Introduction of Change into a Nursing Unit* (Seattle: University of Washington, 1976), p. 10–11, 19.

SHAPING THE ENVIRONMENT FOR PROFESSIONAL NURSING PRACTICE

Creating a positive environment for the professional practice of nursing should be viewed as one of the most critical elements in fulfillment of the nurse executive's role. It is possible even in 1987 to provide cost-effective, high quality care by following the simple equation that satisfied nurses equal satisfied consumers. Although it is not possible to create a perfect environment where harmony is present at all times, it is probable that a nursing organization can develop around a managerial system that emphasizes professional goals and achievements, effectively delegates responsibility and authority, uses the expert talents of practicing staff nurses for monitoring quality control, and promotes excellence through programs of commendation and reward for special achievement.

However, creating such an environment requires shaking off such vestiges of the past as time clocks and the passion for supervision and replacing them with trust, support, and internal and external networking mechanisms. Most important is the willingness to share power with all nurses in an organization, thus empowering them to succeed and achieve personal and organizational goals and finally to help create a more powerful total nursing organization for all.

Efforts to decentralize a nursing organization will have less than the desired results if a spirit of participatory management does not accompany the organizational changes. A nurse executive committed to the belief that the professional nurse is a self-controlled, critical thinker with a desire to grow beyond the limits of a job description will plan the organizational environment to accommodate this vision. Participatory management can be easily implemented in any situation and often serves as a learning experience for nurses who can then move more easily into more formal governance structures. Most nurses will meet expectations and often stretch beyond them, given the opportunity to do so.

The famous football coach Vincent Lombardi once said that the quality of a person's life is in direct proportion to his or her commitment to excellence, regardless of the individual's chosen field of endeavor.[1] If

Nurs Admin Q, 1987, 11(4), 11–35
©1987 Aspen Publishers, Inc.

the nurse executive establishes an environment fostering excellence and, like the coach, guides, encourages, and supports the team towards victory, the rewards for all will be multiplied by the efforts of so many achievers. Their commitment to excellence will raise them above the ordinary expectations of job satisfaction and present new horizons of inquiry, challenge, and expectations that result ultimately in a heightened sense of professionalism.

Various recent nursing studies and best-selling books describe common expectations of employees working in a companies or hospitals they perceive to be responsive and excellent. Very simply these expectations include communication (sharing of information with staff), influence (listening to staff, involving them in decision making), and recognition (providing positive reinforcement).[2] These approaches can be used to build understanding and cooperation that result in a more harmonious environment for delivery of patient care.

Clearly this era of cost containment, ethical considerations, and competition has presented the nurse executive with many new challenges; yet if these challenges are viewed as opportunity rather than calamity, much can be gained for the individual nurse and the professional in general.

The opportunities open to nurse executives can, with their guidance and sincere assistance, also be made available to practicing professional nurses. It may then be evident that, as Ralph Waldo Emerson said, "It is one of the most beautiful compensations of this life that no man can sincerely try to help another without helping himself."[3]

REFERENCES

1. *Motivational Quotes* (Lombard, Ill.: Great Quotations, 1986) p. 1.
2. Buccheri, R.C. Nursing Supervision: A New Look at an Old Role. *Nursing Administration Quarterly* 11, no. 2 (1986): 11-25.
3. *Motivational Quotes,* 20.

—Joan Trofino

PARTICIPATIVE MANAGEMENT

One of the objectives in nursing administration is to promote an atmosphere that enhances each professional nurse's self-esteem and paves the way for self-determination or self-actualization. Participative management assists nurses as they all reach for this goal. As defined by the National Commission of Nursing's Summary Report and Recommendations, 1983, participative management is the style of management in which the leader encourages members of an organization to contribute ideas, opinions, and recommendations. Communication travels in an upward as well as downward manner and group decision making is promoted.[1] Drucker states that increased knowledge and sharing of responsibility do not undermine authority, but rather enhance authority.[2] Communication and decision making are intertwined throughout this nursing division, and the payoff is always gratifying.

Decentralization

Providing the right foundation is essential, because nurses must feel that their nursing managers are sincerely interested in and believe in them. McGregor, in his Theory Y, assumes that people are not by nature lazy, unreliable, irresponsible, or immature.[3] He believes that people can be basically self-directed and creative if properly motivated and permitted to express creativity. Decentralization of Riverview's nursing services—delegating the decision making as low as possible in the nursing organization—has provided a solid base for projects. Eighteen nursing units are managed by clinical coordinators who are department heads and thus have 24-hour responsibility and accountability. Hiring occurs at the unit level and thus appropriately meets the needs of the unit. Each unit has an assistant clinical coordinator (ACC) for each shift who hires, counsels, disciplines, and terminates employees as necessary. Using criteria-based performance appraisals, the ACC evaluates shift employees and recommends merit raises. This first-line manager also assesses the educational needs of the staff and plans appropriate unit inservice programs. Since new employees have the opportunity to assess their supervisor and the working environment before accepting employment, it is not surprising that bonding occurs at this level. This unit-shift identity enhances working relationships and ultimately the quality of patient care.

The clinical coordinators work closely with their assistants to achieve unit goals, promote communication, and identify and resolve problems. Responsive nursing management, which is essential to maintain a collegial environment for the practice of professional nursing, is more than listening to problems and resolving issues on a daily basis. It includes an awareness of changes within the profession that alter the work environment and a vision of what the future might hold. Directors and assistant directors work closely with the clinical coordinators to plan for the future. At this level strategies are developed to prepare for change in today's complex and constantly changing environment.

To complete the decentralization process and to retain clinical nursing positions threatened by a budget reduction of $250,000, the Riverview nursing division

planned in 1982 for the elimination of shift supervisors. The ACCs were in different stages of development, and the shift supervisors assisted them in their maturation within the role and generally performed hospitalwide administrative tasks on shift. Argyris's immaturity-maturity theory states that individuals move on a continuum of growth: When expectations for their behavior change, they move from immature to mature behavior.[4] To accelerate the development of the ACCs, we developed a forum in which education and networking could take place.

A decentralized organizational structure and efforts toward participative management have led to increased socialization among nurses at all levels.

Two years later incumbent supervisors had found new positions within the organization. Each ACC acts on a rotating basis as a resource person on his or her shift for a designated day, usually remaining on the clinical unit to handle administrative questions and concerns. Completion of the decentralization of nursing management heightened everyone's development and paved the way for more decision making at the staff nurse level. A decentralized organizational structure and efforts toward participative management have led to increased socialization among nurses at all levels, a predictable occurrence in the work environment when self-determination is the goal and expected outcome.

Participative management

We define participative management as an effort to maintain an open environment conducive to democratic leadership that promotes problem solving at the unit level and fosters job satisfaction and development of personnel; to actively involve staff members in the development and implementation of nursing and patient care policies, procedures, standards, and activities through participation on nursing and hospital committees and the Nursing Council; and to encourage increased autonomy and authority of each nursing unit through decentralization of the nursing services.

Participative management flows from the executive level to the staff nurse level. Communication, a key element, occurs in both upward and downward directions. Staff nurses are given opportunity and encouragement in an atmosphere of open communication to provide input on the activities of the nursing division and thus to influence all phases of the management process. Primary nursing, an essential component of a participative system, permits nurses the independence to practice professionally and to help make decisions about the specifics of patients' care; thus primary nursing fosters increased professional effectiveness in a climate of self-development.

Nurse management meetings

Participative management has begun with monthly nurse management meetings at which middle nurse managers and nurse administrators collaborate on various subjects according to a published agenda that includes such topics as staffing, staff development, quality assurance, current legislation, and particular in-house concerns. Although formal and chaired by the vice president for patient care services, the meetings encourage open discussion. Ideas, problems, concerns, solutions, and recommendations are presented, decisions are made, and the group reaches a consensus.

Clinical and assistant clinical coordinator forums

Additionally, the clinical coordinators conduct a monthly resource forum for initiating problem-solving procedures and making recommendations to the management group. This forum is chaired by an elected member and has existed since 1978.

Recommendations are also made to the management group by committees of ACCs who meet monthly to enhance their professional growth through networking and education, as they serve as administrative resource persons. Solving problems; sharing individual management approaches, ideas, and experiences; and making recommendations about the clinical areas to nurse management all evolve from this forum. Although the forums were previously guided by an assistant director and a clinical coordinator, they are now chaired by a member of the group who is elected annually. The recommendations and minutes of the clinical coordinator and ACC forums are presented, reviewed, and discussed at nurse management meetings.

Staff nurse involvement

It is expected that all staff nurses will be involved in some way in participative decision making. They may be involved formally as they serve on various nursing committees such as professional practice, staffing forum, nursing council, nursing/pharmacy, nursing research, or quality assurance. Staff nurses may also serve with physicians and administrators on such formal hospital committees as orthopedic collaborative practice, medical/surgical dialogue, or pharmacy and therapeutics. These groups also foster collaborative practice between the nursing and medical staffs.

Today, staff nurses also cochair nursing committees. Initially, clinical coordinators recommended nurses based on their development, background, clinical expertise, and area of practice. Currently, many staff nurses initiate their own requests to serve on a particular committee. They act as representatives of their units, specialties, and the division, sharing the results of committee activities with their colleagues informally and through formal reporting at unit meetings. The input, recommendations, and suggestions of their colleagues are then brought back to the committee.

Although this process takes time, the outcomes of participative management are generally better received by the staff and consequently are more easily and quickly assimilated into practice.

Management by objectives

Riverview's participative style of management is enhanced by the use of management by objectives, which fosters creativity and enhances goal achievement. Management by objectives on an abstract level can be described as "a philosophy of management or administration that seeks to convert organizational goals to personal goals to satisfactory performance outcomes. The organization establishes goals and action plans to attain these goals at the highest level of the organization; then, by pushing the goal setting activity down through all levels of the organization, it ensures that the lower administrative levels understand, accept, and control their own efforts toward the accomplishments of these higher level goals."[5]

The formulation process begins annually at unit level meetings conducted to identify needs, identify new areas to explore or pursue, and share unique and original ideas. Using unit-level suggestions to formulate objectives for the coming year, the administrative staff drafts a statement of goals. The draft is then reviewed both at unit and management levels for content, realism, feasibility, attainability, and acceptability. The goals must be accepted by all members of the nursing division before they are made final and then presented to the hospital president for final review and approval.

Developed by the individual unit, unit-level goals reflect division goals and suggest methods to help nurses attain these goals. Incorporated into the unit-level goals are objectives specific to particular areas of clinical practice that must also be reviewed and accepted by the staff on a particular unit. The ability of nurse managers and staff to attain stated goals is reflected in annual performance appraisals and merit raises.

Since the inception of management by objectives, accomplishments of staff have been noted and credit given where it is due. An annual meeting is held for all members of the nursing staff; hospital administrators, physicians, local legislators, affiliating agencies, and members of the board of directors are invited to attend this presentation of our accomplishments. The nursing division takes pride in demonstrating that nurses contribute positively to achievement of goals and to promotion of quality patient care.

Nursing council

In 1975, a nursing council was formed to strengthen communication and to provide a mechanism for involvement in decision making at all levels in the nursing division. The council's stated objectives were

- to improve communication among all levels of nursing personnel;
- to provide an effective forum for the solution of individual employee problems in accordance with a problem review procedure;
- to identify patient care problems and to present suggestions for possible solutions to nursing management; and

- to make recommendations regarding the formulation of new policies and the revision of current ones.

This committee has always been chaired by a director of nursing. Members are appointed for a period of six months. Service is voluntary, but once an appointment is accepted, attendance and participation are expected.

Over the years many problems have been resolved in this forum. Employees who present suggestions that the committee considers will improve care or curb costs are awarded either an honorable mention or a U.S. savings bond. The need for the Nursing Council continues to be demonstrated by positive evaluations from the membership, who continue to support this mechanism for upward communication.

REFERENCES

1. National Commission of Nursing. *Summary Report and Recommendations* (Chicago: The Hospital Research and Educational Trust, 1983.)
2. Drucker, P.F. *Management* (New York: Harper & Row, 1974.)
3. McGregor, D. *The Human Side of Enterprise* (New York: McGraw-Hill, 1980.)
4. Argyris, C. *Interpersonal Competence and Organizational Effectiveness* (Homewood, Ill.: Ervin Dorsey Press, 1962.)
5. Robbins, S.P. *The Administrative Process* (Englewood Cliffs, N.J.: Prentice-Hall, 1980) p. 171.

—Marguerite Dieffenbach
—Cynthia Marvulli

MANAGEMENT DEVELOPMENT

The philosophy and environment of Riverview Medical Center's nursing division support and encourage autonomy in practice and professional development for all members of the nursing staff. A key element in the success of our decentralized management structure has been a comprehensive and systematic approach to management development. Drucker describes management development as providing those skills necessary for people to do their jobs effectively.[1] The environment at Riverview supports the acquisition of necessary skills and knowledge by all levels of nursing managers.

Development of charge nurses

At Riverview Medical Center management development begins at the staff nurse level. Under the direction of unit managers, staff nurses are guided systematically in the transition to charge nurse. It is expected that all RNs will perform effectively in the charge nurse role within their three-month probationary period. In preparation for this responsibility, all RNs must attend a full-day charge nurse workshop that covers such topics as assertiveness, problem solving, delegation, use of resources, and communication. Clinical coordinators serve as instructors because they are close to the needs of new charge nurses on the clinical units.

In addition to attending the workshop, staff nurses must meet the following specific charge nurse criteria before assuming the charge nurse role:

- fulfillment of staff RN job description;
- completion of probationary period;
- demonstration of ability to solve problems;
- demonstration of ability to function effectively in stressful or emergency situations;
- demonstration of ability to communicate effectively;
- demonstration of ability to assign patient care in normal and unexpected staffing situations;

- demonstration of ability to use personnel and material resources appropriately;
- knowledge of the policies and procedures of Riverview Hospital; and
- demonstration of ability to administer or delegate appropriate nursing care for patients in stable or unstable medical conditions.

These criteria were developed to foster a consistent, comprehensive approach to management development at the charge nurse level and emphasize those abilities and skills necessary to perform effectively as a charge nurse.

Development of assistant clinical coordinators

In keeping with the nursing division's commitment to managerial growth, responsibilities of the assistant clinical coordinator (ACC) have continually expanded. Reporting directly to the clinical coordinator, the ACC coordinates patient care activities in addition to managing a specific shift. Each ACC interviews, hires, and evaluates nursing personnel working on his or her shift and also assumes responsibility for unit scheduling, staff development activities, and attainment of divisional and unit goals.

In addition, these highly skilled first-line managers assume administrative responsibility for the entire medical center when they serve on a rotating basis as resource persons. This innovative system of providing for administrative coverage on a 24-hour basis was implemented in 1983, when budgetary constraints prompted an administrative decision to fill the traditional shift supervisory positions with ACCs whose roles could be expanded to include administrative responsibilities. During a two-year period, ACC's leadership and management skills were carefully developed to prepare them for their new role. The working environment has been purposely structured to foster professional growth and managerial effectiveness within this group.

ACC autonomy criteria

Completed during the three-month probationary period, the following objective criteria have been designed to guide the development of ACCs and to evaluate their progress:

- fulfillment of ACC job description;
- completion of probationary period;
- completion of management course;
- completion of cross-training for and scheduled to work in administrative assistant's role;
- demonstration of ability to handle patient and staffing crises;
- demonstration of ability to communicate effectively with other departments;
- demonstration of ability to solve problems;
- demonstration of ability to use cross-reference index and other resources;
- demonstration of ability to work with other ACCs to solve problems;
- consistent attendance and active participation at designated ACC forum; and
- completion of preceptor program.

Successful completion of these criteria indicates an ability to act autonomously in the ACC role and a readiness to assume the responsibilities of resource person for the entire hospital.

As part of the program to develop ACC autonomy, a two-week period of comprehensive cross-training to the role of resource person is scheduled. During this time, an autonomous ACC serves as preceptor and guides the new manager in carrying out such responsibilities as staffing on a hospitalwide basis, acting as an administrative resource for interpreting medical center policies, and taking responsibility for departmental and intradepartmental problem solving.

Completion of the criteria for ACC autonomy also requires attendance at a comprehensive, four-day management development program taught by Riverview clinical coordinators and nurse administrators and designed to explore skills needed by the beginning manager, such as management by objectives, counseling, negotiation, assertiveness, interviewing skills, and performance appraisal. Structured to include lectures, role playing, and group discussion, this program encourages active participation in the learning process.

Nursing resource manual

Designed to augment existing policy and procedure manuals, this resource serves as a tool to foster independent problem solving. Included in the manual are timely memorandums and guidelines addressing unique problems that may be encountered by the resource person.

ACC forums

Scheduled monthly on each shift, these lively meetings provide ACCs with opportunities for group problem solving, networking, discussion of current issues within the division, and pertinent inservice education. Attendance at forums is required because they promote professional growth in the management role.

The development of ACC forums reflects the expanding scope and responsibility of ACCs. In five years, the purpose and function of the forums have changed significantly. In 1981, forums were implemented on all shifts to enhance communication among ACCs, increase the opportunity for networking, and provide ongoing inservice education. A staff development instructor

By 1987, the ACC forums had evolved into autonomous problem-solving bodies that elect their own chairpersons from among group members.

and clinical specialist cochaired the meetings. By 1987, the ACC forums had evolved into autonomous problem-solving bodies that elect their own chairpersons from among group members. Forum agendas and inservice education programs are now planned by the group. ACC forum chairpersons attend monthly nursing management meetings to report on forum activities, participate in decision making, and provide informational feedback to forum members from the nursing management group.

Development of nurse managers

As at all levels in Riverview's decentralized structure, opportunities supporting professional growth at the department head level have been developed. A 100% tuition reimbursement program for credits leading to an academic degree and support for continuing education are available to all employees. Nurse managers are encouraged to regularly attend management development programs outside the medical center to take advantage of opportunities for networking with professional colleagues.

Monthly clinical coordinator resource group meetings are scheduled to provide a forum for discussion of pertinent issues, proposed programs, and ongoing problems. Results of such discussions may be communicated as recommendations to higher-level nursing management. Clinical coordinators elected by peers to chair the clinical coordinator resource group on a rotating basis enjoy additional opportunities to develop their leadership skills.

Riverview's nursing management group is chaired by the vice president of Patient Care Services and is attended by nurse administrators, clinical coordinators, chairpersons of the ACC forums, and clinical specialists. In addition to planning, reviewing, and making decisions, the group discusses trends in health care, issues in the nursing profession, legislative activities, and advances in developing the nursing organization at Riverview Medical Center.

REFERENCE

1. Drucker, P.F. *Management* (New York: Harper & Row, 1974.)

—Diane Brady
—Mary Jane Shea
—Patricia Gossett

CREATING AN AUTONOMOUS PRACTICE ENVIRONMENT

One of the generally accepted criteria for a profession is that it maintains autonomy over its own practice. It is a unique responsibility of a nurse administrator to create an autonomous practice environment for the staff, one in which the RN can indeed practice as a professional. The creation of a professional environment has been foremost in the evolution of the nursing division at Riverview Medical Center over the past 13 years.

Primary nursing

The primary nursing model is viewed as one in which RNs function to the full scope of their professional role, assuming full authority and accountability for the nursing care delivered to a patient or group of patients over a 24-hour period, from admission through discharge. Primary nursing was adopted in 1977 as Riverview's nursing care delivery system. In preparation for the implementation of primary nursing, a committee researched the literature, made visits to nursing divisions that had implemented the model, and prepared a proposal. Primary nursing was adopted after further discussion with a consultant. Primary nursing has proven most satisfactory for Riverview's staff and patients. The quality of nursing care as documented by quality assurance activities has remained consistently high, while patient evaluation tools have indicated a high degree of patient satisfaction and identification with the primary nurse. Increased autonomy of practice resulting from use of the primary nursing model has fostered professional growth and increased satisfaction and retention of RN staff.

The commitment to primary nursing was clearly demonstrated several years ago when, faced with significant budget cuts, staff nurses requested that the primary nursing model be retained and suggested alternative approaches to budget control. Responding to budget restrictions, the nursing staff reshaped primary nursing into a more contemporary model that supports the autonomy and accountability of the RN and delegates nonprofessional aspects of care to ancillary personnel.

Involvement in developing divisional goals

Just as autonomy in clinical practice is one aspect of the professional practice of nursing, so too is autonomy in shaping the practice environment. Our participative management philosophy and decentralized organizational structure provide an environment in which staff nurses can fulfill their professional role. Management by objectives, in which success is measured in terms of results, supports a professional practice environment. Input from staff nurses forms the basis for the development of annual divisional goals. Staff meet with their clinical coordinators to assess progress in achieving the previous year's goals, identify those that will carry over into the subsequent year, and propose new ones. Goals for the coming year are validated by each clinical unit and accepted or rejected based on their appropriateness. These divisional goals become the basis for developing the more definitive annual goals of each nursing unit. Through participation in goal assessment and goal formation, staff nurses play an active role in shaping the nursing environment in which they practice.

Participation in committees

Another avenue of participation that supports the autonomy of the nurse is committee structure. Consistent with a philosophy of participative management, there is broad-based representation of staff nurses on hospital, medical staff, and nursing division committees. The appointment of staff nurses as active committee members demonstrates the belief that nurses practicing in the clinical setting are best prepared to identify problems and to design solutions, policies, and procedures that will support their practice. Committee participation is viewed as a serious responsibility. A list of committee representatives is posed on each nursing unit.

Quality assurance, staffing forum, nursing council, patient education, and nursing research are committees whose members are predominantly staff nurses. The staff is encouraged to bring suggestions and concerns to peers on the appropriate committee. Staff nurse committee members report on the progress and activities of the committee to their colleagues at monthly unit meetings. Additionally, staff nurses cochair the professional practice and clinical ladder committees.

The professional practice committee is dominated by a majority of staff nurses. Its purpose is to provide a forum for ongoing communication between staff nurses and nursing administration on issues related to clinical practice. The committee fosters staff nurse empowerment through participation in developing, reviewing, and revising the procedures, policies, and standards that guide nursing practice. The committee also recommends corrective action for identified nursing practice problems. Many such problems and issues are identified by division-wide monitors through the quality assurance program. Committee members keep their colleagues apprised of the committee's work and seek their suggestions for future agendas.

The clinical ladder committee was formed to support a current divisional goal—development of a mechanism for recognizing different levels of clinical practice and rewarding the staff nurse who chooses to remain at the bedside. The goal of the committee is development of a proposal that will include job description and criteria-based performance evaluations for each level of practice, as well as operational and financial design. The nucleus of this ad hoc group will serve as the operational committee for implement-

---

The clinical ladder committee was formed to support a current divisional goal—development of a mechanism for recognizing different levels of clinical practice and rewarding the staff nurse who chooses to remain at the bedside.

---

ing the clinical ladder and will eventually evolve into a nurse credentialing committee for the entire division. This is yet another example of the staff RN exercising professional autonomy in shaping the work environment.

Operation of the quality circle concept

The quality circle concept is a mechanism used at both organizational and clinical unit levels to involve staff nurses in the identification and resolution of problems relating to patient care and the environment. This involvement benefits the division in a variety of ways: The front-line nurse has the opportunity to modify the practice environment, thus increasing job satisfaction, enhancing professionalism, and improving patient care. The division is strengthened as nurses fulfill their professional role. All benefit from the creativity engendered by such a system, in which success is measured by outcomes.

Involvement in interviewing prospective managers

Autonomy is also enhanced by the involvement of staff in the appointment of new clinical coordinators (head nurses). Following screening interviews by the personnel office and the director of nursing for the clinical area, a committee of staff nurses and assistant clinical coordinators representing the unit is formed. The unit committee reviews the curriculum vitae of the candidate and composes interview questions that reflect issues and concerns of the staff. Following a formal interview of the candidate, the committee submits a summary of the interview and their written recommendations, which are then forwarded to the director.

This process has proven most beneficial: The staff of the unit have the opportunity to meet and interview the prospective candidate and make their recommendation to nursing administration. The recommendations of the unit are heavily weighed in the final appointment. Candidates have also viewed the group interviewing process positively, welcoming the opportunity to meet representatives of the staff firsthand and to identify congruency of goals. The staff interview process enhances the professional autonomy of the staff by making them a vital part of the decision-making process. It also has the added benefit of providing the newly appointed clinical coordinators with an advance team of staff nurses who can serve as advocates in their transition to the new role.

Staff development

The division's commitment to autonomy of staff nurses is demonstrated in various avenues of staff development. The staff nurse is afforded the opportunity to grow professionally and personally while remaining at the bedside. One such avenue for growth is the preceptor program, in which staff RNs volunteer to assist their colleagues in becoming oriented to the nursing division, to their unit, and to their job responsibilities. Staff nurses also serve as preceptors to nursing students, externs, and radiology students. The nurse preceptor is prepared in principles of adult education, counseling, and evaluation. After successful completion of the educational program, the preceptor is assigned an orientee who assumes the schedule of the preceptor. This program has assisted in maintaining a low turnover rate. In repeated surveys, the preceptors have expressed pride in their role and a sense of satisfaction in assisting their colleagues.

One of the preferred roles of the preceptors is working with externs, guiding future colleagues in adapting to the real world of nursing. The extern program was implemented about five years ago to enhance recruitment efforts and to promote professional development. Senior nursing students are selected for a summer externship of ten weeks. Each student is assigned to a medical-surgical unit with a preceptor and practices in an expanded nursing assistant's role under the preceptor's direction. Two one-week clinical rotations to the specialty areas of their choice are offered to externs. These practical learning experiences incorporate concepts such as prioritization and organization into clinical practice, thus enhancing externs' classroom learning. Included in the experience are educational programs on topics chosen by the externs to meet their identified needs. Many externs have returned to our nursing division following graduation, and some now serve as preceptors themselves.

This year, the Staff Development Department began contracting for qualified staff members to assist in meeting the educational needs of the staff. Managers and staff nurses responded. Criteria were developed for approval to teach programs at various levels, and the applicants were screened for acceptance. Guidance in the development and presentation of programs is provided by the Staff Development Department. Compensation for contractual educators is given in accordance with an agreement separate from that affecting their positions as members of the division. The nurse who elects to function in this role operates as an independent practitioner. The response to this program has been extremely positive. The nurses take pride in and demonstrate commitment to their educational responsibilities. They have expanded their professional role by their own choice, received recognition from their colleagues, and enabled the division to creatively use scarce educational resources. The division logo's motto, "Where Theory and Practice Come Together," is a true reflection of an environment that fosters autonomous practice. The opportunities and support for autonomous practice have stimulated the personal and professional growth of the staff and of the division as a whole.

—Patricia K. Kane
—Susan Palette
—Ruth Strickland

STAFFING AND BUDGETARY CONTROLS

In the nursing division, unit managers are responsible for personnel selection, orientation, evaluation, and termination. Decentralized interviewing and hiring have facilitated matching staff to the appropriate unit and thus have helped to decrease turnover rate and to encourage retention in the division and cohesiveness of unit staff members.

A weekly position vacancy control report is submitted to the staffing office by the clinical coordinators and directors so that available positions can be posted. This alerts the staff to new opportunities within the division and the nurse recruiter to vacant positions.

Riverview's decentralized nursing division is supported by a centralized staffing office. This office assists the unit managers in recruiting on-call staff and in keeping records for payroll and staffing. The staffing office is open 7 days a week from 6:00 a.m. to 12:00 a.m. (midnight) and is handled by nonnursing clericals. This relieves nurse managers from the tasks of telephoning and calculating the payroll, thus freeing them to focus on patient care.

Master schedules are unit based and include a float and full-time equivalency allocation for benefit replacement. On-call personnel are assigned to specific units to encourage their identification with a unit cluster. The use of four-week repeatable schedules provides a consistent schedule for staff members, who have full knowledge of their schedule prior to official posting. Changes and requests are handled at the unit level. Staff members are responsible for development of their own schedules, which they plan among themselves. The assistant clinical coordinator or clinical coordinator approves all time off and all schedule changes with the result that the schedule is consistent but also flexible enough to meet the request of the staff. The clinical coordinator is responsible for staffing on a 24-hour basis.

Cluster unit staffing

Cluster units were formed in 1986 to augment staffing resources by decreasing the need to reassign staff to less familiar areas while allowing for floating between similar units. Unit managers of the cluster meet to plan schedules together and reassign float staff when necessary. Staff have become more efficient and comfortable in the cluster units while expanding their expertise in particular clinical areas of practice.

Assistant clinical coordinators assign themselves to serve as daily cluster representatives. They meet in the staffing office before each shift to review their own staffing requirements and to negotiate with other cluster representatives when reassignment of staff is necessary. Implemented to further decentralize the staffing procedure, cluster staffing promotes better understanding of the staffing function and places additional control for staffing at the unit level.

GRASP implementation committee

In 1986 one of Riverview's goals was to revise and update its patient classification system. An early GRASP (Grace-Reynolds Application and Study of Poland, English Thornton, and Owens) model had been used since 1984. To implement the updated model, the GRASP implementation committee, consisting of representative staff nurses from all areas and shifts, was formed. This committee is responsible for designing and piloting a new tool for measuring nursing workload and patient acuity. At Riverview these data are used to develop statistics on staffing, utilization, acuity, and budgeting. The committee members were educated in the GRASP System process and are quickly becoming experts on the process within their particular specialties. All specialty areas and specialized medical-surgical areas are currently designing and piloting their own patient acuity and workload management charts.

The GRASP implementation committee's responsibility will also include maintaining the currency and relevance of the GRASP tool through biannual review. In this way, the system for assessing acuity will continually reflect patient needs, and data on nursing care hours will accurately reflect the hours of care delivered by nurses. The staff have undertaken this project under the direction of a project coordinator. Because data on patient acuity are used for staffing, budgeting, and workload management, it is imperative that all staff nurses understand and support the system adopted for classifying patients and managing workloads.

Staffing forum

The staffing forum was created to support group problem-solving approaches to staffing issues. The forum allows for staff participation, education, and decision making regarding staffing procedures and is cochaired by the assistant director for staffing and finance and a clinical coordinator. This com-

Input and feedback from this forum guide nurse executives in creating an environment that supports the concept of staff as a vital resource to the division.

mittee has staff nurse representation from each unit and varying shifts.

Discussion topics include position vacancy volumes, recruitment strategies, budgetary status, turnover rate, call-out rates, patient day volume, acuity statistics, proposals for cost containment, economic and health care trends, changes in and updates to the New Jersey reimbursement structure, and feedback related to general staffing. Discussing these topics educates the staff with regard to mechanisms of personnel recruitment, budgeting, and external forces affecting financial structure.

Conversely, input and feedback from this forum guide nurse executives in creating an environment that supports the concept of staff as a vital resource to the division. Without their participation, appropriate use of resources and excellence in care would be only a dream.

—*Marguerite Gelcius*

SHAPING A COLLABORATIVE PRACTICE ENVIRONMENT

Strengthening and supporting physician-nurse relationships has long been recognized as conducive to creating an environment that promotes high quality patient care. The National Joint Practice Commission published guidelines in 1981 for the establishment of joint collaborative practice in hospitals.[1] At Riverview Medical Center, the concept of collaborative practice is supported by the medical and

nursing staffs and by hospital administration. The center's first formal joint practice committee was established in 1983 on the orthopedic service.

Innovative design

While the Medical-Surgical Collaborative Practice Dialogue Group was formally initiated in September 1985, ideas for its development had been germinating for several years. Dialogue between nurses and physicians supported the need for a forum in which issues and concerns regarding medical-surgical patient care could be shared in a collaborative environment.

A proposal that outlined the purpose and organization of a medical-surgical collaborative practice group was developed jointly and presented to the chief medical executive officer by the vice president for patient care services and the chief of medicine. The proposal delineated the purpose and structure of the committee. In keeping with the recommendations of the National Joint Practice Committee, the membership was to be composed of equal numbers of physicians and nurses. To meet the needs of an integrated service environment, a single committee representing all of the medical-surgical practice areas was proposed. Physicians representing a variety of disciplines within medicine and surgery were approached and volunteered to participate on the committee. Nurse members included nursing managers and staff representing the hospital's eight medical-surgical units.

In keeping with the spirit of collaborative practice, it was proposed that chairmanship of the group be shared jointly by a physician and a nurse. This joint chairmanship, to which the nurses felt strongly committed, resulted in the creation of a dialogue group as opposed to a standing committee, since the medical staff bylaws would have required chairmanship by a physician. The committee was accepted as proposed and has been meeting on a regular basis. The group is cochaired by a clinical coordinator (head nurse) and the director of medicine.

The primary goal of the group was to establish a forum in which issues and problems evolving from the medical-surgical areas could be ventilated and resolved. Previously, there had been no arena where nursing and medical staff could address the needs of medical-surgical patients, who comprise the largest volume of clients. Additionally, attention was focused on enhancing relationships between nurses and physicians, thereby supporting high quality health care.

Common goals

One of the initial issues the dialogue group discussed was the increased demands placed on physicians and nurses by cost containment and professional review organizations. This shared concern led to a sense of cohesiveness among the group members. With higher patient acuity and shorter length of stay imposed by the diagnosis related group system of payment, it became apparent that time management was a concern of all. One approach to saving time was the development of a communication sheet to be placed on the front of each patient's chart. This eliminated the need for the nurse to be "on watch" for a physician. This tool reduced tension and saved time for both

---

With higher patient acuity and shorter length of stay imposed by the diagnosis related group system of payment, it became apparent that time management was a concern of all.

---

nursing and medical staff personnel, who now have a standard sheet on which to communicate. All disciplines within the institution have joined in using this tool.

To expedite diagnostic patient testing, specimen packets with reminder signs for collection were developed. These tools have proven effective in timely collection of specimens, supporting the shorter length of patient stay.

Extensive amounts of nursing time were being spent in reversing the order of discharged patients' charts. The cost of this task, accomplished at the unit level, was identified and discussed by the committee. The result was the delegation of chart reversal to the Medical Records Department. Patient concerns relating to the transmission of acquired immune deficiency syndrome (AIDS) through blood transfusions were addressed. Systems in place for patient-directed blood donations were discussed. Both nurses and physicians were educated in policies, procedures, and options available, thereby supporting a consistent approach to patient education regarding the safety of blood transfusions.

The physicians expressed interest in formal programs of nurse recognition. Systems and awards already in place within the nursing division were shared. Other areas such as nurse marketing ventures, turnover rate, budget, and nurse satisfaction were also discussed.

Another approach to better serving the patient population was evident in multidisciplinary review of preadmission testing procedures. The results of a three-month survey of existing procedures and patient satisfaction were shared with this dialogue group. Information gathered on preferred times for preadmission testing and public opinion of the system was analyzed. Investigation of possible changes involved laboratory, radiology, and electrocardiology departments, with input from all department heads.

A patient discharge instruction form was also developed by the group. The nursing discharge summary and patient discharge instructions were combined into a single form. The form was developed to include a chart copy, a copy for the physician, and a copy for the patient. Once again, time has been conserved while providing a high quality tool for patient care.

The group agrees on the need to improve patient education related to understanding of medications and is viewing available patient educational tools. Its goal is to enhance patient discharge instructions with printed information on medication to be continued after discharge.

Disseminating information

Communication of the work and progress of the committee takes a variety of forms. Word-of-mouth communication by both physicians and nurse members is one of the most significant. Formal lines of communication to the medical staff include reports to the Department of Medicine and Department of Surgery by physician members, and then to the medical executive committee. A further reporting relationship to the medical executive staff was established by the appointment of the coordinator for medical affairs to membership on the dialogue group. The fact that a number of physician members of the collaborative practice dialogue group are also members of the medical executive committee further strengthens communication.

Communication to the nursing division takes place through channeling issues and proposals for review to the professional practice committee, a committee of staff nurses, and to the nursing management group for approval and implementation.

A continuing dialogue between nurse members and their colleagues in the clinical area keeps the staff apprised of progress and provides an avenue of input for further topics for discussion. The vice president for patient care services, who attends the medical executive committee meetings, provides a further link in the interpretation of collaborative practice outcomes.

Collaborative practice: A nurse's perspective

As a nurse member of the Medical/Surgical Collaborative Practice Dialogue Group, we can attest to the value that this committee offers the profession. The dialogue group provides a forum in which nurses can collaborate on a professional level with physicians. Sharing and respecting each other's opinions fosters helpful interaction that encourages members to value each other, improves professional relationships, and strengthens relationships with patients. Of the many positive outcomes of this group, one that we have found especially rewarding is the sharing of knowledge and expertise with other nurses and physicians.

With the increase in acuity level, medical-surgical nurses are dealing with more severely ill patients, requiring a broader knowledge base. This committee endorsed additional education and increased interaction and dialogue among physicians and nurses. Physicians have come to the group and to individual members to offer their support and involvement in staff education programs. Educational activities are being accomplished with physician involvement on the clinical units. This approach allows more spontaneity for both nurses and physicians and further enhancement of a collegial relationship.

Sharing information through this collaborative practice group has strengthened relationships and provided a forum that allows nurses and physicians to share their respective ideas to better coordinate patient care.

REFERENCE

1. National Joint Practice Commission. *Guidelines for Establishing Joint or Collaborative Practice in Hospitals* (Chicago: NJPC, 1981.)

—Patricia K. Kane
—Bernadette McCabe
—Joan Bierly

COLLABORATIVE PRACTICE: A PHYSICIAN'S PERSPECTIVE

Riverview Medical Center is a large, full service, nonteaching community hospital where the nursing staff, due to a lack of house staff, has accepted a large share of the responsibility for patient care. Over the past few years, a need for better communication between the physician and nursing staffs became apparent. For this reason, in September of 1985, a Medical/Surgical Collaborative Practice Dialogue Group was formed. This group, which is not an official hospital committee, was formed primarily to improve patient care by promoting a better understanding of the common problems faced by physicians and nurses in delivering quality medical care.

This group is cochaired by a physician and a representative of the nursing staff, who coauthor the agenda with input from the entire committee, which is made up of an equal number of physicians and nurses. In this way, a large variety of topics can be discussed, from very practical problems to more involved philosophical issues that can affect the entire operation of the hospital.

In its first year of existence, this group has proved to be a very successful venture. It is the only open forum in the hospital in which physicians and nurses can discuss common

concerns and also resolve problems about which there may be differences of opinions between these two groups.

Although the committee has no official authority and cannot make policy, it has reported its discussions and recommendations to the individual departments and through them to the executive committee, and thus has effected a significant number of meaningful changes to improve patient care.

Probably the most important byproduct of this collaborative practice dialogue group has been an open forum that provides a congenial and nonthreatening environment for everyone involved, in which matters of common concern can be discussed frankly. This forum has had the net effect of significantly improving relations between two groups that in many hospitals have traditionally had an adversarial relationship.

At Riverview, the collaborative practice group represents a giant step taken toward improving nurse-physician relationships, thus achieving a significant improvement in total patient care.

—Charles Miller

NURSING RESEARCH: ALIVE AND WELL IN A COMMUNITY MEDICAL CENTER

Can nursing research be conducted in a community medical center? Research has long been an endeavor that staff nurses have avoided. Clinical nursing research, important to the growth and development of the nursing profession, should become an essential component of every nurse's practice. At Riverview Medical Center, a professional practice environment encourages the legitimate involvement of the clinical nurse in research activities.

The nursing research committee was formed at Riverview in 1975. Its purpose is to enhance the quality of nursing practice by promoting understanding of the research process and by facilitating the implementation of research studies at this 500-bed community medical center.

The committee, which is composed of staff nurses and nurses in management roles, seeks to fulfill its goal through a variety of activities. Because a majority of the nurses are graduates of associate degree and diploma schools of nursing, one focus of the committee has been to educate its members in the research process by reviewing various types of research and the critical elements of a research proposal. Committee members develop their critical skills by preparing monthly critiques of research articles according to recognized guidelines for evaluating research projects. Members of the committee volunteer to present a study to their colleagues, evaluating the strengths and limitations of the design and its implications for practice. Over the years committee members have presented research studies on subjects ranging from pet therapy to the validation of infant behavior identified by neonatal nurses. This approach has increased committee members' receptivity to research by enhancing their ability to critically assess the implications of its findings for nursing practice.

Staff education

Another important function of the committee has been to increase the staff's awareness of the research process, both through reports of committee activities and through formal educational programs. Nursing research seminars open also to nurses outside Riverview provide a forum for nurse researchers to share the design, realities of implementation, and outcomes of their studies. Attendance at these seminars has slowly increased over the past years, reflecting a growing recognition of nursing research as a vital element of the profession.

Implementation of research proposals

Over the years nursing research committee members have served as the initial reviewers for nursing research projects conducted at Riverview. The staff have been most receptive to nurse researchers and have participated in studies exploring such diverse topics as nurses' abilities to assess behavioral cues of prelingual children and nurses' interactions with hospice patients.

Although many of the clinical studies have been conducted by student affiliates in graduate and doctoral programs, involvement of the staff in actual clinical research has been a positive experience that stimulates interest in the critical evaluation of nursing practice. Studies designed and conducted by staff members themselves have included topics such as anxiety in chemotherapy patients, and the relationship of quality circles, a mechanism for involving staff nurses in identification and resolution of problems, to staff nurse satisfaction.

While much remains to be done, success in establishing support for nursing research in a community medical center has contributed to the shaping of a professional practice environment.

—Patricia K. Kane

FORMATION OF AN ORTHOPEDIC COLLABORATIVE PRACTICE COMMITTEE

At Riverview Medical Center, a 500-bed, acute care community hospital, the nursing division has promoted a milieu for participative management. Staff nurses at Riverview serve on hospital and nursing committees. Therefore, they are a part of the decision-making forces that have an impact on patient care. This environment is the basis for collaborative practice between the nurse and physician.

History

In 1983 the nursing division identified the need to enhance communication between physicians and nurses within a formal structure. Certain key elements necessary for collaboration, such as primary nursing and decentralization, were already in place. Due to homogeneity of the practice setting and the need to incorporate orthopedic medical and nursing regimens, the Orthopedic Department was selected to pilot the initial joint practice committee.

Committee formation

The orthopedic clinical coordinator (head nurse) and the chief of orthopedics served as cochairpersons of the first orthopedic joint practice committee (OJPC). They subsequently selected five nurses and five physicians to be active members of the committee. Within the organizational structure, the OJPC was responsible to a steering committee composed of the president of the medical staff, the president of the hospital, and the vice president for nursing.

At the first meeting goals and objectives were formulated (see box). In subsequent meetings the committee members discussed physicians' and nurses' roles and relationships, as well as methods to improve patient care. They also considered approaches to the establishment of protocols and the implementation of an integrated patient record to be used both by nurses and physicians.

Committee process

Committee members participated in a multifaceted educational process. Articles and publications referring to collaborative practice were compiled and disseminated to all committee members, and an on-site visit was made to a medical center that had an established joint practice committee.

The nurse manager was invited to attend orthopedic departmental meetings. Additional education specifically directed to nurses included programs on group dynamics and joint practice, an educational bulletin board, and workshops to refine nursing documentation.

The committee developed and piloted an integrated patient record and nursing protocols with guidelines for implementation. The protocols and patient record were approved by the orthopedic department but met with resistance when presented to the medical executive committee for hospitalwide implementation. This result indicated the need for improved communication and education regarding the aims of collaborative practice.

Joint projects

Emanating from this committee were various activities that had a direct effect on patient care. The establishment of a satellite physical therapy room adjacent to the orthopedic unit decreased patients' waiting time because they no longer had to wait for trans-

The establishment of a satellite physical therapy room adjacent to the orthopedic unit decreased patients' waiting time because they no longer had to wait for transportation.

Joint Practice Committee Purpose and Objectives

The purpose of the committee is to establish joint or collaborative practice in the hospital—a jointly determined relationship between nurses and physicians who practice here. In collaborative practice, the medical and nursing regimens are integrated into a single, comprehensive approach for optimal patient care.[1]

Objectives

- To act as a pilot for instituting joint practice committees on other units in Riverview Hospital.
- To enhance the quality of patient care on 3 South by elaborating the communication between physicians and nurses.
- To recommend changes in policies.
- To establish policy and procedures for the orthopedic unit.
- To establish collaborative practice in a milieu of mutual trust and practice roles.
- To integrate the medical and nursing care regimens by developing an integrated record and establishing protocols for nursing intervention.

---

portation. In addition, the patients were close to the unit so that nurses and physicians were able to monitor them clinically and note their progress.

A multidisciplinary monitor of the total hip patient's length of stay was also completed. Results of this monitor were shared with the Social Service Department, and comparisons were made with other hospitals. Further monitoring of other aspects of total hip care was developed and implemented. One result of this monitoring activity was an educational videotape that was shown to the Orthopedic Department and subsequently placed in the medical library for reference.

Another project was the implementation of grand rounds. A physician, a primary nurse, a social worker, a home health nurse, and a physical therapist meet every two weeks to discuss various patients. This multidisciplinary approach to patient evaluation offers the opportunity to all disciplines to coordinate patient care while patients are in the hospital and when they are discharged.

Additionally, the committee addressed the issues of education of the staff and patient education. Physicians videotaped inservice programs and sponsored nurses' attendance at orthopedic national conventions. Nationwide nursing turnover rates were reviewed by the group; increasing the volume of open communication was discussed as a means of increasing staff nurse retention. The committee members developed slide presentations and educational booklets for patient distribution. An orthopedic manual, which includes information and treatment pertinent to specific orthopedic disease entities, has been reviewed and revised to reflect current practice. Educational programs evolved from joint quality assurance monitors that had been implemented by the committee.

Effectiveness of the committee

The committee members were highly successful in achieving a majority of their objectives. However, further education is necessary to meet the challenge of and overcome the obstacles to achieving hospitalwide passage of an integrated patient record and of orthopedic nursing protocols.

At each meeting a dialogue continues that fosters open communication and respect between nurses and physicians as well as a heightened awareness of each discipline's plan for care. Any concerns about practice are discussed and appropriate action is taken. The result of this continued collaboration has been an enhanced quality of patient care at Riverview Medical Center.

REFERENCE

1. New Jersey Hospital Association, Council on Professional Practice Task Force. *Recommendations for Collaborative Practice* (Princeton: NJHA, 1982.)

—Dale Barth
—William Halligan

RESEARCH PERSPECTIVES OF A STAFF NURSE

Two years ago, I was invited to serve as a member of Riverview Medical Center's nursing research committee. This experience was exciting for me because I was actively carrying out a research project as a requirement of the master's program in which I was enrolled. Committee membership allowed me to view nursing research from a clinical setting while learning the theoretical process of this complex activity. It truly has been an ideal situation.

Committee participation has enhanced my ability to critique various research proposals and projects and to develop the skills necessary to assist the committee in screening proposals submitted by prospective nurse researchers. Another important benefit of membership in this committee has been exposure to varied levels of researchers. This interaction with nurses involved in

the research process helps to promote a personal commitment to research.

One of the responsibilities of the committee is to plan an annual research seminar. As a staff nurse, I have found that participation in planning this seminar has been an exciting experience. It is rewarding to share with my professional colleagues the benefits of nursing research and the results of research projects.

Serving on Riverview's nursing research committee has been a privilege and a responsibility. It has contributed to my professional growth and has also provided me with another opportunity to contribute to the professional growth of our nursing staff and to improve the quality of patient care delivered at Riverview Medical Center

—Martha Noble

MARKETING

Today's competitive health care market requires innovative approaches to recruiting nurses and marketing a positive image of the nursing profession to the public.

Staff nurse participation is a key element in our marketing program. Members of the nurse marketing committee contribute by participating in public forums, writing for publication, attending recruitment sessions, preparing newsletters, conducting educational seminars, and hosting an open house for prospective candidates.

Developing marketing tools

In recent years the escalating costs of health care, shorter length of patient stay, diminishing nursing resources, and more intensive nursing care needs have greatly affected staff nurses. Additionally, heightened public awareness concerning health and patient rights have created expectations for higher health care. In response to these factors, the marketing committee prepared a marketing/patient educational tool that is still in use. "Today's Nurse," a booklet designed to be easily read by patients and their families, described the various roles of hospital nurses in the 1980s. This booklet also contains a questionnaire that asks specific questions regarding the patients' perceptions of nursing care received. This information, which is tallied and reviewed quarterly, affords a keen insight into the quality of nursing care as experienced by patients.

Marketing by networking

Our professional colleagues also have needs to which we have attempted to respond. Over years of contact with nurses at various meetings and in academic settings and professional organizations. Riverview's image as a progressive nursing division has become known. We have been willing to respond to inquiries from across the state regarding the "how to" of decentralization and middle nurse manager development. Numerous requests prompted us to extend invitations to visit Riverview, an approach that has proved highly successful and has eventually evolved into a marketable seminar format.

Projecting an image

Brochures marketing seminars

We recognized that Riverview's early preparation and offering of management development programs were unique and that the quality of the program and of the nursing division should be reflected in a marketing tool that could be mailed to colleagues in the tristate area of Pennsylvania, New York, and New Jersey. Cur-

rently, ideas for brochures are solicited from nurses preparing the seminar. A graphic artist prepares the sketches, and a professional printer is employed to print the brochures.

As a result of this planning, all brochures marketing Riverview's nursing seminars are identifiable on sight and reflect the high quality we want to promote with our theme, "Quality Is Never An Accident." A fee is charged for our programs; the income earned is channeled into the nursing seminar budget, which provides financial support to our nurses who may wish to attend continuing education programs offered by other agencies and not available at Riverview.

"Accent on Nursing"

A nursing division in which nurse managers and nursing staff support ambitious goals must use several channels of communication. Our nursing newsletter, "Accent on Nursing," which is distributed quarterly to nursing personnel with their paychecks, is written by staff nurses, middle managers, nurse administrators, committee members, and others. Members of the marketing committee serve on an alternating basis as coordinators for issues of the newsletters: they write articles, ask individuals to assist them, meet with the printer, and arrange photo sessions. This newsletter is a means of communicating with the hospital about nursing division interests and activities. Copies of "Accent on Nursing" are distributed to academic institutions, the medical staff, all department heads, the hospital administrative team, members of the board of governors, the nurse recruiter, and the hospital library. The image we are marketing is projected in each of our publications. That image reflects a positive, highly professional organization.

Recognizing excellence

The bedside nurse is the cornerstone of any nursing organization and is, in our system, recognized for outstanding contributions to direct patient care. Once again, we saw the opportunity to foster staff nurse participation in all phases of a project by recognizing excellence in clinical practice. The process of identifying, nominating, and selecting the recipient of the award for excellence in nursing was developed by a committee dominated by staff nurses. The award recipient is selected anonymously by a panel of peers, and while the award serves primarily to acclaim a single nurse for excellence in practice, it also serves to focus positive attention on the nursing division in general during Nurses' Week activities in May. Members of the medical staff and of the board of governors, a keynote speaker, and families of staff nurses attend the ceremony. Representatives of the press are also invited to provide coverage in local newspapers. Again, a positive image of the profession is projected.

Looking ahead

"Shadow a Nurse" program

The image presented by today's nurse should serve as a marketing tool for recruitment of tomorrow's nurse. Marketing programs can be planned to achieve short- and long-term goals. Nurse recruitment is an immediate as well as a long-term goal. Our marketing program is used not only to derive immediate recognition for the nursing

---

The image presented by today's nurse should serve as a marketing tool for recruitment of tomorrow's nurse.

---

division but also to support the advancement and growth of the nursing profession. To this end, our "Shadow a Nurse" program was developed. This one-day program offers high school students the opportunity to spend a day in the hospital and thus experience a typical day in a nurse's professional life. Professionally motivated staff nurses, serving as preceptors, are the best salespeople for nursing. Students returning to their high schools discuss their experiences with peers and, it is hoped, convey to others the positive image of nursing derived from their direct experience with nurses.

Summer extern program

During the summer months we provide an opportunity for nursing students entering their senior year to apply theory and develop basic nursing skills in a program designed both to ease students' transition from classroom to work environment and to supplement regular staff during the peak vacation season.

The selection process is competitive and requires endorsement by the student's academic instructor and an interview with a member of our Staff Development Department. Students may request assignment, for one two-week period, to a unit of their particular interest. A nurse extern job description clearly delineates the scope of practice for externs, who are guided by nurse preceptors.

Several externs who have successfully completed this program have accepted positions at Riverview upon graduation, so this marketing approach has proven to be a successful method of recruitment.

National recognition

In response to an announcement by the program committee of the American Organization of Nursing Executives (AONE) and

Sigma Theta Tau, the international nursing honor society, the marketing committee submitted abstracts of its marketing program for review. Riverview was privileged to be selected to exhibit at the poster session for the AONE annual meeting in Boston in October 1986, and the regional meeting of Sigma Theta Tau in Philadelphia in November 1986. These sessions allowed us to display our marketing tools and to send staff nurse members of the hard-working nurse marketing committee to explain and present our marketing approaches.

Riverview's theme for the poster was "Marketing Nursing: A Community Medical Center Perspective." In addition to marketing our nursing division, our goal was to encourage others to implement a marketing plan. Using a small brochure, we described the visual presentation of our display to nurses from across the country who were then able to take Riverview's concepts back home. Our guest book, signed by many attendees, will be used for future mailings and to respond to requests for information regarding the various programs we have developed.

Although the display items for the poster were selected by members of the marketing committee, the final presentation, using many of our marketing tools, was designed by a professional printer. A slide program was also presented. Individual earphones enabled people to hear a brief description of our marketing program as it had been described at our annual meeting.

Emphasizing divisional accomplishments

The annual meeting of the nursing staff serves several purposes, including communication with staff nurses, hospital administrators, physicians, legislators, board members, and nurse managers. This pre-

sentation, supplemented by visual aids, depicts the accomplishments of the division relative to its goals for the past year; it provides another opportunity to demonstrate that "Quality Is Never An Accident."

—Joan Chack
—Barbara LuBrant

PROFESSIONAL AFFILIATIONS

An environment of participative management encourages all professional nurses to broaden their scope through membership in national or state organizations. Such an environment fosters a striving for excellence.

The nurse executives at Riverview Medical Center (RMC) serve as role models through their membership in various state and national organizations. Their dynamic leadership in the American Organization of Nurse Executives and the Organization of Nurse Executives of New Jersey fostered the creation of the first Council of Middle Nurse Managers (CMNM) in the country. While no other organization has addressed the needs of the middle nurse manager, this unique forum affords an opportunity for networking, education, and dialogue that focuses on health issues and their implication for the middle nurse manager. The opportunity to communicate on legislative issues and economic trends in the health care industry is also most valuable to nursing managers.

The Nursing Division at RMC takes pride in the fact that all the clinical coordinators (head nurses) are members of CMNM. Two of RMC's clinical coordinators have been elected to terms as president of the organization. Nursing administration strongly supports their involvement by encouraging managers to schedule time to attend meetings and programs.

This enthusiasm and desire for professional development is also apparent in the staff nurses, a significant number of whom are active in the professional organizations such as the Nurses Association of the American College of Obstetricians and Gynecologists, the National Association of Orthopedic Nurses, the Association of Operating Room Nurses, the American Association of Critical Care Nurses, the Emergency Nurses Association, and the Oncology Nursing Society.

Participation in these organizations provides an opportunity for nurses to expand their clinical practice through attendance at seminars, workshops, and meetings. This exposure and a supportive environment tend to motivate and challenge nurses to become certified within their area of specialization. Recognition of certification includes a written commendation from the chief executive nursing officer, publication of the achievement in the nursing division newsletter, and a salary increase.

Broadening the scope of the staff nurse and decentralizing the work environment have increased responsibility and accountability for clinical practice at the bedside as is evidenced by compliance with standards set by regulatory agencies.

Each clinical manager ensures that the nursing staff delivers care in accordance with American Nurses' Association Standards, the New Jersey Nurse Practice Act, state Department of Health rules and regulations, and standards established by the Joint Commission for Accreditation of Hospitals. Specialty units incorporate their practice standards as developed by their respective professional organizations. Riverview's staff nurses have gone beyond meeting mandated minimal criteria and have written and implemented standards for care that demand nursing excellence.

The RMC nursing division strives to ensure that excellent nursing care is continuously provided. Such efforts are validated by positive feedback from concurrent patient care monitors, ongoing patient questionnaires, and independent community surveys by hospital consulting firms.

—Elizabeth Kane
—Bernadette McCabe
—Barbara O'Brien

Contributors:
Joan Trofino, R.N., M.S.N.
Vice President for Patient Care Services

Marguerite Dieffenbach, R.N., M.A.
Director of Nursing

Cynthia Marvulli, R.N., B.S.N.
Clinical Coordinator
Medical / Surgical Unit

Diane Brady, R.N., M.S.N.
Director of Nursing

Mary Jane Shea, R.N., B.A.
Clinical Coordinator
Medical / Surgical Unit

Patricia Gossett, R.N., B.S.N.
Clinical Coordinator
Pediatric Unit

Patricia K. Kane, R.N., M.A.
Director of Nursing

Susan Palette, R.N., B.S.N.
Assistant Director
Staff Development and Patient Education

Ruth Strickland, R.N.
Staff Nurse
Medical / Surgical Unit

Marguerite Gelcius, R.N., M.B.A.
Assistant Director
Nursing Finance

Bernadette McCabe, R.N.
Clinical Coordinator
Medical / Surgical Unit

Joan Bierly, R.N.
Clinical Coordinator
Medical / Surgical Unit

Charles Miller, M.D.
Attending Physician

Dale Barth, R.N., B.S.N.
Clinical Coordinator
Surgical Orthopedic Unit

William Halligan, M.D.
Attending Physician

Martha Noble, R.N., M.S.N.
Staff Nurse
Medical / Surgical Unit

Joan Chack, R.N., M.S.
Director of Nursing

Barbara LuBrant, R.N., B.S.N.
Assistant Clinical Coordinator
Medical / Surgical Unit

Elizabeth Kane, R.N.
Clinical Coordinator
Labor and Delivery Unit

Barbara O'Brien, R.N., M.S.N.
Assistant Director of Nursing
Riverview Medical Center
Red Bank, New Jersey

Part III
Study and discussion questions

1. Identify the diverse communications methods described to support the goal of participatory management.
   —What might be the cost-benefit to the institution to justify the level of direct care providers involvement in this communication system?
2. Compare and contrast the management development program with the prevailing total quality management programs being introduced in health care organizations.
   —How does the Riverview program set the foundation for quality improvement processes?
3. Assess the nursing leadership in your organization.
   —How would they have responded to the budgetary constraints imposed upon the N.J. Hospitals in the mid-1980s?
   —Would you consider eliminating shift supervisors as a part of your vision? What rationale supports your decision?
4. Identify the steps in the development of goals and objectives used at Riverview.
   —What principles are used in the process?
   —Who is involved? What stake holders?
   —Who is held accountable?
   —How would you develop your goal-setting process or plan for nursing care throughout the organization?
5. Reflect on their motto "Where Theory and Practice Come Together." What does that mean to you?
6. Collaborative practice continues to be an illusionary goal in many settings. What strategies worked well at Riverview? What can we learn that would be transferable to other settings?
7. Research is the foundation of nursing practice. In what way were staff nurses involved? What cost/benefit to the customer, the patient?

Part IV
Achieving excellence

Rhonda Anderson, R.N., M.P.A.,
C.N.A.A.
Vice President
Patient Operations
Hartford Hospital
Hartford, Connecticut

How have we defined excellence? What is the measurement of our ability to achieve excellence? The nursing literature is replete with articles highlighting centers of excellence, describing excellence as it relates to a good quality assurance program in nursing, and indicating excellence and quality are synonymous. In the last ten years, *NAQ* has published many outstanding articles on all of the above topics. Over the years, the quality/excellence curve has transitioned from a risk management to a CQI approach. The early nursing programs of quality assurance were centered on a single event and problem-focused. The goal was to develop and implement a solution that would ensure the single event never occurred again. this approach seemed to lead us to myopic evaluation of a sentinel event having no effect of ensuring quality or excellence. It was an episodic intervention of our practice.

Following this approach to quality assurance, the focus was on process. How were we doing things and how did we follow the steps of the process?

As we monitored process, we became more encompassing in our approach. This helped us to begin thinking about nursing interventions and their impact on patients. We, however, spent too much time on measuring the process and forgot we were doing so to achieve an outcome.

As one now reads about quality, there are two themes: outcomes management and continuous quality improvement. Both seem sound and logical. They should lead us to a culture of excellence if we are identifying what we are trying to accomplish in the care of a patient and then measure if we have achieved that outcome. If we believe we can always do better and strive to continuously improve our present state, then complacency and stagnation won't become the norm. What will emerge is an organization of excellence. An organization that is congruent in its thinking and one in which the mission is constantly being propelled in a forward motion. Peter Senge would say we have moved from events, blame, and guilt to understanding the influence of a system of care.

No department or profession can single-handedly or single-mindedly cause the hospital of the future to be excellent. A hospital will be excellent if it knows its customers and understands what the customers want from their hospitalization. Clinical, utilization, and patient-desired outcomes will have to be met. In order to do so, professions and departments will have to integrate their plans for care of a patient and will have to develop their system of care together.

Many hospitals today are designing this new way to provide care to their patients. Everything is centered around the patients' needs. Providers are aware the systems thinking model supports the growth of the whole. The cultural threads of continuous learning and continuous improvement are women throughout the fabric of the organization.

This integration leads to an attitude of visioning the whole and trying to always improve—stretching toward meeting the goals and mission of the organization. Nursing can participate in creating an excellent organization if there is congruence in forwarding the hospital's mission, extraordinary quality, outstanding nursing practice, and highly satisfied patients.

Achieving excellence at the University of Florida

Many more can achieve [excellence] than now do. Many, many more can try to achieve it than now do. *And the society is bettered not only by those who achieve it but by those who are trying.*[1]

CONCERNED BY an absence of high standards of performance in American institutions, Gardner described the problem in his landmark book, *Excellence, Can We Be Excellent and Equal Too?* His description of excellence is developed in terms of the tension between egalitarianism (also known as equalitarianism) and individualism, a tension that characterizes every society, but none more so than American democracy.

Egalitarianism is the belief that all people are intrinsically equal and that individual differences should be leveled by protecting the less talented, and by curbing the aggressive and more highly skilled people. Individualism, on the other hand, emphasizes each person's achieving and excelling through competitive individual performance.

Describing the conflict between the two, Gardner states: The "two souls" in the breast of every American are the devotion to equalitarianism and the attachment to individual achievement. If you say to an American that all men should be equal, he will say "Of course!" And if you then say we should "let the best man win," he will applaud this as a noble thought.... The idea that the two views might often conflict doesn't occur to him.[2]

There is virtue in believing in both. Indeed, a commitment to the dual values, in moderation, is a necessary ingredient of healthy democracies and democratic organizations. But there are drawbacks and dangers in the two and awareness of these is essential for understanding what is involved in excelling.

THE DRAWBACKS OF EGALITARIANISM

In the extreme, egalitarians view individuals of great ability, energy, and intellectual force—men and women who are excellent at what they do—as troublesome. The social pressure to be "down to earth," to be folksy, to not threaten another's self-esteem, in short, to do noth-

Nurs Admin Q, 1988, 12(4), 15–38
©1988 Aspen Publishers, Inc.

ing that arouses envy, is a manifestation of how uncomfortable people are with individual differences in status, especially when those differences are related to intelligence and talent.

Describing egalitarianism wrongly conceived, Gardner states, "Carried far enough it means lopping off any heads which come above dead level. It means committee rule, the individual smothered by the group. And it means the end of striving for excellence with has produced mankind's greatest achievements."[3]

Egalitarianism in moderation is best exemplified by minimum wage laws and the right of all to vote. Carried to the extreme, however, good people are kept down, situations where individuals can excel are avoided, and if differences do emerge, disparities in status are sidetracked.

THE DANGER IN INDIVIDUALISM

The opportunity for everyone to realize the promise of the creative talent with which he or she was born is part of the American dream, at least, that is, for those with the native ability and stamina to excel. But what of those with less energy, intelligence, and verve? Where a commitment to individualism is extreme, unbridled ambition can be devastating, as the weak fall prey to more aggressive individuals. In any society or organization there is only so much room at the top. If the emphasis on individuals' excelling is exaggerated, life and work for the majority become a jungle, because few are able to function effectively for any length of time under highly competitive circumstances. In this case, rivalry and insecurity are as destructive and as discouraging of excellence as the mediocrity and apathy characterizing organizations where egalitarianism is overdone.

ARE NURSES TOO EGALITARIAN?

Speaking from the vantage point of someone who has been a nurse for 30 years, I believe if nurses err, it is by trying to treat everyone the same. Their tendency is to emphasize uniformity, to keep things equal rather than competitive, and to favor short-term stability, hoping the mediocrity that almost inevitably follows can somehow be overcome by well-meaning fairness.

One factor suggesting that equality may be overdone has to do with the majority of nurses being women. If the feminist literature is to be believed, many women are not especially competitive. Another factor is that in the service professions equal treatment for all is highly valued. Until recently, the idea of competitive marketing and pricing was rarely discussed. Third, there is the longstanding plea in nursing for leadership. In groups highly committed to equality, people do not rise to the top and they do not lead. Indeed, there is no top. Everyone is at the same level and on an equal footing, as they tend to be in nursing where leaders who are the caliber of Nightingale or Robb are almost impossible to spot.

LEADERSHIP AND TALENT

Bloom, in his 1987 best seller, *The Closing of the American Mind,* suggests that with the changes accompanying the social chaos of the 1960s, Americans have had a dangerous and detrimental tendency to suppress many of the possible ways individuals can be distinctive. Because of this trend, their understanding of how to foster genius and leadership has been dulled or lost altogether.[4] In nursing, there is no shortage of talent. The problem is that where the emphasis on equality is overdone, people are slow to recognize the geniuses in every sphere who are eager to excel.

In a free society as pluralistic as America, active, committed leadership by the talented and gifted is needed in every domain. Professionals are needed to pursue their special interests and fulfill their civic responsibility in a variety of useful and creative ways. Where egalitarianism is *not* carried to an extreme—in organizations and societies—such individuals can be nurtured and used effectively. Talented, ethical leaders will proliferate because they are valued and trained. Alfred North Whitehead warns, "The race which does not value trained intelligence is doomed."[5]

The demand for intelligent leaders is enormous at this stage of nursing's evolution as a professional discipline. Creative thinkers, innovators, individuals who are technically competent, and nurses capable of sound judgment and broad perspectives about problems facing the world are needed today perhaps as never before. They are needed in nursing administration to create high-performing health care organizations. Shortell states that people in the best health care systems lead by giving meaning to people's lives; effective leaders know what others value and make decisions accordingly. In addition, excellent leaders stretch themselves; they are committed to the extraordinary. They maximize learning by doing what others consider undoable, by inventing and using strong information systems, and by giving people autonomy.[6]

Excellent organizations have a well-recognized culture with a system of shared values and norms. The best organizations are spiritual: People in these systems transcend the mundane in everyday life. Administrators in excellent organizations have the skill to develop strategies that enable employees to compete sensibly and to be uplifted by their work.[7]

● ● ●

Highly capable first-line, middle-, and top-level nurse administrators who are respected in their communities and who work in organizations considered excellent have been selected to contribute to this "On the Scene." Each author describes a unique sphere of nursing administration, its problems and opportunities, and the judgments involved when trying to be excellent. The authors describe, too, how they avoid extreme competition, and how they balance recognition of distinctive individuals with even treatment and recognition of everyone's intrinsic worth.

The setting is Gainesville, Florida. The three organizations are the Veterans Administration Medical Center (VAMC), Shands Hospital of the University of Florida, and the College of Nursing at the University of Florida. In the first article, a staff nurse who is a patient care manager describes a system that defines quality from the consumers' point of view, then builds responsibility for quality control into every aspect of each employee's performance.

The second article is a head nurse's analysis of the imaginative strategies used in a nursing home care unit to overcome a loss of confidence among the professional staff. Considered a center for excellence, the unit is described in terms of morale, talent, and motivated performance.

At Shands Hospital, assuming responsibility for the total hospital each evening is a special challenge. In the third article, the author articulates an ideology and describes how nursing and administrative theory are used to make sense of the complex events in a large, fast-moving medical center. Identifying outstanding caregivers, finding constructive ways to inspire others, and creating an organization that is spiritual—one that brings meaning to people's lives—are addressed.

In the fourth article, the author, who is currently the acting director of children's health at Shands Hospital, describes trying to be excellent in a temporary position. Little has been reported about the pros and cons of filling in as a manager on an interim basis. The author develops a model describing factors that are well worth worth considering when thinking about accepting an acting position.

Graduate education for nursing administration is the topic of the fifth and final article. Nursing administration is a focus of study in at least 75 schools of nursing in the United States. The author discusses how faculty make the difficult decision about who will be admitted and how they foster superior performance through competitive exercises designed to encourage logical thinking, concise writing, and public speaking. Taken together, the articles present a model for excellence that is useful at all levels of practice.

REFERENCES

1. Gardner, J.W. *Excellence, Can We Be Excellent and Equal Too?* (New York: Harper & Row, 1961) p. 133.
2. Ibid., 6.
3. Ibid., 15.
4. Bloom, A. *The Closing of the American Mind* (New York: Simon & Schuster, 1987.)
5. Whitehead, A.N. *The Aims of Education and Other Essays.* New York: Free Press, 1929, p. 14.
6. Shortell, S.M. High Performing Healthcare Organizations: Guidelines for the Pursuit of Excellence. *Hospital & Health Services Administration* (July-August 1985): 7-34.
7. Ibid.

—Beverly Henry

A QUALITY ASSURANCE PROGRAM TO ACHIEVE EXCELLENCE

The word "excellence" strikes a responsive chord in staff nurses and board members alike. The idea of excellence evokes wide-ranging interest, in part because market analyses in the health service industry demonstrate that there is a strong connection between outstanding service and portion of market share.

In today's highly competitive marketplace, without a means for achieving and demonstrating a quality of service that is well above average, an organization's survival is at risk. To be successful, institutions must also be excellent. But what is meant by excellence? How is excellence defined and identified in health service organizations? How is excellent quality actually achieved and how is evidence documented in an understandable format?

The variable quality of nursing care

The words "quality" and "excellence" are synonyms, according to Roget's thesaurus. In a number of dictionaries, quality is defined as "great excellence." But in nursing, quality means different things to different people because of the variable nature of the work nurses do. Nursing care is not provided in a factory with unchanging combinations of standardized raw materials that are routinely processed to achieve predictable products. Rather, nursing is done in diverse settings for a vast array of recipients, using numerous resources and many technologies. Excellent care, therefore, involves complex activities and varies as a consequence of social and economic values and the technologies in each setting.

The values held by providers and recipients of health services are central to the development of useful definitions and standards of quality. A valid definition reflects the values of caregivers and the values of the receivers of services in any given situation.

Standards or criteria are the yardsticks by which quality care is measured. Appropriately applied through a strong quality assurance (QA) program, standards provide direction for caregiving activities. Outcome criteria represent the level of quality sought in a situation. Without standards to measure the outcomes of activities that have been performed, there can be no rational assessment of what has been achieved and who has excelled.

Customizing standards

Recent guidelines published by the Joint Commission for Accreditation of Healthcare Organizations (Joint Commission) mandate that standards in hospitals vary to reflect community and societal expectations, as well as the values and unique circumstances of providers and recipients. Summarizing the many factors influencing the development of standards, the nurse administratively responsible for the implementation of the QA program at the Veterans Administration Medical Center (VAMC) notes, "All program activities are a reflection of community and professional standards; of the hospital mission, philosophy, and values; of the doctrine of the reasonable person; and of societal expectations exemplified by accreditation requirements" (A. Urquhart, pers. com., December 1987).

VAMC has made a concerted effort to establish unit-specific, highly individualized QA programs under an umbrella QA system developed for the total institution. In a decentralized program such as the one in Gainesville, Florida, which begins on each nursing unit, individual and institutional values are acknowledged inasmuch as standards are tailored to the mission and capability of each unit and service. Standards in a nursing home care unit may vary significantly from the criteria set by nurses caring for patients in highly specialized surgical intensive care units. In nursing homes, for example, a high premium is put on long-term collaborative planning that involves patients and their family providers. For in-

tensive care, on the other hand, high-level technological skill and the ability to function effectively in emergencies for the immediate short term are of the highest value. Because such a plethora of factors are relevant to quality care, identifying excellence is highly complex. Achieving it is even more so.

Achieving excellence

VAMC has a well-deserved reputation as an outstanding institution in the community, region, and country. But how does a large government-funded hospital, operating in an atmosphere of restrained federal spending, provide high-quality service on a day-to-day basis? The McKinsey 7-S Framework developed by Peters and Waterman in their study of excellent organizations is useful for responding to this question.[1] The framework is composed of seven interconnected elements. Shared values are central and connect to all remaining parts of the model. The framework suggests that understanding how excellence is achieved in an organization requires analyzing each of the seven factors and the connections among them.

Shared values, structure, and strategy

Peters and Waterman stated unequivocally that every excellent organization in their study was clear about what it stood for and took value shaping seriously. Moreover, having the right values was obviously linked to effective, high-quality performance.[2] At VAMC, a document entitled *Values* has been developed and published. Shared with all staff and clients, it states, "We believe in the absolute necessity of quality care, and in furthering and increasing competence at all levels and in all units of the organization. We believe in a constant search for excellence...We believe in each other."[3]

The QA program at VAMC is structured to decentralize authority and responsibility for assuring quality from the hospital director to the staff nurse providing direct care to patients and families. An associate chief nurse is responsible for chairing the QA committee in the department of nursing. The strategy is to integrate activities for quality control into the everyday practice of all employees.

In this sense, every nurse is entrusted with the responsibility for accomplishing the goals of the QA program. When departmentwide activities and standards are needed, special task forces and ad hoc groups are formed and given the responsibility for collecting the necessary information and developing the appropriate umbrella plans that each nursing unit can adapt, depending on its special goals and services.

Each nursing unit has a philosophy and purpose that fits within the larger philosophical framework of the nursing department, which is aligned with the values and mission of the institution. Standards and desirable outcomes of nursing interventions have been developed for each unit. The responsibility for monitoring compliance with the standards varies according to the structure and functioning of the various nursing units. On some units, nurses volunteer. On others, nurses are assigned responsibilities for quality assurance, and on others, the head nurses assume responsibility.

Systems, staff, skills and style

A comprehensive system for ensuring skin integrity was recently implemented at VAMC and illustrates the interrelationship of systems, staff, skills, and style in high-performing organizations. Through a system of reporting patient changes, a nurse was able to identify what seemed to be an unusually high incidence of loss of skin integrity. Information about the problem was communicated to the chairperson of nursing's QA committee. Subsequently, data were collected to determine the frequency and extent of problematic occurrences, and to differentiate problems that existed at the time of admission and those acquired during the hospital stay.

Because of the applicability of the problem to many patient care areas, it was deemed an appropriate target for action. First, a system was devised to identify the stages of loss of skin integrity. Second, protocols describing nursing interventions were developed for each of the stages using information from the nurses on all units throughout the hospital. Third, a teaching program was devised to highlight the problem, discuss the protocols, and improve the knowledge and skill of all nurses providing care.

At the same time, monitors were designated on each nursing unit to check for documentation of impending or progressing skin care problems. The monitors also assessed the nursing staff's adherence to the interventions prescribed in the protocols. Data were collected by the monitors, and trends and comparisons were developed for individual patients and units by medical diagnosis and length of stay.

Clinical specialists and staff educators made site visits to each nursing unit to query the staff about their knowledge in diagnosing problems and using the protocols, the explanation of which had begun in the formal training sessions. The unit visits brought to light further deficits in understanding. Therefore, a second teaching program, taking a new approach to skills development, was initiated. Head nurses on all units selected one member of the staff to attend the second series of classes. The person selected was typically someone who exhibited a special interest and could ultimately become the expert in integumentary systems for the entire unit.

To develop the skills of the staff, the special classes focused on identifying patients at high risk, instituting preventive regimens of care, and reporting further problems. Nurses who attended monitored the system on their unit and served as consultants to others. In addition, these specially trained experts became members of a committee designed solely to monitor skin care problems. Members of the committee are now preparing standardized care plans for prevention and treatment. Because of their specialized skill, members also review all new product and equipment applications pertaining to skin integrity.

Throughout the development of the system for improved patient care, the style of the nurses who have been involved has been highly participative. Involving large numbers of staff, from diagnosis of the problem through implementation and evaluation of the new program, has encouraged a free-flowing exchange of useful, innovative ideas. Morale has stayed high and the self-confidence of all staff has increased immea-

Each nursing unit has a philosophy and purpose that fits within the larger philosophical framework of the nursing department, which is aligned with the values and mission of the institution.

surably as new skills have been acquired. High standards have been set and maintained using democratic organizational structures and strategies that have applauded improvements in care.

Documenting high levels of quality care

Defining and achieving high-quality services are commendable achievements. Means must also be found, however, to communicate what has been accomplished. Clear, concise documentation in a format where data are easily used and retrieved is of paramount importance.

The nurses at VAMC have devised ways to simplify documentation and communicate care plans to ancillary staff, to accrediting boards, and to each other. Some units have nursing orders in a checklist format. These were devised by the primary nurses and are kept at the patients' bedsides. The nonprofessional staff have only to read through the checklist to learn what type of care has been prescribed, then initial the appropriate item when care is complete. The primary nurses assume responsibility for monitoring what is documented and the care that has been given.

On some units, forms have been devised to record items of special significance, such as patient falls, medication errors, and patient complaints. Included in each patient's chart, the form facilitates data collection about special problems, contributing factors, and resolution. Retained by the head nurse, information compiled from the forms provides an objective indicator of trends in patient care problems on the unit.

At VAMC, personnel in the quality assurance section are available to assist with documentation. As the administrator responsible for the hospitalwide QA program explains, "The staff here do quality work. Our department helps make that quality explicit through written standards and criteria. We help the staff use standardized formats that smooth communication when viewed by representatives of accrediting agencies" (R. Walker, pers. com., November 1987).

Quality assurance at the Gainesville VAMC integrates quality control and everyday nursing practice. Attention to standards and goals, and careful documentation, increases skills and develops talent throughout the institution.

REFERENCES

1. Peters, T.J., and R.H. Waterman, *In Search of Excellence* (New York: Warner Books) 1982.
2. Ibid.
3. Gainesville Veterans Administration Medical Center, *Values* (Gainesville, FL: Gainesville Veterans Administration Medical Center, 1987) p. 1.

—Mary F. Brallier

Jane O'Donnell, B.J. Palotsee, Karen Putney, Richard Walker, and Audrey Urquhart contributed to this article.

PROMOTING EXCELLENCE THROUGH PRIMARY NURSING IN LONG-TERM CARE

Excellence in a long-term care setting is rarely addressed in nursing. Unfortunately, much has been written about mediocre, or worse, persistently poor care, lack of professionalism, and low morale. This article refutes some of the negativism by showing

that through diligent effort, nursing homes can maintain high standards.

Opportunities and problems

Five years ago, three east was perceived as one of a number of well-functioning nursing units in the medical center. The unit had a reputation as a good place to work. Staff turnover was low, and many of the nursing problems often associated with long-term care, such as nosocomial infections, pressure sores, and sensory deprivation among patients, were minimal. Quality assurance reports indicated that nursing care plans were developed in a timely manner. Patients received better than average care and documentation of that care was commendable.

On three east, nurses had many opportunities to expand their knowledge and understanding of care for the elderly. The physical plant was new and equipment was of the latest design. Human and technical resources were ample, but nursing practice on three east, while up to standard, was not excellent. The task, therefore, was to determine what was standing in the way of achieving excellence, to develop a plan of action for raising the standards, and to assess the extent to which improvements had been made.

Diagnosis was first: The problem as the staff and I perceived it, was related to the recent influx of inexperienced registered nurses (RNs) and to the way primary nursing was practiced. While, theoretically, the model of practice was primary nursing, in actuality, the emphasis was on getting tasks—largely related to the physical aspects of care—done in the shortest possible time. Unfortunately, primary nursing on three east had disintegrated to a point where all members of the staff, both professional and nonprofessional, functioned in nearly the same way. Clearly, there was a crisis of ineffectiveness.

Ancillary rule

Initially, I observed that the less proficient RNs simply depended heavily on the licensed practical nurses (LPNs) and nurse assistants (NAs). Over time, however, dependence of the RNs on the ancillary personnel had grown excessive, to the point where the RNs abdicated their responsibility as leaders and credited the LPNs with far more knowledge than they actually had. The RNs either did not understand or did not accept their role as accountable primary nurses. They functioned more as technicians, a fact that was apparent from the number of knee-jerk reactions that occurred when problems arose, and from the less than ideal solutions that were formulated for long-range patient care interventions.

Consequently, within a short time after the implementation of primary nursing, the RNs lost confidence in themselves and the nonprofessional staff lost confidence in the RNs. Morale suffered. With the perception among the ancillary staff that the RNs could not or would not lead, a power vacuum was created that the ancillary staff quickly filled. Thereafter, important judgment calls as well as everyday decisions were unduly influenced by the LPNs, who, while having many years of valuable work experience, had only limited theoretical knowledge to assess and diagnose nursing problems effectively.

With a shift in the power base from the professionals to the nonprofessionals, conflicts and power struggles posed a nearly constant problem. All members of the staff complained about the absence of strong leadership, saying the unit's objectives were unclear and that they were frustrated.

The challenge

When things go wrong, the leader (in this case, the head nurse) must take responsibility and move as swiftly as possible to set things right. As Drucker notes, the leader "sets the goals, sets the priorities, and sets and maintains standards. The leader's first task is to be the trumpet that sounds a clear sound."[1]

The clear sound "trumpeted" on three east was that quality care would continue, but those accountable for that care, the primary nurses, would be in charge. This was the challenge: to put an end to the inertia among the RNs and develop them as leaders and as expert care providers. Our aim was to clarify the roles and functions of all personnel on the unit, then to develop each staff member to the maximum of his or her clinical and managerial capability. Priority was given to developing an appreciation of what each staff member could contribute by what Norton calls the "congeniality of excellences": having knowledge of one's abilities and comparative advantages relative to those of others, appreciating each other's abilities, and complementing each other rather than competing.[2]

At times, the task of reform seemed formidable. Yet, as Gardner notes, "The most powerful moving forces in history are...highly motivated people and their ideas of what is worth living for and striving for."[3] The staff and I were highly motivated by the challenge and by a number of ideas about how best to capitalize on the many available resources.

Clarification and alignment of roles

First, the assistance of the unit preceptor was sought. At the Veterans Administration Medical Center (VAMC), nurses widely recognized for their high levels of competency serve as expert clinical consultants. The unit preceptor and I formed an alliance to develop a three-month plan to restore the balance of power by developing the leadership skills of the RNs, thus enabling them to be accountable for care.

Priority number one was to meet individually with each member of the nursing staff and describe the plan of action, followed by a careful, systematic review of job descriptions specific for each level of personnel. The messages was clear: Staff who had been performing below standard would measure up; and those who had exceeded their organizational prerogatives would back down. Within the parameters of their positions, all were expected to be excellent. That was the new standard.

Change on three east began at the top of the hierarchy. The head nurse worked hard to create an environment conducive to excellent performance, "in which there can flourish not only individual genius but...the collective capacities of all."[4] Each firstline nurse manager was expected to find every conceivable opportunity to foster creativity, risk taking, and autonomy. Consistency and honesty were the watchwords. Energy and time were committed to defining roles and developing the RNs' managerial skills. Excellence was viewed not only as perfection but also as striving for perfection.

The head nurse and preceptor met with the RNs to reclarify the primary nurse role. Time was invested in defining primary nursing, what it is and what it is not. Training programs were developed and used when need was indicated by substandard performance.

Reinstatement of the RNs

Once the roles were clarified, all patients were assigned to an RN. Primary nurses were responsible for presenting an indepth case study on each patient to the total staff, every two weeks. Presentations included a complete chart review of the physiological, social, and psychological aspects of the patients along with the care plans that had been designed. The presentation was intended to expand the primary caregivers' knowledge, build their confidence in managing caseloads, and enhance their credibility with the ancillary staff.

Primary nurses became the main source of all information regarding patients and, other than in emergencies, no new patient care interventions were used without consulting primary caregivers. The autonomy and authority of the primary nurses were fostered and upheld. In addition, each primary nurse gave appropriate hands-on care. Providing direct care enhanced the RNs' ability to analyze problems and needs and anticipate outcomes. As a consequence, members of the ancillary staff listened to and followed what primary nurses had to say.

Development of primary teams

To fully use and enhance the skills of the LPNs each of the technical nurses was carefully teamed with a primary nurse as an associate. Cooperation in the team was enhanced through frank discussions about common problems related to delivering care to elderly patients. The continuity of care afforded by the primary nurse and their associates helped counter the earlier knee-jerk approaches to problems and provided consistent guidance to the nonprofessionals.

During end-of-shift reports, the entire staff participated in discussions designed to enhance care. No problem was considered too insignificant. No suggestions were considered worthless. At times, it was the NAs who suggested the "perfect" solution to a nagging problem, and it was the primary nurses who acknowledged the contribution and implemented the recommendation.

With the clarification and realignment of roles, there was less opposition to change and less of a need to waste time in power plays designed to circumvent or undermine authority. With the RNs fully accountable for patient outcomes, and the ancillary staff included in decision making, tolerance increased and a congeniality of excellences surfaced. With recognition of each other's unique talents, the synergy needed for achieving excellence was created.

Leadership and achievements

Gardner asks, "Is it possible for a people to achieve excellence if they don't believe in anything?"[5] The philosophy of three east has long attested to a belief in primary nursing as a way of achieving the best possible care. Although there are elements antagonistic to high standards, there is also an aspect of human nature that sets and strives to meet them. Staff on three east sought a leader who valued caring and collegiality. They sought a head nurse who believed in their ability to achieve outstanding service.

> *With the clarification and realignment of roles, there was less opposition to change and less of a need to waste time in power plays designed to circumvent or undermine authority.*

Rewards and awards

Many good things have happened since excellence was made the norm. Three members of the staff have enrolled in academic programs to earn higher degrees in nursing; four have gotten American Nurses Association (ANA) certification in their clinical specialties; three have been promoted; four have been awarded outstanding performance ratings; and nine are members of influential committees in the medical center.

The excellence of three east is widely recognized. Interactions between nurses and physicians are collaborative. Physicians seek primary nurses for advice before prescribing new medical regimens. Patients who were once labeled "difficult" are now more amendable to therapy, and improvements in their health are often noted. Primary nurses feel keenly their responsibility as advocates and promote the welfare of their patients. Of significance, too, is the high level of satisfaction expressed by the staff in their personal growth and development.

Excelling together

Not long ago, I shared a report of the success on three east with a peer group of head nurses and emphasized the need for vigilance, saying, "Nothing is ever finally safe and every important battle is fought and refought."[6] Tears welled in the eyes of one person. For a moment, I wished I could give her a simple, straightforward formula for success. But there is no best recipe. I suggested instead that she begin with herself—her dreams, goals, and visions—and an estimation of her assets—and go to the staff and be frank about what they could become. Others might find, as I did, that many have been patiently waiting for us to develop ourselves and our organizations. But it should be noted that "the real organization you are working for is the organization called yourself. The problems and challenges . . . you are working for 'out there' and the one 'in here' are not two separate things. They grow toward excellence together."[7]

REFERENCES

1. Drucker, P.F. Leadership: More Doing than Dash. *The Wall Street Journal* (January 6, 1988).
2. Norton, D. *Personal Destiny: A Philosophy of Ethical Individualism* (Princeton, N.J.: Princeton University Press, 1976.)
3. Gardner, J.W. *Morale* (New York: W.W. Norton, 1978) p. 41.
4. Collier, A.T. Business Leadership and a Creative Society. In *Executive Success*, ed. E.G.C. Collins (New York: Wiley, 1983) p. 172.
5. Gardner, J.W. *Excellence* (New York: W.W. Norton, 1984) p. 10.
6. Gardner, *Morale*, 153.
7. Pascale, R.T. Zen and the Art of Management. In *Executive Success*, ed. E.G.C. Collins (New York: Wiley, 1983) p. 517.

—Karen Putney

The author thanks Jane O'Donnell, Audrey Urquhart, Joyce Hauner, preceptor, and the staff on three east for their assistance.

ACHIEVING EXCELLENCE IN HOSPITALWIDE NURSING SUPERVISION

Being administratively accountable for the services provided between 3:00 P.M. and midnight in a 476-bed medical center hospital has given me insight into what it takes to ensure that clients receive the highest possible quality of care. My world view has been shaped largely by two bodies of knowledge: first and foremost by that in nursing, and second by management science.

Like Jean Watson,[1] a prominent nurse theorist, I view nursing as a human science and as an art in which each nurse is a coparticipant with another in the human care process. "Another" may be a patient, or, in the case of a nurse administrator, the nurses with whom one works. Instilling meaning and hope, cultivating sensitivity toward others, and developing trusting relationships are the key ideas in Watson's perspective, as are systematic problem solving and promotion of interpersonal learning.

Many of these ideas are prominent in the human relations perspective of management. Theorists who have made major contributions to the field, especially Maslow and Argyris, heavily emphasize human needs, relationships, sensitivity, learning, and trust.[2,3] Other major contributors to management knowledge such as Pondy and Peters and Waterman, have, like Watson, contributed to understanding how values, beliefs, and traditions give meaning and purpose to people's lives in high-performing organizations.[4,5]

Caring in a complex technological setting

Caring is deep in the roots of nursing and in the traditions of human service,. Nurses put a high premium on caring for others in empathic, warm ways even when confronted with the pressures of a highly technological environment where demands for greater levels of productivity conflict with the human need for care.

Human dignity and altruistic values

Nursing takes a humanistic stance toward people who are ill or in need. Watson states, "Caring calls for a philosophy of moral commitment toward protecting human dignity and preserving humanity."[6] Excellence is created in human-to-human caring relationships between nurses and patients, and between nurse administrators and those being supervised, when the subjective meaning of the experiences of each are empathetically shared, understood, and acted on. Underlying this high value on meaningful, trusting relationships is a concern for the importance of humanistic values in an age when a premium is also placed on the rapid advancement of automated technologies. As Watson notes, "The concept of caring is not merely characterized by certain categories or classes of nursing actions, but as ideals, which persons desiring care and persons (nurses) doing those actions hold before them."[7]

Nurse administrators face the challenge of interpreting the value of human caring to hospital administrators and ensuring that explicit statements of a belief in the value of human dignity are incorporated into every hospital's statement of mission. Collier, author of *Management, Men and Values,* wrote, "It seems to me that . . . executives ought to aim at articulating an ideology that, in addition to being an accurate expression of management goals, is a little closer to the personal and even religious aspirations of the people than anything we have espoused in the past."[8]

A belief in caring, almost a religious aspiration, is exemplified by the committed young nurse taking full responsibility for a critically wounded patient in an intensive care unit. The high technology—electrical monitors, waveforms, and life-support machines—is one aspect of care. The other is the nurse's humaneness and transcendent awareness of all that can be done. The magnitude of the injuries is nearly overwhelming. But the nurse works quietly, self-assuredly, to the limits of his or her potential, aware, too, of the anxiously waiting family. Human-to-human caring is taking place in spite of the enormous demands on the resources of patient and caregiver. The nurse, by sharing deeply the life and death of another, is achieving excellence, perhaps without realizing it. For the nurse, caring is the essence of nursing.

The contagion of excellence

Caregiving that brings meaning and purpose to people's lives has an uplifting effect on the standards and performance of others. This effect can be called the "contagion of excellence" or the reciprocal nature of excellence. Nurses performing at the peak of their intellectual and physical ability engender outstanding achievements in others. The joy and pride of witnessing what is possible are infectious.

Caught up in the daily whirl of meeting and budgeting, nurse administrators are sustained by the accomplishments of caregivers. Supervisors have excellence re-created within themselves by the magnificent obsession of outstanding nurses who strive to make a difference, to excel, by going far beyond ordinary expectations. Supervisors, in turn, are equally responsible for re-creating in the staff, through their integrity and skill, a vision of all that nursing can be. Nurse administrators must represent the finest leadership by bringing order out of chaos with a steady, creative approach to problem solving.

Just as the nurse executive who is vice-president serves as a model of excellence to middle managers (among who are supervisors), supervisors in turn are models of sensitivity and caring to nurses at the bedside. At ease with themselves, effective supervisors with hospitalwide responsibility move throughout the institution conveying critical information from the executive office to the staff, monitoring levels of practice, and acknowledging the performance of those who excel.

Components of success

"Employees are the stuff of which success is made."[9] Believing in the potential for greatness within people and recognizing the special talents in each person characterize successful supervisors. Availability is also a key to success.

Managing by walking around

Good supervisors are readily accessible. As Peters and Waterman note, the nation's best-run organizations demonstrate "management by walking around."[10] The best supervisors are on the firing line where the

> **Effective supervisors are not secretive: They do not purposely hide information.**

action is. Consequently they have firsthand information about the problems that need solving and how best to find useful solutions. In addition, because they are where the action is, good supervisors learn to talk the language of the people with whom they work. Knowing the special-purpose languages of employees throughout the hospital means that information can be communicated correctly and efficiently.[11]

When supervision is effective, staff nurses feel that what they have to say and the way they say it are understood. They feel cared for, protected, and supported. Aware that the problems unique to certain units and times of day will be accurately transmitted to policy makers, staff nurses have faith and trust. They understand the supervisors because they know them. Good supervisors and staff nurses share common experiences through collegial, empathic exchanges.

Effective supervisors are not secretive: They do not purposely hide information. The pressure of highly complex, nearly constant work in hospitals does not leave a great deal of time for detailed reporting about the changes on every single unit. But understanding and empathy can be conveyed in an amazing number of nonverbal ways in which caring supervisors who are visible on the nursing units are adept.

Being positive and hopeful

When there is a problem related to staffing, being adept at verbally reassuring the staff of their ability to cope and focusing on what can be done, rather than on what cannot be done, go a long way toward reducing tension and being productive. By staying focused on caring and working cooperatively, supervisors are better able to bring a sense of hope to those with whom they work about what can be accomplished with the resources available.

Leaders do not invent excellence in others. They unlock it.[12] They work with the special talent in each person using a variety of strategies to unleash the wealth of untapped creative energy. Because of their belief in human potential, they radiate confidence and motivate others even in dire circumstances.

Strategizing

Emergencies and less than ideal circumstances are a normal part of the supervisor's everyday work life. Being prepared for volatile situations is essential. Through advanced strategizing, all nurse administrators are better able to manage the unexpected. For example, when an electrical failure leaves the hospital in nearly total darkness, it is essential to know all personnel and where they can be reached. Knowing which engineer to call and where to find emergency battery-operated lighting spells the difference between life and death.

During emergencies, the value of hospital rounds to establish rapport with all employees is reinforced. Identifying who the strong, reliable performers are in every department, from the telephone operators and security guards to the administrators on call, is essential.

Organizing with care as the focus

For excellent organizations, work in all departments is designed with authority and decision making vested in the caregiver and receiver of care; patients and nurses "own" the methods of care. Nurses in decentralized organizational systems own the problems and make the decisions about innovations. Structures in high-performing organizations are not fixed and unmalleable: A good structure, be it a nursing unit, a cluster of units, or a department, contains diversity, opportunities for change, and openness that supports new employees learning and making mistakes. When people get involved with problems, understand and live them, and find ways to solve them, they have a chance to feel useful and an opportunity to exhibit excellence. Small cohesive groups become the strong building blocks of the total organization.

Leadership in management

Managers who are also leaders create an atmosphere of approval and security in which employees feel free to express themselves without fear of censure or ridicule. Effective managers accept different points of view in varying contexts and do not make hasty judgments. They encourage sensitive, empathic approaches to conflict and learning. The work of supervision is for the staff, not for management. The more supervisors care about human-to-human giving, the more they are likely to share by teaching and acting as mentors.

In mentor relationships young nurses learn to take risks. They learn to relate to people in intuitive, productive ways. Being a mentor is more than socialization. It is a special exchange in which both parties develop their knowledge and skill, and each develops as a leader.

Caring calls for a philosophy of moral commitment toward protecting human dignity and preserving humanity. Leadership that is caring calls for a commitment to sharing the fruits of success. When sharing and teaching, nurse administrators create a cooperative trusting system where the mission is human service.

Nurses look to leaders to find acknowledgment of their having managed the demands of their job well. Nurses respect in others those qualities they seek in themselves—to have a purpose, to be complete, to have high intentions, and, above all, to care.

REFERENCES

1. Watson, J. *Nursing: Human Science and Human Care, A Theory of Nursing* (Norwalk, Conn.: Appleton-Century-Crofts, 1985.)
2. Maslow, A. *Motivation and Personality* (New York: Harper, 1954.)
3. Argyris, C. *Reasoning, Learning and Action* (San Francisco: Jossey-Bass, 1982.)
4. Pondy, L.J. Leadership Is a Language Game. In *Leadership Where Else Can We Go?*, eds. M.W. McCall and M.M. Lombardo (Durham, N.C.: Duke University Press, 1978.)
5. Peters, T., and Waterman, R. *In Search of Excellence* (New York: Warner Books, 1982.)
6. Watson, *Nursing*, 31.
7. Ibid., 34.
8. Collier, A. Business Leadership and a Creative Society. In *Executive Success*, ed. E. Collins (New York: 1983) p. 170.
9. Johnson, J. Failure Is a Word I Don't Accept. In *Executive Success*, ed. E. Collins (New York: Wiley, 1983) p. 104.
10. Peters and Waterman. *In Search of Excellence.*
11. Pondy, Leadership Is a Language Game.
12. Gardner, J. *Excellence, Can We Be Excellent and Equal Too?* (New York: Harper & Row, 1961.)

—Barbara S. Williams

The author thanks Sharon Daniels, Barbara Donaho, and Marjorie Katz.

STRIVING TO EXCEL AS AN ACTING NURSE ADMINISTRATOR

Many organizations have an interim period—often a lengthy one—between the time one manager leaves a position and another begins. For the interim, an acting manager is appointed to maintain and promote the smooth operations of a unit or department. Someone must also act on an interim basis when a manager is absent for a short period of time ranging from a few days to several weeks. Such absences may be due to illness, vacation, maternity leave, or sabbatical. Most nurse administrators have assumed an acting position at some point in their careers. Yet little information is available about how to function successfully, about the kinds of decisions that are contingent on the accessibility of the regular person in charge, and about the strategies that may be useful relative to the time frames involved.

Time and reasons for being away

A pertinent factor is the length of time spent functioning in an acting capacity. Whether it is for a few days, weeks, or months makes a significant difference in the decisions and actions that are taken. Which problems are tackled, which decisions can be made in the short term, and which decisions can wait until the full-time manager returns are central, daily questions. Judgments regarding the necessary personnel changes to facilitate staffing on the following shift will have to be made expeditiously. But a decision to appoint a number of top-flight nurses to a special task force for a project due six months hence generally can be delayed until the manager who is away returns.

If a long-term leave is involved because of illness, resignation, or termination, it is important to have information about the circumstances of the departure. When people leave because they are sick, there is concern for their well-being. If they leave to accept other positions, the feelings among those left behind run the gamut from congratulatory to wretched. In any case people who are gone are usually missed; being sensitive to these feelings is essential.

Accessibility

A related factor is the accessibility of the full-time person. Is he or she readily and immediately available, for example, working at home? Or is the person only somewhat available, such as away at a conference where a message can be picked up? Or is the manager largely unreachable, for example, visiting a foreign country and accessible only in case of dire emergency? Knowing where the person is, the duration of time until return, and the reasons for the leave affect the decisions that are made.

If there is a problem of major proportion and vacationing executives are easily reached, a wise substitute notifies them about a problem before they first hear of it on the evening news. If the manager is severely ill, on the other hand, even information about an impending crisis is best held and communicated only when he or she returns.

Opportunities in a long-term interim role

When the person being replaced is away for many months or has resigned, there are numerous opportunities to develop the needed knowledge and skill pertaining to the role. A word of warning, however: It is important to keep in mind that an acting position is a temporary one even though weeks in the position may stretch into months, as they frequently do.

Serving in an acting capacity is often required for middle- and executive-level positions where the jobs are highly specialized and the supply of well-qualified candidates is low. The search process for executives can easily take up to a year during which time many applicants will be identified and subjected to lengthy interviews, only to be rejected. During this period, the person filling in is kept busy assisting with recruitment. As time consuming as this may be, it is time well spent. Much can be learned from what applicants have to say in the course of being interviewed.

A great deal can also be learned by an incumbent—from the vantage point of an interim manager—about the reactions of coworkers to each of the applicants. If an acting manager decides to throw his or her hat into the ring and seriously compete for the position, serving for the interim is an opportunity for the person to demonstrate to the satisfaction of superiors and subordinates alike that he or she is up to the task. It is also a valuable time to learn about the responsibilities of the position, the types of problems entailed, and the people involved. It is a good time, too, to decide whether the position is one worth holding. Responsibility in an acting role affords one the unique opportunity to experience first-hand much of what is good and bad about a job, and to identify what it takes to excel.

Drawbacks to a temporary assignment

Working with incomplete information, competing with rivals for the full-time appointment, and having to return defeated to one's former position if not selected are among the less attractive, more grinding aspects of a temporary assignment. Excelling depends to a great degree on being able to gather pertinent information quickly without causing a furor and without threatening others. Scanning the environment for sources of necessary data and locating the people and various databases needed to make intelligent decisions are critical activities. But deciding which questions need asking, gaining access to vital resources, and synthesizing large amounts of new data are stressful.

Moreover, competing for top-level positions can be both time consuming and disappointing. All management jobs take high levels of physical and intellectual stamina. But functioning in an acting capacity can consume twice the usual amount of energy if one is actively lobbying for a position and at the same time carrying the responsibility for it.

When filling in, administrators have total responsibility but partial authority. Acting administrators are treated differently, as something temporary, even disposable, a perception that is subtle but potentially damaging in the final competition. After one has held a position for an extended period of time, it is disheartening if a competitor wins out, and readjusting to a former role or to yet another position can be extremely wearing. Because of the significant number of drawbacks it is prudent to assess the magnitude of changes and carefully think about whether the position is a challenge in the right measure.

When filling in, administrators have total responsibility but partial authority.

Management style

Once one has accepted a position as acting administrator, a salient factor contributing to success in the role is management style—one's own and that of the person being replaced. Ideally the styles should be similar or complementary, especially if the time involved will be of fairly long duration, and assuming that the former person was effective.

If styles are widely disparate, it will be hard for those being supervised to make the necessary short-term adjustments. It can be difficult to routinely work for an authoritative manager and then be temporarily assigned to someone who is laisséz-faire: one day having an administrator who makes decisions and the next day working for someone who expects autonomous decision making is confounding. Even where styles are similar, decisions will constantly be compared to those made by the one who has been replaced or to employees' best guesses of the way problems would have been handled.

Differences in management style, however, will be less irritating if the incoming and outgoing managers spend time together discussing problems and approaches to solving them. In some cases, where an administrator has resigned or is planning to retire, it is a good idea to have the senior person serve as preceptor. This type of preparation for the role is one of the most effective ways for staff to gradually grow accustomed to the successor and for the incoming person to learn the subtleties of the job.

If a manager has been fired or has been asked to resign, the situation is different. When one's predecessor was ineffective and has left problems behind, a new management style is exactly what is needed. It is necessary to bite the bullet, make changes, and get things on course.

Networks and agendas

Regardless of the circumstances, many factors come into play for an acting administrator. Those discussed are summarized in Figure 1. The figure also presents factors related to effectiveness and satisfaction in the acting administrator role, networks and agendas. Networks of individuals and groups who can provide resources are changed whenever a position changes. This is equally true for acting positions. To think otherwise is folly.

Relationships with peers are altered and the new arrangements are sometimes awkward. Hearsay that was once shared may no longer be appropriate for casual lunchroom conversation. In fact, it may no longer be possible to socialize to the same degree with former associates. It is uncomfortable when rumors are only partially valid and coworkers who were once peers clamor for news that now must be kept confidential.

Relationships with superiors change as well. As Gabarro and Kotter note, one of the central players in a manager's network is the boss.[1] In an acting position there is usually a new boss. With this change come new styles and demands. If the boss is highly entrepreneurial, informal, and intuitive, and one is accustomed to accomplishing tasks bureaucratically and formally, adaptations must be made. Effective administrators, whether temporary or permanent, manage this important resource deliberately and skillfully.

When working in an acting capacity, especially at the middle and executive levels, success also hinges on being able to quickly add new members to one's network. The resources needed to excel are in flux when positions change. Success depends on identifying the resources that are needed—locating the equipment, information, money, and people—and quickly adding to the network what is required for effective perfor-

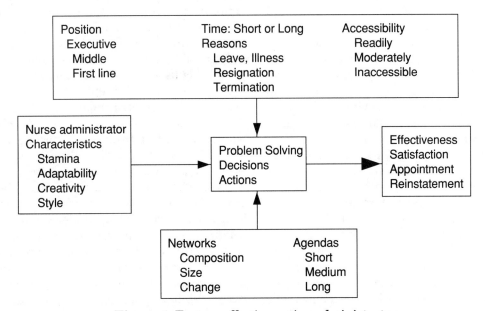

Figure 1. Factors affecting acting administrator.

mance in the new job. The most successful managers in a wide variety of organizations are those who engage in the largest number of network-building activities designed to create strong relationships with a wide range of influential people.[2]

In doing so, however, managers who excel may have to alter their agendas. Acquiring resources quickly because of the immediate problems that are encountered often has to take precedence over activities for the medium or long range. Setting agendas may have to be reactive and incremental if many of the functions in the position are new, or if the organization unit is in a crisis. Where little is known about the demands of a position, or when crises occur, rational-deductive approaches may have to be replaced with what Lindbloom calls "muddling through."[3]

Excelling

New networks and revised agendas are prerequisites for success. Equally as contributory are the behaviors common to all successful managers: listening, synthesizing pertinent data, making decisions in a timely manner but not jumping the gun, and being visible. Adaptability is also important. The work world is competitive. Adapting to the give and take of solving problems is necessary for anyone who wants to advance to the positions at the top of an organization. The nurse in an acting position who is also competing for the job needs a strong sense of identity and solid self-esteem to adapt and successfully cope with the changes and challenges.

Trust in oneself and in others is a must. Before there is interpersonal trust, however, there is testing. This is a normal part of any relationship, whether temporary or permanent. It is essential to recognize that an interim is a time of uncertainty. Self-

confidence and a belief in the dignity of all makes trust possible and once trust is established, people excel.

REFERENCES

1. Gabarro, J.J., and Kotter, J.P. Managing Your Boss. *Harvard Business Review* 58, no. 1 (1980): 92-10.
2. Kotter, J.P. *The General Managers* (New York: Free Press, 1982.)
3. Lindbloom, C.E. The Science of 'Muddling Through.' *Publication Administration Review* 19, no. 2 (1959): 78-88

—Dorothy H. Barrus

Marjorie Katz and Linda Sortino Kenwood contributed to this article.

MASTER'S OF EDUCATION DEGREE FOR NURSING ADMINISTRATION

Only high ability and sound education equip a man for the continuous seeking of new solutions.[1]

High standards of knowledge and skill are the core of the programs for nursing administration where the goal is to educate students for the life-long seeking of new solutions. Standards are the level or degree of quality that is expected. The standards used to sort out who gets what kind of education is a highly sensitive topic in a nation as democratic as ours. In fact, as Gardner notes, "The sorting out of individuals according to ability is very nearly the most delicate and difficult process our society has to face."[2]

As painful as sorting out students may be, it is, nevertheless, a task for which we are responsible. Excellence in academic nursing administration means having a clear vision of what the standard for a well-educated nurse administrator is. Excellence also involves faculty who are willing to assume the accountability for setting educational agendas—agendas that require both teachers and students to stretch to the limits of their ability.[3]

Who is admitted

Anyone who has been a member of an admissions committee has experienced the painfulness of sorting and selecting people based on ability. In the interest of being fair, of giving all applicants a chance to discover themselves, it is dangerously easy to postpone, wherever possible, the closing of the schoolhouse door. But in the process, we lower standards and rob society of an excellent educational system, substituting instead one that is highly equalitarian but mediocre.[4]

At the University of Florida, standards used by committee members to decide who will be admitted include a minimum grade point average of 3.0: a combined verbal and quantitative score of 1,000 or above on the Graduate Record Examination (GRE); strong recommendations from employers and undergraduate advisors; and evidence of defined career and research goals. Applicants for nursing administration are also expected to have a minimum of one year's management experience.

Preadmission interviews

Prospective students in nursing administration are advised to meet with a faculty member for a preadmission interview. Although it is not mandatory, the interview is strongly recommended, especially to those who have any question about the likelihood of their being admitted. During the interview, which lasts about an hour, faculty describe the courses, expectations, and the existing research programs relevant to an applicant's scientific interest.

Prospective students are encouraged to spend the extra time it takes to develop their admission forms in careful, thorough ways, thinking through, perhaps more extensively

than they had in the past, specifically why they want to study nursing administration. It is made clear to applicants that competition for admission is keen. The probability of being admitted is discussed openly and frankly.

Critique of applications

Faculty may also spend time examining drafts of a student's admission application. In the course of these critiques, a deeper understanding is developed of each student's ability to think and write. Beginning with the preadmission interview, faculty assess an applicant, not only as a candidate for admission to the master's program, but also as a potential candidate for doctoral study, and then structure advising accordingly. The educational track of high achievers is greatly facilitated by planning for doctoral study early: Master's electives can be selected with an eye toward a doctoral minor, and a research topic with thesis and dissertation stages can be planned.

Individual guidance

What of the weaker applicant, who is less likely to be admitted? Educational systems in democracies are responsible for upholding high standards, but they are also responsible for providing the right kind of education for each person. As Gardner notes, "The good society is not one that ignores individual differences but one that deals with them wisely and humanely."[5] Based on this belief, faculty are committed to identifying individual differences in levels of readiness for graduate study and then developing custom-made assistance for prospective students.

Assuming applicants qualify with respect to grades, references, and goals, we often provide the most individualized guidance for the GRE. When an applicant has questions about improving examination scores, we direct him or her to books designed to help prepare for the test, as well as to commercial testing agencies, and to local community colleges where courses are offered that are designed to review the content of entrance examinations.

It is with respect to the GRE that the sorting and shifting are most painful. Nurses who otherwise have a strong application—with good grades and years of recent management experience—sometimes complain bitterly that the required score for the GRE is excessive and ask that it be waived. While there are limits to what examinations can predict, our experience has shown that students who score highest on the GRE perform best in the program.

In our program, there is a heavy emphasis on advising each individual applicant. Faculty feel the time is well spent. Once students are admitted, they know what to expect, what the standards will be, and what the competition is, so there are few unfortunate surprises. Applicants who do not succeed in getting admitted are humanely directed to other types of educational systems—to community colleges and other state schools or to extension programs—where their knowledge and skill are more aligned with the purpose of these alternatives.

Performance goals

Developing future nurse administrators with more than just technical competence is the goal. In a major public university such as the University of Florida, we are concerned with short-term needs in the state for more effective management of nursing services. We are equally concerned, however, with producing talent that will create a great civilization. To prepare students for positions after graduation, as well as for leadership in the profession and in society, faculty insist on careful thinking as demonstrated

in good writing and speaking.

Emphasis on writing and articulating ideas verbally is especially heavy in courses in organizational behavior, nursing administration theory, and human resource management. To develop depth of judgment and a perspective that broadly comprehends problems in organizations and society, students are expected to read widely from the professional and classical literature and to contribute actively to seminars by addressing problems of major consequence.

Herman Finer made these comments about nursing administration three decades ago, and they are still true: "It is urgent that the vision of the profession be lifted from petty and verbal questions and be focused on matters of principle rather than on mere symptoms."[6] If education for nursing administration is to be professional and scientific, as opposed to technical and vocational, then careful, clear thinking and development of the student as a responsible, mature person need to be paramount. To equip students in nursing administration with the critical qualities of mind and character needed to understand principles and cope with major organizational change, the school places heavy emphasis on intelligent, logical thinking, and the use of good English.

Writing well in nursing administration

Willingness to put one's thoughts on paper, whether as an administrator or as a

---

If education for nursing administration is to be professional and scientific, as opposed to technical and vocational, then careful, clear thinking and development of the student as a responsible, mature person need to be paramount.

scientist, is an essential aspect of professional accountability. Good writing is as necessary for success in an administrative role as it is in an academic one. Many nurse administrators find it difficult to express themselves in writing; they generate windy, confused, overlong memorandums and reports that aggravate hospital administrators. Patients suffer too when nurses in administrative positions cannot convey their ideas quickly and easily using fetching language that people take to heart.

Students in our program are forced to actively practice writing. (And "forced" they often are: Writing is hard for most people and requires the greatest diligence and perseverance.) We believe, as Finer does, that, "the person who cannot express himself in writing is lacking in ideas or is lazy."[7] Development of writing skills, therefore, is done in a variety of ways throughout the program. Quizzes are not used, but unplanned writing exercises are. In addition to the writing of short and long essays, on the average of every two to three weeks, students develop their skills to write resumes and business letters, as well as memorandums, reports, research proposals, and theses.

The standards for content and format of written assignments are shared with students at the beginning of each term, and are then used to determine grades. Correct spelling and punctuation and standard grammar and syntax are the basic criteria. A high premium is put on writing where the logic is clear, where the language is concise, and where the ideas are new, interesting, and useful.

Students are also expected to demonstrate an understanding of which kind of language to use for various kinds of audiences. Nurse administrators who mistakenly use the jargon and special language of nursing when writing to or talking with physicians or members of the board are in danger of failing to achieve their goals. This is the point we make to students: Sensitivity to written and verbal language is essential in the art of nursing management.

Speaking well and reading widely

The nurse administrator who speaks well thinks clearly. To help students think intelligently, we find ways to encourage them to read broadly. The majority are well versed with respect to nursing knowledge. Once they are admitted, therefore, their reading is first focused on nursing administration and then on the best research in management science.

Professional reading alone, however, is not sufficient, especially when the educational background of many students is narrowly technical. To enlarge students' world views and to expand their understanding of an array of life experiences, faculty expect students to broaden their knowledge of society, governments, and world problems by reading good and great literature. Required reading includes Plato's *Republic,* de Tocqueville's *Democracy in America* and Machiavelli's *The Prince.* In the human resources management course, students are given the option of reading a dozen great books and analyzing the implications of the problems historically faced by people for contemporary health service.

Reading widely is accompanied by an emphasis on speaking in a variety of contexts. Students are expected to contribute to every class discussion. For those who initially are not as well versed as others, the expectation, nonetheless, is that they talk by asking questions, reflecting aloud with those who do speak, and taking the risk of expressing their opinions about what others have said.

Students are expected to express themselves in a way that contributes to the continuity of group discussions without overtalking. (Class sizes of about 10 make active participation possible.) When someone reneges, faculty meet with the student on an individual basis and suggest mechanisms that are useful for becoming a fully participative class member. At the close of class sessions, each student is given a grade that reflects the faculty's assessment of the substance of what he or she has said, the quality of speaking, and the extent to which what was said contributed to the advancement of understanding by the group. Weekly assessments continue, however painful and time consuming they might be, until everyone performs fully and effectively.

Other opportunities provided to help students develop as speakers are individual and group presentations in class and group facilitation exercises. Interviews with potential preceptors for assignments to clinical units and summary conferences are also used. At the conferences, an analysis of clinical problems is presented to faculty and preceptors in terms of nursing and management theory.

All faculty members have worked as executives. From personal experience, they realize that the work life of a nurse administrator is highly verbal. Managers typically spend from 75 percent to 90 percent of their time talking with others[8,9]; hence the heavy emphasis on encouraging students to develop the self-confidence with public presentation that being an administrator who is a spokesperson for nursing requires.

Standards that stretch us

Faculty are responsible for what is taught in schools. Sensibly, good teachers in professional disciplines such as nursing listen carefully to what people in practice tell them about the problems at work. Students' expectations are attended to as well. But in being sensitive to real life problems and adapting course content to students' likes and dislikes, excellent educators do not relinquish their intellectual authority. The buck stops with them as far as being responsible for what it is that is worth knowing, defending, and believing. Caving in to vocational pressures to condone watered-down curriculums, to marketing pressures to increase enrollments, or to political pressures to admit undisciplined students may characterize some of American higher education.[10] These same failures must not, however, describe education for nursing administration.

Nurse administrators say the problems they face are so complex as to almost defy solution. High standards in education for nursing administration are set for students because to a one, each is capable of solving problems and trying to be, and being, excellent.

REFERENCES

1. Gardner, J.W. *Excellence, Can We Be Excellent and Equal Too?* (New York: Harper & Row, 1961) p. 35.
2. Ibid., 71.
3. Fiske, E.B. "Colleges Are Called Failures at Teaching Humanities Courses." *New York Times* (November 26, 1984).
4. Gardner, *Excellence*.
5. Ibid., 75.
6. Finer, H. *Administration and the Nursing Services* (New York: Macmillan, 1952) p. 320.
7. Ibid., 296.
8. Gronn, P.C. Talk as the Work: The Accomplishment of School Administration. *Administrative Science Quarterly* 28 (1983): 1-21.
9. Kotter, J.P. *The General Managers* (New York: Free Press, 1982.)
10. Fiske, Colleges Are Called Failures at Teaching Humanities Courses.

—Beverly Henry

Contributors:
Beverly Henry, R.N., M.S.N., M.P.A.,
  Ph.D.
Associate Professor
College of Nursing

Mary F. Brallier, R.N., B.S.N.
Staff Nurse
Veterans Administration Medical Center
Master's Student
Gainesville, Florida
College of Nursing

Karen Putney, R.N., B.A.
Head Nurse
Nursing Home Care Unit
Veterans Administration Medical Center
Master's Student
Gainesville, Florida
College of Nursing

Barbara S. Williams, R.N., B.A.
Nursing Supervisor
Shands Hospital
Master's Student
College of Nursing

Dorothy H. Barrus, R.N., M.S.N.
Acting Director for Children's Health
Shands Hospital
Doctoral Student
College of Nursing
University of Florida
Gainesville, Florida

Excellence

Barbara J. Brown, R.N., Ed.D.,
F.A.A.N., C.N.A.A.
Editor
Nursing Administration Quarterly

Excellence is a term used from the time we are very young. Each of us is encouraged to achieve the very best for whatever the endeavor is throughout our lives. Grades in school are based on the highest value of excellence. Competition in sports is based on excellence. Even in one's home environment, the Good Housekeeping Seal has a meaning of excellence, as does a blue ribbon won at a state fair. Each connotes excellence.

Excellence in nursing has a value of surpassing, exceeding, excelling, having a superior nursing staff, or nursing endeavor, and being recognized for our qualities. The Magnet Hospital Report recognized 41 hospitals as having the best environment for nursing practice, thus being able to attract and retain nurses. I had the good fortune of being the nursing administrator in two of those Magnet Hospitals: Family Hospital, Milwaukee, Wisconsin, and Virginia Mason Hospital, Seattle, Washington.

More recently, Virginia Mason Hospital was recognized among the best hospitals in America out of 64 hospitals in the United States and was praised as having exceptional nursing staff. In a patient survey, the nursing staff received excellent marks, with 96 percent of the survey population saying that the nurses were sensitive to the needs of families and visitors.

Development of such nursing staffs and recognition as a magnet hospital require a particular discipline of excellence in nursing leadership. Vision, imagination, knowledge, and a degree of intelligence in applying the knowledge in a practically useful way to convert an environment are all attributes in creating nursing excellence. The effectiveness of knowledge in the work setting is defined by the results. The results are then visible to peers for awards such as that given to Virginia Mason Hospital.

Although the goal to achieve such blue ribbon status can be present, the pragmatics of implementing the goal become a real administrative challenge. When faced with particular implementation dilemmas

Nurs Admin Q, 1976, 1(1), vii–ix
©1976 Aspen Publishers, Inc.

in providing leadership to a nursing service in order to achieve excellence, many barriers come to mind. Most important is the individual nurse leader who is having a difficult time changing from an autocratic managerial style to one of professional clinical leadership. Such an individual was part of my team in 1984, and the difficulties encountered were so severe that the chief physician asked that that individual not be continued as a leader for the units of responsibility.

It is easy for a nurse administrator to remove an individual when a physician or administrator requires such removal. It is far more difficult to coach, to guide, to search for ways in which a comprehensive plan can change the individual as well as the nursing staff.

In reflecting on developing clinical excellence in nursing, I am drawn to 1985 when such a challenge confronted me as an administrator. The individual was an excellent person, but needed counseling and direction on how to proceed. This counseling resulted in some very specific guidelines for all clinical leaders in that practice environment to move forward in clinical excellence. It seems appropriate as we address our passion for excellence in nursing to present some practical, applicable guidelines.

1. Plan specific continuing education programs each year to focus on the clinical specialty service for which you are clinical leader.
2. Develop specific inservice training on each clinical service, including nursing personnel in the planning and presenting. The sessions should be multidisciplinary and should include physicians, physical therapy, respiratory therapy, pharmacy, nursing, and all disciplines involved with the clinical specialty the session is addressing. Notices of inservice training should go to all nursing staff and other departments as appropriate.
3. Develop a comprehensive plan for collaborative practice committees. Each nurse leader needs to meet regularly with the chairperson or chief of the section that predominates on the clinical service in order to establish the agendas for the collaborative practice committees. The focus should be on the standards of practice for each specialty service, (e.g., respiratory care, neurology care, endocrinology care, gastrointestinal care) and enhancing the implementation of the physician's plan for specific clinical patient care and enactment of the nursing care plan.
4. Look at opportunities to broaden collaborative practice committees to include representatives from other allied health disciplines such as pharmacy, respiratory therapy, physical therapy, and any other discipline or administrative service.
5. Establish special task forces to look at patient teaching needs and clarify the responsibility for positive reinforcement in a team effort to enhance the outcome of patients and review and develop more comprehensive patient plans.
6. Evaluate the communication between pharmacy, dietary, and other disciplines and nursing per patient population. Utilize nursing/pharmacy or nursing/dietary or other appropriate ancillary discipline committee to increase the collaborative efforts to each interdisciplinary department.
7. Plan nursing grand rounds to focus on clinical services. Make these nursing grand rounds available to the entire nursing work force. Focus on

highlighting excellence, sharing with others their excellence in practice.

8. Attend specific medical staff and house staff (if a teaching hospital) meetings when appropriate. An example would be a chest service conference. Try to assign the primary nurse whose case is being discussed at the clinical conference.

9. Implement multidisciplinary quality assurance programs to review the process and outcome of patient care in a collaborative team effort.

10. Review and evaluate the total discharge planning and the team relationship for discharge planning for each clinical service.

Much could be added to these guidelines. However, these are the exact guidelines that formulated action plans for clinical excellence for 1985 for each clinical service at Virginia Mason Hospital Nursing Services. These guidelines plus the comprehensive team effort of all nursing leadership people as well as the total team effort between physicians, nurses, and administrators led Virginia Mason to receive recognition as a top hospital. Indeed, the nursing staff is exceptional and will continue to be as long as there is application of knowledge, concentration on the priorities of patient care, and effective self-discipline in managing and leading nursing toward excellence. These priorities apply in any work setting.

As we have set forward a goal to become a center for nursing excellence in the Middle East at King Faisal Specialist Hospital, several priorities need to be addressed. One is the vision for the future. A five-year long-range plan has given direction to the future for excellence similar to that used in previous settings. We also strive to maintain a posture of proactive decision making rather than reactive. We recognize each situation as an opportunity for change and redirection rather than taking each situation as an adversity to be overcome. This attitude enables us to keep a high level of self-direction for goal accomplishment toward the future; we set high aims every day. In general, time management, integration of ideas, and consolidation of efforts all lead to providing the opportunity to develop that priceless valued center for excellence in nursing.

Part IV
Study and discussion questions

1. What are the components of an excellent organization and an excellent nursing department? If they are different, why? How can they be integrated to achieve a common vision?

2. How are Quality Assurance principles and TQM/CQI principles similar or different?

3. What are the pros and cons of an organization mastering a particular author's CQI process versus integrating some TQM/CQI concepts into the organization?

4. Can nursing implement a TQM/CQI program without the entire organization? If yes, how? If no, why not?

5. How does one transition the culture and thinking of an organization to TQM/CQI?

6. How can a meaningful CQI program be developed so staff effect changes in their practice and improve care to patients?

7. What are the benefits of implementing a TQM/CQI program in hospitals?

Part V
Nurse/physician/administrative relationships

Doris M. Armstrong, R.N., M.Ed., F.A.A.N.
Nurse Administrative Consultant
Avon, Connecticut

The purpose of Collaborative Practice continues to be to improve patient care. Fundamental to this system of providing care are close interactive relationships between nurses, physicians, and administrators, where trust and mutual respect are essential. These inter-relationships have been expanded in recent years to include all professional disciplines in the health care team. The professional nurse continues to be the appropriate integrator/coordinator of care for patients.

As professional models of nursing practice have been implemented within the collaborative framework, more opportunity for autonomy is experienced by professional nurses. In order to be successful, the environment and systems within which the nurse practices must be supportive of the collaboration of all professional disciplines and demonstrate a commitment to patient centered care.

While the original work of the National Joint Practice Commission (NJPC) did not include evaluation data to demonstrate the cost/benefit of collaborative practice, such analysis is essential in the current economic environment and in the foreseeable future. The efforts of the NJPC, now more than a decade later, represent significant steps forward in collaborative relationships and practice and offer valuable guidance in the redesign of hospital systems. Redesign of models of collaborative practice implemented in the 1980s are now being introduced with renewed focus on a patient centered system of care which includes regular reviews of performance, quality, and cost.

Collaborative practice at Hartford Hospital

Beverly L. Koerner, R.N., Ph.D.
Associate Professor of Nursing
Chairperson, Department of Nursing
University of Hartford
Hartford, Connecticut

Doris A. Armstrong, R.N., M.Ed.
Assistant Director, Hartford Hospital
Director, Department of Nursing
Hartford Hospital
Hartford, Connecticut

*D*URING THE PAST DECADE nursing practice has undergone significant changes. Scope-of-practice acts have been revised, and primary nursing has been instituted in many health care agencies. These changes have resulted in an overlapping of nurse and physician roles and an interdependence between nurses and physicians, and they have clarified the independent functions of the nurse. These changes have been recognized by the National Joint Practice Commission, as shown in the following statement.

The accumulation of knowledge and the expansion of techniques and skills able to be utilized in the care of individuals and in the prevention, treatment and cure of disease has necessitated or resulted in a realignment and readjustment of nurse and physician roles.[1]

It is clear that for health care delivery to be effective and efficient, nurses and physicians must collaborate to jointly determine role functions. Hartford Hospital, a 1,000-bed acute care facility in Hartford, Connecticut, recognized the need for collaboration and in 1977 began planning to implement collaborative practice. In that year a Joint Practice Committee was established to enhance the quality of the interface between nurses and physicians.

The Hartford Hospital Joint Practice Committee (HHJPC) is composed of equal numbers of nurses and physicians, and the associate executive officer. Two of the physician members had been previously involved in the State Joint Practice Committee established by the Connecticut State Medical Society and the Connecticut Nurses' Association. The HHJPC was created for the following purposes: (1) to clarify the interactive roles of the nurse and physician and

Nurs Admin Q, 1983, 7(4), 72–81
©1983 Aspen Publishers, Inc.

their relationship with other professionals; (2) to problem solve patient care issues and explore accountability of the nursing and medical staffs; (3) to foster understanding and effective collaboration between members of the nursing, medical, and administrative staffs; and (4) to facilitate activities of clinical service patient care committees as they cross departmental lines.

In the early years of the HHJPC, members spent time building trust and familiarizing themselves with the nurses', physicians', and administrators' collaborative efforts already in existence, primarily in the ambulatory care setting. Administration was supportive of developing a system of collaboration to foster professional practice and had worked with nurses and physicians to achieve these goals. It readily became apparent to the HHJPC that in order to establish true collaborative practice, efforts needed to be concentrated on one demonstration project unit. In order to implement such a project, a grant would be required.

Since the four demonstration projects of the National Joint Practice Commission were successful,[2] it was felt that the Hartford Hospital project should be designed as closely as possible to those projects. Specifically, this would require informing observer health agencies about what was being developed and having them critique the plans. In addition, it was recognized that specific criteria had to be collected from which the hospital would be able to determine the cost of entering into collaborative practice. If this demonstration project were successful (and there was every indication it would be), collaborative practice would expand to other units in the hospital. A major medical unit was chosen for the demonstration unit.

As in any new venture, timing and the right people were important keys to success. The nursing assistant director for medicine who was a member of the State Joint Practice Committee was eager to participate in this venture, as was the physician assistant director for medicine. The head nurse was an outstanding employee who had fulfilled the new role of the head nurse particularly well and was most eager to be involved in this project. The chief of medicine was supportive as were staff and attending physicians.

The opportunity to work with a nurse educator prepared with a doctorate in measurement and evaluation facilitated the development of the criteria for evaluation. The educator was knowledgeable in the strategic planning that was ongoing in nursing, and was supportive of the efforts being made toward a system of professional nursing practice. It was recognized that nursing by itself could not develop such a system and that much more integration and collaboration with physicians and hospital administration were necessary. The groundwork for the Collaborative Practice Project was supported by the nursing, medical and administrative staffs of the hospital and by the board of trustees.

DEVELOPING THE EVALUATION DESIGN FOR THE DEMONSTRATION UNIT

Commitment was made to the collaborative practice demonstration unit. The combined hospitals fund provided seed money for a project coordinator and an evaluation consultant. Given this level of support, a

It was recognized that nursing by itself could not develop such a system and that much more integration and collaboration with physicians and hospital administration were necessary.

plan for evaluating the project was formulated several months before implementation of the project. The project evaluator met with staff and administration to identify outcomes of collaborative practice.

Renzulli's Key Features Model[3] was used to design and implement the evaluation and to organize the variables to be evaluated. This model provides for a multivariate approach to analyzing factors affecting the project as well as collecting data from multiple sources. The focal point of the Renzulli model is identification of key features or those areas that are to be evaluated. The evaluator of the Collaborative Practice Project Evaluation (CPPE) identified ten key features or variables from a review of the literature,[4] interviews with staff administrators, and ongoing observations of potential problem areas.

Data were to be collected from the project unit and two additional comparison units. One unit was deemed to be comparable with the demonstration unit in terms of staffing ratios, types and education of staff, structural supports, types of clients, and related pathology. Both units were 27-bed medical teaching units. Because of the geographic proximity of the two units, a third unit was used to compare certain attitudinal data. Brainstorming sessions were held to identify specific items for instruments that might be sensitive to the differences in the "treatment" (i.e., collaborative practice and primary nursing). For example, since the majority of the patients on the demonstration unit were elderly, an instrument to measure patient satisfaction was developed and pilot tested on elderly clients in Florida and Illinois. Interpreters translated the instrument into Spanish, Portuguese, and Italian. The tool included the following questions, which were thought to be sensitive to the new job description written for the primary nurse.

- Do you know the name of the nurse who primarily took care of you and planned your care?
- Did your primary nurse involve you in planning and taking care of your needs?
- How often did you receive an explanation of your treatments such as X-rays and other tests?

Similarly, a physician attitude survey and a nurse attitude survey were developed to measure role conflict, autonomy, decentralization, nurse-physician relationships, etc. A stratified random sample of attending physicians and all interns and residents was given the physician survey. All RNs and LPNs on the demonstration and comparison units were given the nurse survey. Currently, the data from these surveys are being stored on computer tape and will be compared with data collected at 6- and 12-month intervals.

Several standardized instruments are being used to measure other key features, such as the Leader Behavior Description Questionnaire,[5] the Job Satisfaction Index[6] and the Hospital Attitude Survey.[7] Using a time-series format, data are being collected (1) prior to implementation of the project, (2) at six months and (3) at 12 months. Retrospective process and outcome record audits are being used to look at the quality of delivery of care. These audits are addressed later in this article.

The cost/benefit dimension is being compared on the two units from October 1 to March 20, 1981, prior to implementation of the project and April 18 to September 30, 1982. (Cost/benefit factors are presented in Table 1.) It is hoped that comparison data for the two hospital units will show significant differences on these cost-benefit variables. In summary, the evaluation of the project was planned prior to its implementation. A comprehensive model that provides for ex-

Table 1. Cost/benefit factors

Patients	Personnel	Nursing units
Nursing hours per patient day per job category	Total hours budgeted for nursing unit by job category	Number of beds
Average patient classification	Actual full-time equivalent personnel by job category per nursing unit	Occupancy
Number of diagnostic tests ordered	Personnel transferred into and out of nursing unit	
	Average nursing salary rate per hour per job category	
	Nursing salary costs per patient day per job category	
	Nursing salary costs per nursing unit by job category	
	Illness, vacation, and absenteeism by job category	
	Average time for intershift report	
	Education and length of employment by job category	
	Education costs of orientation	

amination of multiple variables was used to design the evaluation, and several instruments were developed that are expected to differentiate outcomes attributable to collaborative practice.

ESTABLISHING INDEPENDENT NURSE FUNCTIONS

The American Nurses' Association Statement of Functions[8] outlines general areas of independent role functions that professional nurses may implement without physician orders. These functions have been used in defining nursing practice in the United States. For example, the Connecticut Nurse Practice Act defines nursing for the registered nurse as:

Diagnosing and treating of human response to actual or potential health problems . . . and executing medical regimens prescribed by a

licensed or otherwise legally-authorized physician or dentist.[9]

New York State has added the statement that a nursing regimen shall be consistent with any existing medical regimen.[10] The last statement is particularly relevant to the implementation of primary nursing and collaborative practice. It is a major premise of this article that the independent functions that are the components of primary nursing are intricately linked with the functions that are interdependent with physician functions and together these form the basis of collaborative practice.

Another example of this interrelatedness of functions is presented in the Washington Nurse Practice Act.[11] This act acknowledges other functions requiring education and training which the medical and nursing professions both recognize as proper nursing functions. What are germane to this discussion are the ethical and legal implications of the various definitions of nursing practice and how these interface with primary nursing and collaborative practice. The following discussion focuses on four related concepts: (1) clinical expertise, (2) accountability, 3) risk taking, and (4) interdependence.

The role of the primary nurse, a crucial component of collaborative practice, mandates clinical expertise to assume responsibility for 24-hour care of the client and to comprehensively coordinate all aspects of service delivery. Thus the nurse is asked to implement new behaviors and skills—specifically, the issuing of nursing orders that are derived from the previously defined independent functions. Clarifying the boundaries or limits of the nursing role is imperative for both RNs and LPNs. As Creighton notes, "if a patient sues a nurse on a charge of malpractice and attempts to recover damages, the patient has to prove that the nurse's negligent act occurred during, or resulted from, her performance of a nursing function and that she violated the standard of care in her performance of that function."[12]

A case that illustrates violation of the standard of care is Barber vs. Reiking.[13] An LPN administered a polio booster shot to a two-year-old boy which resulted in a broken needle remaining in the boy's buttock. Because the licensing law for professional nurses specified that LPNs could not legally give inoculations, the courts ruled that the LPN did not possess the required knowledge and skill to administer the inoculation. As this case illustrates, no physician or RN can expand the functions for the LPN beyond those defined in state licensure laws.

Likewise, a physician cannot expand the functions of the RN beyond those defined by licensure laws and more specific rules and regulations of the Board of Nursing.

Without clear delineation of nursing scope of practice, gray areas between medicine and nursing will continue to exist. Questions will always arise as to whether a specified order is a nursing order or a medical order. For example, an independent function of the nurse is health teaching. Yet many institutions still require a physician's order for teaching or for referral to a clinical nurse specialist in diabetes or oncology. Who is accountable in this instance if the teaching is not accomplished? The nurse is accountable as is demonstrated in the case of Kyslinger vs. United States. A nurse provided instruction (to both the wife and her husband, who had kidney disease) on "the operation, maintenance and supervision of treatment during the 10 months in which he underwent biweekly hemodialysis in the hospital."[14] When the husband died two years after home dialysis, the trial court ruled that the widow failed to prove that she and her deceased veteran husband were given inadequate instruction.

These cases demonstrate the importance of defining what a nurse does, that is, what her work is, as well as the importance of nurse-physician collaboration in implementing a comprehensive, coordinated plan of care for the client. This need becomes even more critical where state boards of nursing have inadequate rules and regulations to define the practice of nursing.

At Hartford Hospital, primary nurses are becoming interdependent with physicians through collaborative practice so that they can clearly define and implement their independent functions. This process is essential as Lower notes:

> Primary nurses are stepping into the realm of collaborative partnership with physicians and finding that they are not necessarily wanted there. Many primary nurses expressed feelings of placing their heads on the chopping

block whenever they wrote a nursing order until the idea worked on was accepted by the physician.[15]

Whereas the New York State Practice Act, previously mentioned, mandates that a nursing regimen shall be consistent with an existing medical regimen, clearly the physician and nurse must collaborate to deliver health care to the patient. If areas of nurse-physician practice are clearly delineated prior to implementation of primary nursing, and physicians are assured of nursing's consistency with the medical plan of care through simulated patient care examples, risk taking will be lessened for the nursing staff. For example, a physician who understands nurses' clinical decision-making processes for a simulated case study may support that as a prototype for subsequent patients. Nurses will have the written and verbal endorsement by physicians for those independent functions defined by the American Nurses' Association, which by law as well as consequence to the patient must be interlinked with the medical regimen in acute care settings.

At Hartford Hospital, a committee of nurses and physicians involved in the Collaborative Practice Project met with the hospital risk manager to develop guidelines for the scope of nursing practice on the project unit. Nurses defined areas of practice, heretofore gray areas, that could be functions of nurses but were currently controlled by physicians. They presented these to the physicians for discussion and negotiation. For example, nurses needed a physician's order to initiate a referral to the diabetic clinician or to the nutritionist. They also could not implement certain procedures such as catheterization of a female patient without a physician's order. The nurses presented a strong rationale for why these functions could be performed independently by the nurse, and the com-

mittee developed and endorsed a list of scope-of-practice behaviors for nurses. With this type of game plan formulated in advance, there was little chance of an occurrence of the "chopping block syndrome" noted by Lower. Such a game plan is also consistent with the Washington Nurse Practice Act which states that functions that nurses and physicians both recognize as proper to be performed by nurses are within the scope of nursing practice.

There is no doubt the key words here are *discussion, negotiation* and *compromise*. Nurses and physicians are both likely to resist change—nurses because they are asked to assume more responsibility with subsequent accountability for functions, and physicians because they are giving up some perceived turf. As Orem notes, the ability to make and maintain a valid nursing focus is directly related to the nurse's education and experience.[16] Those RNs with limited education and experience will form the basis of associate nurses at Hartford Hospital. They will be prepared to care for a patient in cooperation with the primary nurse who has more advanced education and experience. The important point is that "each nurse is legally responsible for the level at which she undertakes to work. In other words, if a nurse with lesser education and capabilities undertakes the work of a nurse with advanced preparation and experience, she is legally held liable if she fails to perform as a nurse with advanced preparation and experience."[17]

Part of the committee's role is to inform physicians of the nursing functions generally accepted by the nursing profession and the legal consequences of a failure to uphold these. Lastly, the committee can be the arena for resolving nurse-physician conflicts on scope-of-practice issues that may potentially jeopardize the care of the patient.

COLLABORATIVE PRACTICE RECORD KEEPING

Expanded roles for nurses require major adjustment in role behaviors and legitimization of the new behaviors in institutional policy. Enactment of primary nursing and collaborative practice also requires the documentation of the nursing and medical regimen in the patient record. A joint record system requires that nurses and physicians use the same data sheet to create progress notes and that nurses and physicians collaboratively develop a plan of care using a problem-oriented record developed by Lawrence Weed for the patient. As the head nurse of the collaborative practice unit at Hartford Hospital noted, a joint record facilitates the sharing of patient information and promotes a continuous dialogue concerning patient needs and changing status. Prior to this, physicians and nurses wrote in separate sections of the record as though they were charting on two different patients.

A joint record system requires that nurses and physicians use the same data sheet to create progress notes and that nurses and physicians collaboratively develop a plan of care.

An essential ethical and legal issue is safeguarding the patient by establishing standards of nursing and medical care. Nurses and physicians at Hartford Hospital have established standards of care for patients with congestive heart failure. These standards are a component of the evaluation design of the Collaborative Practice Project. The nurses have established a protocol for nursing judgment related to congestive

heart failure that includes independent functions such as monitoring of current status and health education. The physicians have delineated the critical elements of the medical regimen for this disease. Records of patients with congestive heart failure from the collaborative practice unit and from the comparison unit will be tagged for a process retrospective record audit. A committee of physicians and nurses who are not directly associated with the project will review the records for implementation of the protocol as well as the quality of nursing and medical care delivered. The committee also will look for the congruence between the nursing and medical regimens as a function of improved communication because of collaborative practice.

Another component of the evaluation design for the project is related to an outcome retrospective audit of patient records on the collaborative practice unit and the comparison unit. Within a 12-month period, medical record technicians will audit a random selection of 100 records from each unit. Certain key indicators that were thought to be sensitive measures of the differences in patient care outcomes caused by collaborative practice have been identified by a committee of nurses and physicians. Some of the indicators are number of laboratory tests per client, number of transfers to intensive care, number of codes and deaths, number of discharge plans, and number of hospitalized days. Both the process audit and the outcome audit promote staff accountability and provide useful data for improving patient care.

Creighton states that nurses should realize the value of complete charting in avoiding negligence actions against them.[18] For example, in Jenkins vs. Bogalusa Community Medical Center, a hospital patient got out of bed unassisted, fell, and fractured his hip. He later died of a pulmonary embolism following hip surgery. It was noted in this case that nursing was responsible for recording the fact that a patient had been told of medical orders restricting his activities and that needed nursing assistance would be provided. This information was documented in the patient chart, and no damages could be recovered since contributory negligence was found on the part of the patient. The nurse is personally liable in a civil action if a patient is injured because of the nurse's incompetence or carelessness. A nurse action that shows reckless conduct or disregard for human life is construed as gross negligence and is viewed as criminal.

Keeping records of nursing and medical regimens and subsequent responses of the patient is a key element in accountability. Collaborative practice should strengthen the planning and execution of care, causing

demonstrable change in patient status. The evaluation plan for the Collaborative Practice Project seeks to measure change in the quality of health care delivery and in patient outcomes.

TRUE COLLABORATION ENHANCES EFFICIENCY

While data collection for the Collaborative Practice Project study is incomplete, subjective observations indicate that identified outcomes are being realized in a positive manner. Patients report that they are more involved and satisfied with their care; and nurses, physicians, and administrators are enthusiastic and optimistic about the project. It has been said that when nurses and physicians truly collaborate, efficiency and effectiveness are enhanced.

REFERENCES

1. *Statement on Medical and Nurse Practice Acts* (Chicago: National Joint Practice Commission, February 1974.)
2. Applebaum, A. Commission Leads Way to Joint Practice for Nurses and Physicians. *Hospitals* 52, no. 14 (1978): 78–81.
3. Renzulli, J. *A Guidebook for Evaluating Programs for the Gifted and Talented* (Ventura, Calif.: Ventura County Superintendent of Schools, 1975.)
4. *Nursing Administration Quarterly* 5, no. 4 (1981): 1–111.
5. Stogdill, R. *Leader Behavior Description Questionnaire.* Form XII (Columbus, Ohio: Ohio State University, 1962.)
6. Smith, P. *Job Description Index* (Bowling Green, Ohio: Bowling Green State University, 1975.)
7. Holloway, R. *Hospital Attitude Survey* (Chicago, Ill.: Holloway Health Management Group, 1978.)

8. American Nurses' Association Statement of Functions. *American Journal of Nursing* 54, no. 7 (1954): 868–71.
9. Conn, Gen. Stat. §20–87A (1977) p. 36.
10. Creighton, H. *Law Every Nurse Should Know.* 4th ed. (Philadelphia: Saunders, 1981) p. 23.
11. State of Washington. Law Regulating the Practice of Nursing, cited in Creighton, *Law Every Nurse Should Know,* p. 23.
12. Creighton, *Law Every Nurse Should Know,* p. 36.
13. Ibid., 26.
14. Ibid., 25.
15. Lower, J. After Primary Nursing Is Implemented: Then What? *Nursing Administration Quarterly* 5, no. 4, (1981): 17.
16. Orem, D. *Nursing Concepts of Practice* (New York: McGraw-Hill, 1971) pp. 1–2.
17. Creighton, *Law Every Nurse Should Know,* p. 146.
18. Ibid., 114–18.

Personal, organizational and managerial factors related to nurse—physician collaboration

Anna C. Alt-White, R.N., M.S.N.
Assistant Professor of Nursing
Catholic University of America
Washington, D.C.
Doctoral Student
University of Maryland
Baltimore, Maryland

Martin Charns, D.B.A.
Associate Professor of Organizational
  Behavior and Management
School of Management
Boston University
Boston, Massachusetts

Richard Strayer, Ph.D.
Vice President
Serafini Associates
Cupertino, California

OVER THE LAST DECADE the nursing literature has focused a great deal of attention on improving nurse-physician collaboration. The National Joint Practice Commission (NJPC) significantly contributed both to this literature and to improving nurse-physician collaboration throughout the country.[1-6] In addition, a number of other articles have emphasized a shift from the traditional physician-dominated relationship to a more balanced nurse-physician collaborative relationship.[7-10] Based on these articles, nurse-physician collaboration can be defined as the process whereby nurses and physicians work together in the delivery of quality care, jointly contributing in a balanced relationship characterized by mutual trust.

However, there has been little systematic research directed toward the factors that encourage collaboration. Instead, most studies have focused either on different approaches to joint practice and its implementation, or on the effects of collaboration. The study reported here was conducted to examine the personal, organizational, and managerial factors that contribute to nurse-physician collaboration on patient care units. The patient care unit was chosen as the focus for this study because it is the primary inpatient location where physicians and nurses need to work together to provide services to patients. It therefore provides an optimal setting for examining the factors that contribute to collaboration.

Nurs Admin Q, 1983, 8(1), 8–18
©1983 Aspen Publishers, Inc.

FACTORS CONTRIBUTING TO COLLABORATION

The health care and organizational literature suggests a number of factors that potentially affect the establishment and maintenance of reciprocal relationships between nurses and physicians. These factors may be broken into personal, organizational and managerial groups.

Personal factors

Given the emphasis that has been placed on baccalaureate nursing preparation, it is appropriate to investigate whether personal factors are related to the amount a nurse collaborates with physicians. One would expect greater collaboration by nurses with baccalaureate education than by those with a diploma or associate's degree. Such broader educational background should provide the basis for a more professional practice of nursing, a broader view of nursing responsibilities and thus greater collaboration.

A second personal factor expected to relate to nurse-physician collaboration is nurses' length of experience. With greater experience generally comes more skill and confidence, as well as greater opportunities to h̶ built a working relationship with physi̶ ̶ns.

Organizational factors

The two organizational factors that the literature suggests may be related to nurse-physician collaboration are the use of primary nursing and whether the unit provides critical or noncritical care.

Primary nursing is one of the five elements intended by the NJPC to enhance collaboration.[11] It pinpoints staff nurse responsibility for patient care and provides the opportunity for professional nursing.

Because it specifies a single nurse as responsible for a given patient's care on the unit, it limits the number of people with whom a physician talks to obtain information. This makes it more likely that physicians will contact the primary nurse with regard to patients who the nurse see as his or her patient. It follows that if a unit uses primary nursing, physicians will have increased working contact with individual primary nurses.

There may also be differences in collaboration on critical and non-critical patient care units, since each type of unit has unique characteristics. For example, in critical care units nurses usually work in a small geographical space, are familiar with and use sophisticated medical technology, have more frequent contact with physicians and work with fewer auxiliary personnel, and the patient-nurse ratio is smaller. In addition, the staff has the expectation that all of the patients are critically ill at some point during their say in the unit. On the other hand, in non-critical care units nurses work in a larger geographical space, the patient-nurse ratio is larger, nurses rely less on medical technology to carry out patient care, physicians are generally less available, and more auxiliary personnel are present. In addition, on non-critical care units the patients' conditions are on a continuum ranging from being critically or terminally ill at one end of the spectrum to being healthy enough to be discharged from the hospital at the other end of the spectrum.[12]

The two organizational factors that the literature suggests may be related to nurse-physician collaboration are the use of primary nursing and whether the unit provides critical or noncritical care.

Managerial factors

The study considers three managerial factors that are potentially related to nurse-physician collaboration. The first of these, approaches to coordination, has been identified as an important managerial factor that affects communication between professionals.[13,14] March and Simon suggest that there are two broad categories of coordination: coordination by plan (programmed) and coordination by feedback.[15] They argue that organizations develop programmed responses to various stimuli and that when a novel stimulus is encountered, problem solving has to be initiated. Programming, then, reduces the need for an organization to exchange information. Feedback methods, on the other hand, increase an organization's ability to process information because they involve person-to-person contact and allow for greater variability of response.

Programming involves various forms of standardization.[16,17] Those commonly found in health care are the following:

1. standardization of work—where activities to be performed are specified ahead of their actual performance through the use of rules, schedules, plans, protocols, etc.;
2. standardization of skills—where the training and skills necessary to perform activities are specified.

Feedback mechanisms, which transfer information in a richer, more adaptable way, include the following:

1. supervision—in which information is exchanged between two people where one is responsible for the actions of the other in a hierarchical relationship;
2. mutual adjustment—the exchange of information between two people not having a formal hierarchical relationship;

3. group coordination—in which the exchange of information takes place among three or more people in a group setting.

Charns et al.[18] found use of all types of coordinating approaches to be related to patient care unit effectiveness.

The organizational development literature has repeatedly identified the communication process in a given work setting as being another influential factor in determining the extent of collaboration. One would expect that this also would be true in the context of nurse-physician relationships. The greater the openness and mutual respect between care providers, the more one would anticipate a higher level of collaboration.

The third factor thought to relate to collaboration, however, in reverse, is organizational stress. If an organization does not provide adequate support to its staff, in terms of equipment, salaries, or staff resources, professionals will become disenchanted and not invest the energy needed for collaborative effort. In addition, if the bureaucracy is so cumbersome that it is a barrier to collaborative accomplishment, staff will adjust by diminishing their effort. Thus organizational stress would be expected to have an inverse relationship to collaboration.

METHOD

Background of the study

The study is one in a multiphase action research project conducted in a large, eastern university teaching hospital. The purpose of the overall project is to evaluate patient unit effectiveness and to make recommendations for improvements. One of the major components of the project is the study of coordination among health care professionals. The work reported in this article is part of that project and examines nurses' perceptions of factors that contributed to nurse-physician collaboration.

Subjects

In total, 446 nurses from 46 patient care units responded to an extensive questionnaire that focused on aspects of patient care units. Units in the hospital were organized according to medical specialty, which in turn generally determined the type of patients admitted to units. Included in the total were 226 nurses from six medical-surgical, adult, critical care patient units and 16 non-critical care units.

Nursing questionnaires

The nurses working on the patient care units provided data in three different areas pertinent to the study. First, they reported on the types of coordinating mechanisms that were most useful in performing their jobs. Second, they responded to a number of items concerning the functioning of the unit, developed from the Charns et al. measure previously used with nursing professionals.[19] Four factors were measured; staff satisfaction, communication process, organizational stress and nurse-physician collaboration. The last factor was used as the measure of collaboration in the study. Last, demographic information was collected on each respondent, including educational background and years of nursing experience. Educational background was coded into three categories: (1) A.D. or diploma, (2) B.S.N. or (3) M.S.N. or greater.

Additional data

Each unit was also assessed by nursing administration to reflect the extent to which it had implemented primary nursing. Units were coded as: (1) not using primary nurs-

ing, (2) in process of implementing primary nursing or (3) using primary nursing fully. Adult medical-surgical units also were coded as 0 or 1 to reflect whether they were non-critical care or critical care units, respectively.

RESULTS AND DISCUSSION

The three types of factors expected to be related to nurse-physician collaboration were analyzed as shown in Tables 1 to 3.

Personal factors

As shown in Table 1, a weak inverse relationship was found between collaboration and nurse's length of employment at the

Table 1. Correlations between nurse–physician collaboration and nurse personal characteristics, organizational and managerial factors

Factor	Pearson correlation with collaboration
Nurse personal characteristics	
Length of employment at hospital	−.09*
Nursing preparation	−.02
Organizational factor	
Use of primary nursing	.16***
Managerial factor	
Communications process on unit	.20***
Hospital climate that facilitates work	.34***
Satisfaction	.26***

*Significance better than .05.
***Significance better than .001.

hospital, and no statistically significant relationship was found between collaboration and educational preparation of the staff nurse. These results are somewhat surprising. First, the lack of relationship between nursing educational preparation and collaboration with physicians indicates that educational preparation alone does not relate to more or less collaboration. This finding does not mean that baccalaureate nursing education cannot contribute to collaboration. It does mean that in this hospital it is not sufficient alone to cause it.

Although collaboration between nurses and physicians was expected to increase with the length of a nurse's experience in the hospital, the findings were the opposite. Nurses with greater experience in this hospital actually collaborated less with physicians. This may be due to two factors characteristic of the particular hospital studied. One factor is reflected in the extremely low turnover rate at the hospital. Largely due to the personnel benefits of the hospital, staff are encouraged to remain in the employ of the facility even when they are extremely dissatisfied. In this situation, their motivation to work productively is quite low. This is an example of the distinction between an individual's decisions to join and remain in an organization and to produce.[20,21] The organization's liberal benefits, which are unrelated to any nurse's job performance, are what Galbraith has termed a *systems reward.* [22] They do not encourage productive work behavior; they do encourage staff to remain in the organization. Thus on units with low collaboration are staff with high length of service who are locked into their jobs. It is especially important to note these effects of liberal personnel benefits and other systems rewards, for they may be used by more organizations to address problems of nurse retention in times of favorable general economic conditions, but this is done at significant other cost to an organization.

A second possible explanation for the lack of a positive relationship between length of experience and nurse-physician collaboration is the low levels of involvement of the medical staff in patient care activities. One would expect that experienced nursing staff would have greater opportunity than inexperienced staff to get to know physicians with whom they needed to work. This could be one important basis for collaboration. However, few medical school faculty attending physicians had significant patient care responsibilities in this hospital. For example, less than one of every six members of the school's department of medicine admitted patients to this hospital. Physician coverage was provided largely by house staff. The house staff rotated frequently and had patients on numerous units at any given time. Many of them did not know the names of the nurses caring for their patients. It did not matter how long the nurse had worked at the hospital, for the opportunity did not exist for physicians and nurses to develop working relationships. Although these findings present a rather discouraging picture of the hospital, several other factors were found to be related to collaboration.

Organizational factors—primary nursing

A significant positive relationship was found between a unit's use of primary nursing and nurse-physician collaboration (see Table 1). This is consistent with the literature on primary nursing, and the findings represent one of the few empirical tests of this relationship.

Critical care versus non-critical care units

Since it was expected that the physical layout of critical care units and the acuity of patients on those units would encourage medical and nursing staffs working together, the reported amount of collaboration was compared between critical care and non-critical care units. The means of reported collaboration on the two types of units are shown in Table 2. As expected, greater collaboration with physicians is reported by nurses in critical care units than in non-critical care units. To understand this phenomenon in greater depth it is useful to examine the work behavior of physicians and nurses and see how that relates to collaboration. This is seen in the data on approaches to coordination and other managerial factors.

Managerial factors

Three managerial factors also were found to be strongly related to nurse-physician collaboration. The first, communications process on the unit, reflects the degree to which communication on the unit is open, that conflict is managed productively rather than avoided or smoothed over, and that meetings are a useful forum for discussing issues. This finding is consistent with expec-

Table 2. Nurse–physician collaboration in critical and non-critical care units

Type of unit	Mean collaboration reported by nurses
Non-critical care adult units	−.11
Critical care adult units	.20

Difference between means significant for p better than .01. Note: Collaboration scores standardized across all respondents in hospital to yield hospital mean of 0.

An effective nurse administrator would be wise to divide efforts between improving those factors directly controlled within the department and influencing physicians, hospital administration, and support departments.

tations that effective communication on a unit contributes to collaboration. The converse may also be true. When people are able to collaborate, the inherent trust in that working relationship contributes to the open and effective communication process.

An even stronger relationship was found between collaboration and organizational stress. Where nurses felt the hospital did not hinder getting the work done, they also reported greater collaboration with physicians. On the other hand, when nurses felt that it was "difficult to get equipment and supplies needed" to do their work, and it was "frustrating to work here," they also reported low collaboration with physicians. Again, from this comparative study of units, we cannot determine whether collaboration leads to the feeling that the hospital facilitates getting work done, or vice versa. It is likely, however, that when faced with the frustration of not being able to get supplies and equipment and of encountering red tape in dealing with administration and support departments, the sense of being able to do a good job is reduced. Along with this sense of futility is a lowered motivation to collaborate.

This possibility should be noted in efforts to encourage collaboration. Many of the factors that limit collaboration are not directly controllable by nursing. An effective nurse administrator would be wise to divide efforts between improving those factors directly controlled within the department and influencing physicians, hospital administration, and support departments to provide the support that contributes to a climate within which collaboration can occur.

Coordination

Displayed in Table 3 are correlations between approaches to coordination and reported nurse-physician collaboration. In reviewing these data, it is helpful to recall that nurses were asked to rate the extent they used the various mechanisms in performing their work when faced with unfamiliar situations.[23,24] The mechanisms are arrayed in the table in the conceptual categories discussed above. In reviewing the findings in Table 3, it is striking that nearly all of the mechanisms are significantly positively related to nurse-physician collaboration and none are negatively related. As might be expected, direct discussion between nurses and physicians shows the strongest relationship with collaboration.

However, a number of other interesting findings emerge, First, several mechanisms that concern coordination within nursing also are related to nurse-physician collaboration. These are discussion with head nurse, discussion with other clinical (staff) nurses and use of nursing rounds. Most likely, this is a reflection of the phenomenon that well-run units have good coordination both within nursing and between nursing and medicine. It may reflect that good nursing coordination contributes directly to nurse-physician collaboration. Since the other mechanisms (use of nursing manual, team meeting and shift report) which should facilitate coordination within nursing show no significant relationship to collaboration with physicians, strong support does not exist for this later argument.

Several findings concerning relationships between standardized approaches to

Table 3. Pearson correlations between nurse–physician collaboration and approach to coordination

Approach to coordination	Correlation with collaboration
Standardization of work	
Hospital policy manual	.09*
Nursing manual	.06
House staff manual	.17***
Unit policies and protocols	.13**
Patient care plans	.08*
Standardization of skills	
Nursing school education	.11**
Orientation	.24***
Inservice education	.22***
Supervision	
Discussion with head nurse	.13***
Mutual adjustment	
Discussion with other clinical nurse	.15***
Discussion with interns	.17***
Discussion with residents	.27***
Discussion with attending physicians	.20***
Group methods	
Communications book	.17***
Medical records	.08*
Team meetings	.05
Shift report	.05
Nursing rounds	.14**
Medical and nursing rounds	.14**
Interdisciplinary rounds	.00

*Significance better than .05.
**Significance better than .01.
***Significance better than .001.

coordination and nurse-physician collaboration contradict common wisdom and have important implications. Many management researchers and practicing managers have assumed that standardization is antithetical to fostering effective communication and stifles professionals. Yet we find strong relationships between various forms of standardization of both work and skills and nurse-physician collaboration. In recognizing that standardization of skills is actually education, inservice or on-the-job training, and orientation, the relationship between these forms of standardization and collaboration is not surprising. In fact, it is reassuring to know that when staff nurses can depend on their education and training, they also collaborate more with physicians. It is also interesting to note that orientation and inservice education, which take place within the hospital, are much more strongly related to collaboration with physicians than is nursing school education.

Within the category of standardization of work are the most unexpected findings. References to various forms of procedures, plans, policies and protocols are positively related to nurse-physician collaboration. This supports the view that standardized approaches to coordination can facilitate rather than hinder collaboration. Furthermore, the strongest relationships are between collaboration and nurses' use of house staff manual and unit policies and protocols. No significant relationship was found between use of nursing manual and collaboration.

The relationship between collaboration and use of house staff manual has at least two possible explanations. On the one hand, it might reflect that when nurses know the policies and protocols that the house staff are following, they are able to work with them more effectively. On the other hand, the finding might reflect that the house staff manual contains protocols that help the nurses perform their work. This in turn

contributes to their being able to collaborate more effectively with physicians. The overall findings indicate that those policies and protocols that facilitate accomplishment of the work of any given patient care unit contribute to collaboration between nurses and physicians on that unit. The nursing manual and hospital policy manual, which typically contain more general policies and are not as helpful in addressing specific work requirements of any given unit, are less related to collaboration.

Overall, the most important implication of these findings is that the specific requirements of different patient care units, which vary with differences in the work of those units, should be addressed with specific procedures, policies and protocols. These findings are consistent with the earlier work of Charns et al.,[25] and Charns and Strayer,[26] and are further elaborated in Charns and Schaefer.[27]

Satisfaction

The relationship between nurse satisfaction and nurse-physician collaboration also was investigated, and the correlation between these two factors is shown in Table 1. A significant positive relationship exists between them. Although the direction of causality cannot be determined, arguments can be made for causality acting in both directions. First, collaboration can lead directly to satisfaction, or it can act by improving job performance which in turn contributes to satisfaction. Second, more satisfied nurses might be more likely to put in the effort to collaborate with physicians. Since it takes both nurses and physicians to behave in ways that lead to true collaboration, and it is not completely controllable by nurses alone, we would expect that satisfaction is more a product of collaboration than vice versa.

CONCLUSION

By investigating personal, organizational, and managerial factors potentially related to collaboration, the study provides some insights into areas that appear to facilitate collaboration. As the general pattern of results indicates, attention needs to be given to factors beyond those characterizing individual nurses or even those that are direct responsibilities of nursing. Rather, broad organizational and managerial factors also have important

relationships to collaboration. Prominent among these factors is the profile of methods of coordination used on a patient care unit, including the use of policies, procedures, and protocols, and training and orientation.

While further research is needed to be able to provide a more extensive base for generalizing the findings and for more rigorously testing the direction of causality, these findings do suggest areas for attention by nurse administrators seeking to improve nurse-physician collaboration.

REFERENCES

1. Applebaum, A.L. Commission Leads Way to Joint Practice for Nurses and Physicians. *Hospitals* 52 (July 16, 1978): 78–81.
2. Blackwood, S.A. At This Hospital, the Captain of the Ship is Dead. *RN* 42, no. 3 (1979): 77–93.
3. Devereux, P.M. Essential Elements of Nurse-Physician Collaboration. *Journal of Nursing Administration* 11, no. 5 (1981): 19–23.
4. Devereux, P.M. Nurse/Physician Collaboration: Nursing Practice Considerations. *Journal of Nursing Administration* 11, no. 9 (1981): 37–39.
5. Ritter, M.A. Nurse-Physician Collaboration. *Connecticut Medicine* 45, no. 1 (1981): 23–25.
6. Vaughn, R.A. Collaborative Practice. *Nursing Management* 13, no. 3 (1982): 33–35.
7. Christman, L.P. Nurse-Physician Communications in the Hospital. *International Nursing Review* 13, no. 4 (1966): 49–57.
8. Selmanoff, E.D. Strains in the Nurse-Doctor Relationship. *Nursing Clinics of North America* 3, no. 1 (1968): 117–27.
9. Bates, B. Doctor and Nurse: Changing Roles and Relations. *New England Journal of Medicine* 283, no. 3 (1979): 129–34.
10. Phillips, J.R. Health Care Provider Relationships: A Matter of Reciprocity. *Nursing Outlook* 27, no. 11 (1979): 738–41.
11. Devereux, Essential Elements of Nurse-Physician Collaboration.
12. Strauss, A. The Intensive Care Unit: Its Characteristics and Social Relationships. *Nursing Clinics of North America* 3, no. 11 (1968): 7–15.
13. Charns, M.P., et al. *Coordination and Patient Unit Effectiveness.* (Paper presented at the annual meeting of the Academy of Management, San Diego, August 1981.)
14. Charns, M.P., and R. Strayer. *A Socio-Structural Approach to Organizational Development.* (Paper presented at the annual meeting of the Academy of Management, San Diego, August 1981.)
15. March, J.G., and H. Simon. *Organizations* (New York: J. Wiley, 1958.)
16. Van de Ven, A.H., et al. Determinants of Coordination Modes within Organizations. *American Sociological Review* 41 (April 1976): 82–97.
17. Mintzberg, H. *The Structuring of Organizations* (Englewood Cliffs, N.J.: Prentice-Hall, 1979.)
18. Charns et al., *Coordination and Patient Unit Effectiveness.*
19. Ibid.
20. March and Simon, *Organizations.*
21. Charns, M.P., and M.J. Schaefer. *Health Care Organizations: A Model for Management,* chap. 8 (Englewood Cliffs, N.J.: Prentice-Hall, 1983.)
22. Galbraith, J.R. *Designing complex organizations* (Reading, Mass.: Addison-Wesley, 1973.)
23. Charns et al., *Coordination and Patient Unit Effectiveness.*
24. Charns and Strayer, *A Socio-Structural Approach.*
25. Charns et al., *Coordination and Patient Unit Effectiveness.*
26. Charns and Strayer, *A Socio-Structural Approach.*
27. Charns and Schaefer, *Health Care Organizations.*

The changing health care environment: Challenges for the executive team

Luther Christman, Ph.D., R.N.,
F.A.A.N.
Professor, Dean Emeritus
College of Nursing

Michael A. Counte, Ph.D.
Associate Professor
Health Systems Management
College of Health Sciences
Rush University
Chicago, Illinois

*T*HE EXECUTIVE TEAM is a cluster of roles designed to facilitate the attainment of an organization's goals and purposes in an effective and efficient manner. In hospitals, the chief goal is patient care in all its various forms. Education and research may be additional goals in hospitals that are positioned to assume these endeavors. Because the delivery of care is not a static condition, the structure and management of hospitals is ever changing with consequent effects on managerial roles.

The design of the executive team is contingent on the type of organization to be man-aged and the outcome expectations of stakeholders. Hospitals are in an environment of constant change that is propelled mainly by the massive expansion of science and technology.[1] When burgeoning science converges with a strong emphasis on cost control, tension and strain arise that create uneasiness within the system. Other variables such as quality of life, ethical concerns permeating the system, competition between and within health care institutions, growth of the elderly population, preventive health care practices, and general uncertainty of how and what changes at both the macro and micro level may occur without much warning add to the scope and pressures of management.

The nature of the hospital experience creates pressure as well. Persons do not wish to be ill. Thus, there is a negative value on illness and patients are likely to enter hospitals with some resentment of their fate and uneasiness about their future. Each patient brings an idiosyncratic combination of symptoms and pathology. In addition, the general life style of each patient is conditioned by individual variables such as socioeconomic status, education, religious belief

Nurs Admin Q, 1989, 13(2), 67–76

system, ethnic heritage, race, and gender, and a host of personal predispositions to act that contribute to the management problem around each patient as well as in the aggregate. Responding to patient needs is and always has been difficult.

EVOLUTION OF HOSPITAL CARE

Hospitals have had a slow evolution. Their early roots are embedded in the religious pilgrimages in the Age of Faith. Commercial inns did not exist. Religious organizations assisted in hostel care, functioning mainly on generous gifts from wealthy patrons. Gradually their function extended to the sick and homeless, and nursing and medical care became a necessity. Most care, however, remained in the home so that adequate nursing care, food, and shelter could be provided by the family. Transformation to the modern form began with the work of Pasteur and Nightingale. Surgical care especially needed the hospital environment and the desirability of in-hospital care slowly was extended to other disease states. The value of hospitals began to reach new heights when medical research had its beginnings. Hospitals became an essential center of medical development.[2] Impetus was given to research after the publication of the Flexner Report.[3]

For most of the first half of this century hospitals were not complex. Health care in general was more simplistic. Science and technology advanced at a slow and controllable pace.[4] Hospitals and the health care systems were customarily benevolent in nature compared to the economic entities they have become. Hospitals were managed by physicians, nurses, clergy, financial experts, and business people.[5] Service to the public was the theme, which may be one reason hospitals were exempt from the provisions of the Taft-Hartley legislation for so

many years. This legislation exempted hospitals from the wage and hour regulations established by law at the federal level. Because complexity was of such a low order, few requirements were placed on those who managed. The first graduate program in hospital management was offered by the University of Chicago in 1934. Programs grew slowly and it was not until 1946 that the Association of University Programs in Health Administration was formed by the six programs then in existence. It was not until 1964 that a paid association staff was inaugurated. Nursing preparation for advanced clinical practice had a similar slowly evolving history.

The Hill-Burton Act catalyzed the construction of hospitals and provided a demand for more people prepared in management to run these facilities.[6,7] Concurrent with this expansion, an emphasis was placed on clinical research and the first major expansion of scientific research began.[8] In addition, health insurance programs began.

The main preludes to modern complexity were under way when all these new conditions were viewed as a whole. Staffing the hospitals to manage the increasing range of activities to care for patients began to be troublesome. Industrial engineering tactics were used to address these deficits.[9] Single-task or limited-task specialist positions were created in increasing numbers.

Changes in organizational structure increased intraorganizational strain and the phenomenon of territoriality. The ability to coordinate and manage effectively around every patient became less certain because of the larger number of different types of workers with limited job descriptions. The traditional chain of command became suspect as a means of organizing the work where the likelihood of unpredictable events was so high. Additional strain was imposed by the rise in malpractice litigation. This may have been used by patients to cope with the large number, variability, and impersonality of workers they encountered while hospitalized.[10]

STRUCTURE OF HOSPITALS

In its basic simplicity a hospital is a clinical-nonclinical entity. While the popular perception of a hospital is that it is a therapeutic (clinical) facility, it also has a large hotel-like component. In addition to their disease states, all patients bring the peculiarities of their respective life styles to the hospital. Both have to be managed proficiently or patients develop perceptions of poor care and unsatisfying hospital experience. Both the clinical and nonclinical components of care are full of unpredictable events and the probability of an uneventful stay for any one patient is quite low. Furthermore, articulation of clinical and nonclinical entities is unlikely to occur except by chance. In a structure with a large number of job titles, such as hospitals have, the role incumbents tend to portray are often parochial and reactive in their behavior.[11]

Given this clinical-nonclinical focus of activity around every patient, what type of management structure is required? In hospitals, authority often clashes with responsibility. To keep conflict in a reduced state, the organizational structure should permit flexibility and accountability to be parallel characteristics. The early classic approaches were prototypes of the "closed system" ideology. The bureaucratic model closely associated with Max Weber, the matron-militaristic model of Florence Nightingale, and the scientific management approach of Frederick Taylor are examples of the closed model design. The human relations model of Elton Mayo, the exchange model of George Homans, the open systems model of James Thompson, the decision-theory model of Herbert Simon and James March, and the sociotechnical approach proposed by investigators at the Tavistock Institute of Human Relations and by Charles Perrow are all of an open systems nature.[12]

To serve the total demands that arise from the presence of each patient, the structure must be responsive and flexible. Given the serious, if not frequently awesome, nature of the total activity around each patient, how can this effort best be attained? An open systems form of management is a model that permits more facilitation of people's roles as managers. The open systems models tend to be flexible and permit shared power. The hospital administrator, chief executive physician, and chief executive nurse are in a parallel power structure reporting to the chief executive officer, who may emerge from any of these groups. In this power-sharing format they are in enabling positions to supplement and complement each other to reduce the stress involved in managing all the contingencies of care, clinical and nonclinical, as they arise in their multiplicity of permutations and forms.

If power is viewed as the ability to shape social outcomes, the exercise of power is elusive unless it occurs within some type of identified structure. To make social power work for the common good, it is necessary to use organizational designs that make it feasible for the members of each major component of the organization to express their competencies in ways that facilitate the

If power is viewed as the ability to shape social outcomes, the exercise of power is elusive unless it occurs within some type of identified structure.

roles of persons in other parts of the organization. Open systems models, if properly created, have a rich promise for enabling the management team to be proactive. The members of each major component should have both equity and parity. In this instance, equity is defined as having a stake in the outcome, whereas parity means having equal or similar power with other major influential persons.

Open systems models encourage both symmetry and balance. These organizational components can be arranged so that power can be arrayed horizontally and vertically to achieve a design that permits effective role expression and at the same time expedites the steady forward movement of the organization. Symmetry connotes a high degree of similarity in the placement of decision-making centers in the organization; balance indicates the formation of constructive alliances between the professions and disciplines.

This interprofessional power sharing appears to be particularly appropriate to the complexity of a "people processing" organization. To personalize the care of each patient it appears wise to decentralize the decision-making process and minimize layers of decision making within the organization.[13] Theoretically, this form of organization permits a quick response item to demands as they arise. It also facilitates the focusing of resources more specifically on each patient. This can be done by ensuring that rapid response design is in place at all levels of the organization so that issues can be resolved quickly and harmoniously. Thus, initiative and energy can be channeled productively for the benefit of patients.

Before attempting to predict the future of the executive team in health care organizations, one must understand current and anticipated environmental changes that are critical to their survival.

ENVIRONMENTAL CHALLENGES FACING THE EXECUTIVE TEAM

During recent years, health care organizations have been buffeted by a series of changes that are both widespread in scope and rapid in occurrence.[14] These changes have in general increased the need for the executive team to develop both short-term and long-term strategies to ensure the very survival of the institutions they manage. To accurately portray this situation and the dilemmas health care executives frequently face, it is necessary to survey a select sample of macro-level changes and the resulting challenges facing health care executives.

Medical and managerial technology

As various authors[15] have described, the proliferation and diffusion of technological innovations since World War II have been profound. Such innovations have had a major, well-documented impact on clinical heath care services.[16] What is less well recognized, however, is that the managerial sector of health care organization is also incorporating new technologies such as medical information systems[17] and productivity management systems developed in manufacturing industries[18] to improve organizational efficiency and effectiveness.

Reimbursement and public policy

During the 1980s, a new set of concerns generally focused on the issue of cost containment have dominated the field of health care public policy. The introduction of prospective payment for inpatient services (diagnosis related groups) may be only the beginning because similar types of reimbursement systems are now being developed for inpatient mental health services, rehabilitation services, ambulatory health care services, and long-term care. A new emphasis is emerging on the concept of value (or optimizing quality and price). There is also a possibility that the issue of national health insurance will be resurrected with the recent change of administration at the federal level.

Health professions

Contemporary changes in the demand for registered nurses and their supply have been well documented. Most health care executives have probably faced a shortage of registered nurses in one or more service areas and are aware that the supply of candidates to nursing programs has diminished for a wide range of reasons. Equally important is the fact that the supply of physicians is rapidly increasing despite shortages in certain geographical areas (underserved areas) and clinical specialties. Physicians in search of employment in desirable areas may begin to intrude on occupational areas that heretofore have been primarily occupied by hospital administrators and registered nurses. Eventually, there also may be a pronounced shortage of personnel in certain allied health fields such as physical therapy and medical technology.

Aging of the population

There is widespread acknowledgment that the aging of the American population, projected well into the next century, will be accompanied by a changing age structure of the population (flattening out of the typical pyramidal distribution) and changes in the demand for health care services.[19] However, many myths still abound concerning both the aging process and older persons.[20] Thus, the impact of an aging population is unclear.

Competition among health care organizations

The introduction of prospective payment systems that limit reimbursement on the basis of preestablished payment schedules tied to a person's diagnosis and perhaps an excess capacity of hospitals in certain communities have been linked to sharply higher rates of competition among health care organizations and in particular, hospitals.[21] With ever-tightening restrictions on use of hospital inpatient services from various sources ranging from government agencies to business coalitions, there are many projections that competition will only intensify in the foreseeable future.

Consumer and payer expectations

Consumers and payers of health care services (private and public) are increasingly interested in selecting how and where medical services are provided. They also appear to have higher expectations of what services are provided inside and outside the hospital. Thus, consumers basically want a more active role than they typically have been provided.

Organizational accountability

Historically, it was assumed that by virtue of their missions, hospitals and related health care organizations provided certain services to society and local communities that justified exemption from the constraints faced by other types of organizations. In recent years, criticism has emerged that the social benefits provided by health care organizations (provision of public services to the community such as poison control and free care for the indigent) may not equal the costs incurred by society through exemption from local tax rolls. Hospitals in

Utah now have to face a means test prior to being exempt from local taxation. Thus, there is now questioning of the tax-exempt status of health care organizations when they had been automatically exempt.

Acquired immunodeficiency syndrome

Although there is still controversy regarding the prevalence of acquired immunodeficiency syndrome (AIDS), its future proliferation, and its potential costs to society, there is widespread acknowledgement that the problem is serious. Its impact in various areas ranging from costs of treatment to burnout of clinical personnel are and will continue to be significant. With no cure in sight and a steady growth in the incidence of cases in the population, the impact of AIDS will need to be monitored. In the future other types of epidemics may come on the scene with similar confounding outcomes.

Delivery of health care services

Fueled by different factors such as emerging technologies and new practice styles, important changes are occurring in the delivery of health care services. Consumers appear to be more interested in receiving health care services on an ambulatory basis and health care professionals have succeeded in meeting this demand. There is little question that more procedures and a wider range of procedures will be performed on an outpatient basis.

CURRENT AND ANTICIPATED ISSUES FOR THE EXECUTIVE TEAM

All the forces delineated above will directly or indirectly influence both the present and future structure and functions of health care organizations. Hospitals are the major players in the health care industry because of their size and number but in the future other types of health care organizations (such as health maintenance organizations, preferred provider organizations, free-standing ambulatory care facilities, and perhaps forms not yet in existence) may predominate. Nevertheless, there are a number of critical issues that the executive team is beginning to experience and will continue to face in the foreseeable future.

Hospital closures

Competitive pressures and changing reimbursement patterns described above have prompted the demise of hundreds of hospitals during the last five years. The threat of closure appears to be particularly significant in medically underserved urban and rural areas. There is not any indication that small hospitals in medically underserved areas will be receiving any large infusion of financial assistance in the near future because payers continue to limit the growth of inpatient use and reimbursement for those persons who are hospitalized. Thus, the dilemma of closing a hospital or merging it with a larger facility will continue to be a major concern of the executive team.

Moral and ethical concerns

The rapid growth of medical technology now enables health care professionals to sustain a patient's existence for an indefinite period. Questions are now being posed to health care executives that address the quality of a person's life who is being sustained by such technology. Also, limits on reimbursement for certain procedures such as organ transplantation may lead to rationing. The executive team will need to work with clinical staff to develop ethical

> *The executive team will need to devote greater attention to the issue of social accountability to local communities and their populations.*

and acceptable responses to such vexing issues.

Financial concerns

Especially during the last several years there has been a growing indication that hospitals and other types of health care organizations may face severe future constraints on their financial performance. Thus, they will need to constantly develop new methods to obtain more for less. Unfortunately, diminished financial performance also decreases an organization's slack resources, which are used to buffer it during stressful periods, to develop new programs, and to acquire new technologies.

Board governance

Historically, hospital boards have served in an advisory capacity in many areas such as organizational strategic planning and, on occasion, internal hospital operations. There is a growing indication that the function of such boards may well be changing to a more active role. Thus, more attention needs to be directed toward issues such as board member education regarding organizational strategies and activities so that members can fully enact their emerging greater involvement. Also, the composition of boards may need to be broadened to satisfy user and payer expectations.

Social obligations

As mentioned earlier, pressures are growing on health care executives to demonstrate

that they truly deserve exemption from taxation if they are not-for-profit corporations. Thus, the executive team will need to devote greater attention to the issue of social accountability to local communities and their populations. In other words, they need to prepare their case in advance and be involved integrally in the development of legislation that addresses this issue at the local, state, and federal levels. Nonprofit hospitals may find it necessary to make more public the allocation of resources dedicated to charitable care.

Multi-institutional systems

Since there is little reason to project that the growth of multi-institutional systems will diminish in the future, the executive team will need to learn how to manage within such systems. There likely will be both a downside and a upside to life in such systems. For example, health care executives within a constituent organization may have decreased decision-making autonomy in certain areas such as strategic planning while their access to capital markets may be improved.

Management and integration of diversification

A major strategy hospitals have used to respond to environmental changes such as the introduction of prospective limits on the reimbursement of inpatient services is to engage in greater diversification. In most instances such diversification has involved the development of new programmatic initiatives outside the organization but closely related to the current activities of the organization (e.g., home health care, free-standing ambulatory facilities, mobile diagnostic service, and similar forms of care). There has been less movement into non-health care commercial activities such as real estate management, restaurants, and service stations. The key issue now is not the development of such diversified enterprises but rather their effective management, including increased integration and decisions about when to divest an organization of such activities.

Organizational performance

There is little if any question that there will be steadily increasing pressure on the executive team in health care organizations to satisfy the needs and expectations of various organizational stakeholders both within and outside the organization. To accomplish this significant task, the executive team will need to focus greater attention on the goals of the organization, the annual objectives, and the empirical assessment of organizational performance in a wide range of domains. This will necessitate an augmented focus on monitoring indicators both within the organization (e.g., efficiency indicators) and outside the organization (e.g., market share assessment, bond ratings, and similar economic indicators).

Movement from health care administration to health care management

Members of the health care executive team in the future will need to function more in the capacity of managers than administrators. The issues faced by contemporary health care executives are simply too vexing and ever changing to allow for reliance on standard operating procedures, time-honored traditions, or a business-as-usual orientation. Instead, health care organizations will continue to grow to resemble industrial organizations as they acquire cost accounting systems, develop productivity assessment methods, pursue strategic planning, use product-line man-

agement, and introduce increased automation.

Emergence of self-renewing organizations

Although most health care executives acknowledge the importance of periodic planned organizational change activities to the survival of their organizations, a new orientation may well develop in the future. More specifically, health care organizations may adopt total organizational change philosophies that are oriented toward continual improvement of an organization's functioning at every level rather than a specific issue such as improved customer relations. This type of total organizational approach to constant change and innovation within organizations is used already in other types of manufacturing organizations and may become more prevalent in the health care field.

Growth of the clinical management interaction

As health care executives become more interested and involved in monitoring the clinical activities that occur within their organizations, the interaction between health care executives and clinicians will become increasingly important. This change will gradually diminish the current structural and functional separation of hospital medical staffs, nursing staffs, and managerial personnel. If there is not improved communication and eventual cooperation among these groups, it will be difficult for hospitals to adapt to increased external constraints on quality assurance activities, utilization management, and reimbursement of clinical services. Lack of concurrence within the executive team will diminish the organization's ability to respond to these challenges.

General situation

Recent changes in the environments of health care organizations pose significant challenges to the health care executive team. As Brown recently noted: "This last decade will go down in history as one of the most exciting decades in the organization and delivery of medical care. Tremendous pressures are building up for consumer-oriented changes that will make quality medical care available at lower cost."[22(p.85)]

The final question to address, then, is how the executive team may need to change to meet the trends and issues described above as well as those they have only begun to comprehend.

FUTURE OF THE EXECUTIVE TEAM

The nature and composition of the executive team will continue to be patterned to fit the changing nature of the health care system. Even if the rate of increment in scientific expansion remains constant, which is unlikely, the massive accumulation of scientific content will be enormous by the turn of the century. The potential for a major overlap of knowledge between physicians and nurses with clinical doctoral degrees indicates the possibility of much greater shared knowledge between them. It is to be expected that clinical designs of care will become much more sophisticated as a direct outgrowth of the accumulation of scientific knowledge, the accompanying technology, and the better professional preparation of both physicians and nurses.

The upsurge in enrollment in colleges and universities probably indicates that the emergence of the postindustrial knowledge era is well understood by the youth of the country. Not only are satisfying work and steady employment tied to better education but also many aspects of the quality of life. The understanding of how to develop better life styles to live in a healthier way is certain to be an outcome. This will become more evident if public policy ever mandates the integration of health education in kindergarten through grade 12 and beyond as an effective way to reduce illness and to promote good health as a valuable tool in reducing and controlling health care costs.

One of the outcomes of a better educated population will be increased consumer expectations. The increased level of sophistication of consumers of health care services necessitates highly competent clinicians working in easily accessible and consumer-responsive organizational structures. Organizational designs will be under continuous surveillance because public advocacy will be more thoroughly developed, information via the media more rapid, and peer review more scientifically accurate. Those who are managers will have to be in a steady proactive state to be effective.

The lengthening of the life span of the population, especially among those over 85, poses interesting problems about how they will be cared for because of new sets of problems. The frail elderly will have multiple diagnoses. The longer life span may permit more genetic disease to be expressed due to diminishing resistance. It may be that some form of clustering of residences (townhouses, condominiums) will take place over time so that health care and other services can be integrated in a satisfying and economical way. Many, if not most, of the health care services will be delivered in various forms of outpatient care, such as health monitoring, ambulatory clinics, and home health care services. Coordinating these services to maintain reasonably high levels of health and to anticipate health problems will be a major function of management. Sophisticated computer programs will assist in following each person enrolled in a particular service.

Furthermore, the rich potential for fully automated hospitals to remarkably change staffing requirements on both sides of the equation—clinical and nonclinical—must be considered. Devices in the development stage or ready for the market are regularly reported. Technology is in a relatively new state but it will reach maturity quickly. While some of the intraorganizational strain might be reduced if automation lessens many of the unpredictable situations, there still will be a need for imaginative management. It appears that clinical outcomes will be the strongest emphasis of the future. This heightens the likelihood that chief operating officers may be selected largely from the clinical professions. It is the well-prepared clinicians who can envision the future with clarity and who can build programs that can assimilate new knowledge as rapidly as it becomes available.

The steady development of out-of-hospital care programs lend insight to the future. Only the very acutely ill may need hospital-ization as other forms of care are developed and become accepted. The number of hospitals will decline (or at least bed size will shrink) as the combination of automation, economics, and increasingly technical clinical practice emerges. Additionally, the changing life styles of the population as they adopt illness prevention and health maintenance behavior patterns will be a strong variable that may lessen demand on the health care system. In addition, the major changes in therapeutic precision for diseases or conditions either unmanageable at this time or poorly treated because of the lack of development in drugs or vaccines will be responsive to ambulatory care.

The future of the hospital may lie in coordinating the allocation of resources and serving as a health information center rather than solely as in-house care setting. Those interested in health care management, who are preparing for a future in this area, should anticipate being a vested participant in an every-changing care structure. The excitement of influencing and managing change may be the main incentive in opting this career path.

REFERENCES

1. Lessee, S. *The Future of the Health Sciences: Anticipating Tomorrow* (New York: Irvington Publishers, 1981.)
2. Burling, T., et al. *The Give and Take of Hospitals: A Study of Human Organization* (New York: G.P. Putnam's, 1956.)
3. Flexner, A. *Medical Education in the United States and Canada: A Report to the Carnegie Foundation for the Advancement of Teaching* (New York: The Foundation, 1910.)
4. Cockerham, W. *Medical Sociology.* 2d ed (Englewood Cliffs, N.J.: Prentice-Hall, 1982.)
5. Schulz, R., et al. *Management of Hospitals,* 2d ed (New York: McGraw-Hill, 1983.)
6. Christman, L. The Role of Nursing in Organizational Effectiveness. *Hospital Administration* 13, no. 3 (1968):248–55.
7. Christman, L., and M. Counte. *Hospital Organization and Health Care Delivery* (Boulder, Colo.: Westview Press, 1981.)
8. Christman, L. The Role of Systems Engineering in Meeting the Nursing Challenge. *International Nursing Review* 17, no. 4 (1970): 320–25.
9. Christman, L. New Frontiers Facing the Professional Nurse. *University of Michigan Medical Center Journal* 32, no. 2 (1966): 77–81.
10. Illich, I. *Medical Nemesis: The Expropriation of Health* (New York: Pantheon Books, 1976.)
11. Christman and Counte, *Hospital Organization.*
12. Ibid.
13. Seeman, M., and J.W. Evans. Stratification and Hospital Care: II, The Objective Criteria of Performance. In *Medical Care: Readings in the Sociology of Medical Institutions,* eds. W.R. Scott and

E.H. Wolhart (New York: Wiley, 1966.)

14. Brown, M. The 1990s: Just Around the Corner, *Health Care Management Review* 13, no. 2 (1988): 81–86.

15. Pryor, D.B., et al. Clinical Data Bases: Accomplishment and Unrealized Potential. *Medical Care* 23 (1985): 623–47.

16. Lincoln, T., and R. Korpman. Computers, Health Care and Medical Information Science. *Science* 210 (1980): 257–63.

17. Imirie, J. Information System Needs of University-Based Hospitals. *Computers in Healthcare* 5, no. 1 (1984): 44.

18. Walters, W., and T. Lincoln. Using Information Tools to Improve Hospital Productivity. *Healthcare Financial Management* 41, no. 8 (1987): 74–78.

19. Mechanic, D. Challenges in Long-Term Care Policy. *Health Affairs* 6, no. 2 (1987): 23–34.

20. Dychtwald, K., and M. Zitter. "Looking Beyond the Myths of an Aging America." *Healthcare Financial Management* 42, no. 1 (1988): 62–66.

21. Noether, M. *Competition Among Hospitals* (Washington, D.C.: Federal Trade Commission, 1987.)

22. Brown, "The 1990s: Just Around the Corner.", 85.

The nurse executive role: A leadership opportunity

Margaret L. McClure, R.N., Ed.D.
Executive Director of Nursing
New York University Medical Center
New York, New York

*T*HE TURBULENCE inherent in the
health care system today seems to have
reached legendary proportions. Moreover,
there is every evidence that these conditions
are likely to continue, unabated, for the
foreseeable future. Such an environment
requires skillful leadership for our institutions to survive and thrive. As a consequence, it seems appropriate for those of us
in nursing to devote some time and attention to the role of the nurse executive, since
that individual has become increasingly
significant in the leadership of health care
delivery.

THE NURSE AS CAREGIVER

Oddly enough, it may be most useful to
begin our discussion by briefly examining
the role of the nurse before moving on to the
role of the nurse executive. One analytic

approach that is particularly helpful is to
divide the role into two highly interrelated,
yet separate, subsets: the *caregiver* and *integrator* roles. The caregiver role, which is, of
course, the one that nurses learn from their
earliest professional training, involves
meeting the following patient needs:

- dependency needs (bathing, grooming,
  toileting, feeding, safety);
- comfort needs (physical and psychological);
- monitoring needs (vigilance to signs
  and symptoms, including appropriate
  response based on the data obtained.
  This monitoring role should be made
  more explicit to others because it is, in
  fact, the area in which the nurse must
  exercise the greatest knowledge, judgment, and skill; it is also the function
  that keeps patients safe. There is an
  inverse correlation between the quality of the nurse's capability as a monitor and the extent to which patients
  suffer preventable, untoward conse-

This article was presented at the First International
Nurse Executive Institute, Florence Nightingale
Foundation, London, England, October 1987.

Nurs Admin Q, 1989, 13(3): 1–8
©1989 Aspen Publishers, Inc.

quences during the course of their care);

- therapeutic needs (medications, treatment, dressings); and
- educational needs (including the fostering of coping mechanisms).

THE NURSE AS INTEGRATOR

The integrator role is examined and described less explicitly in the literature and in the educational process. The label for this role comes from the work of Lawrence and Lorsch, two organizational theorists who describe complex organizations as being composed of a great number of highly specialized departments that deal with one particular aspect of the commodity or service being produced. Within each of these specialized departments a set of standards, norms, and work habits develops; in effect, such a department frequently evolves into a sort of subculture, often separated from the goals of the larger organization. As a result of this separation, all complex organizations develop integrator roles. Integrators are individuals who, by virtue of their special position, have the knowledge necessary to integrate all of the input from the specialized departments in such a way as to result in a satisfactory, complete product. In other words, they have the responsibility for tying together all of the disparate parts that must eventually combine to make up the whole.[1]

This analysis is exceptionally helpful when it is used to examine health care settings. A hospital, for example, is an extremely complex organization divided into a large number of highly specialized departments. Without question, many of these develop the characteristics of a subculture. Nursing, of course, is one such specialized department. On the other hand, it is the professional nurse who is, and who has always been, the integrator. Because of the moment-to-moment clinical knowledge that she or he possesses regarding the patient's needs for services from the other specialized departments, only the nurse is in a position to serve as integrator.

Many authors and nursing leaders have failed to appreciate both the importance and the power of the integrator role. They have seen the caregiver/integrator subsets clearly enough but have mistakenly labeled the former "nursing the patient" and the latter "nursing the system." They have failed to recognize that the integrator role is one of the highest forms of patient advocacy and that it is impossible to be a truly fine caregiver without being a truly fine integrator. Excellence in the execution of both of these subsets results in excellence in nursing care.

Nurses are not the only people who have failed to understand the essential importance of their contribution as integrators. Hospital administrators and members of other disciplines are equally guilty. In the case of hospital administrators, however, enlightenment regarding this particular role is crucial, because only they have the power to ensure appropriate and timely responses from those other departments whose work nurses are, in effect, integrating. Administrative support, then, is fundamental to the delivery of the total patient care package.

While the discussion has focused thus far on the hospital, there is certainly a great deal of evidence to support the notion that these role subsets of caregiver and integrator apply equally well to community nursing and other outpatient settings.

With this background in mind it is easy to see that nursing administrators come to their positions highly qualified, owing in no small measure to their experience as integrators. Who else better understands how all of the intricate patches fit together to create the whole quilt of patient care? Because of this understanding, nursing directors make a unique contribution to the executive suite because they are more familiar with the product than are their administrative peers (who are almost always nonclinical) and also with the role and contribution of all clinical and nonclinical departments.

PHYSICIANS AS ADMINISTRATORS

One of the trends that we in the United States are beginning to experience is the rebirth of physician/administrators. Their medical backgrounds lend credibility and understanding to their dealings with the support departments that are clinical in nature. As a result, they are able to provide important insights into decision making that is related to these areas. It should be understood, however, that most physicians have never filled the role of integrator, since their experience with the nonclinical side of health care is virtually nonexistent. In contrast, the nurse has spent a professional lifetime dealing as much with the laundry, food service, and maintenance departments as with the laboratory and radiology departments.

Although this idea may be controversial, this author suggest that those of us who work on hospital staffs in the United States have mistakenly viewed physicians as also having a staff role. Not only have physicians not had experience as integrators, but most have not had experience as staff members. In fact, it may be that we would begin to deal more realistically with this group of professionals if we viewed them as customers. After all, hospitals have little or no direct access to patients. Instead, they offer an array of services to physicians so that they may, in turn, offer them to *their* patients.

This point of view seems to be enormously helpful in explaining a set of relationships that are often troublesome to all of the various players in the scene, from the trustees to the parking attendants.

THE DUAL ROLE OF THE NURSE EXECUTIVE

Against this backdrop the role of the nurse executive, somewhat analogous to the role of the staff, is dual in nature. First, she or he must be a leader in the clinical discipline of nursing. Clearly this requires that the individual have both an experiential and an educational background in nursing. Included in such a mandate is the ability to conceptualize practice, making the application of theory possible, and lending insight and vision to the evolution of nursing within the particular setting involved.

Second, the nurse executive must be an administrator. It is well known that nurse executives generally have responsibility for the largest number of staff and more than half of the operating budget in most health care settings today. In other words, they are held accountable for multimillion dollar operations that have serious consequences for many thousands of patients.

None of the above is new, except that we are now confronting a health care economy that is shrinking, rather than expanding as it was for many years. The American public have made it clear that they do not intend to accept the escalating prices of the care that

It is well known that nurse executives generally have responsibility for the largest number of staff and more than half of the operating budget in most health care settings today.

most professionals want to deliver, and it seems evident that this statement could also be made regarding the citizens of Great Britain. Thus difficult decisions are being made in virtually every area of service in an effort to reduce the cost of care.

In this environment, the role of the nurse executive becomes even more critical than it has been in the past. Many people have come to recognize that patients are admitted to inpatient facilities because they need nursing care and are discharged when it is determined that their nursing needs may safely be met in alternative situations. The pressure to move patients more quickly out of inpatient settings, then, is a pressure to find alternatives to delivering nursing care in hospitals and nursing homes. In the United States we are being forced to discharge patients earlier either by assisting them to become self-sufficient sooner or by referring them to agencies that can meet their needs, preferably within their own home environments. This movement has serious consequences for nurse executives in every setting.

This trend has been going on for a substantial period of time, but it has accelerated in recent years. The result has been sicker patients within our hospitals and nursing home facilities and sicker patients within the community. And as the reimbursement monies continue to shrink, one can predict that we will be compelled to cut costs more while taking care of the more acutely ill.

TRANSFORMING VS. TRANSACTIONAL LEADERSHIP

Given these role definitions, the most important quality that nurse executives must develop and continually refine is that of becoming "transforming" leaders. This is a term gleaned from the work of James MacGregor Burns. Certainly most of us are familiar with the classic leadership thinkers; Burns, however, is a writer who has made his contribution to the literature relatively recently, and his work offers a slightly unique slant. The title of his book is, quite simply, *Leadership.*[2]

Burns identifies and analyzes two kinds of leadership:

1. *Transactional:* leadership that is based primarily on material rewards for both the leader and the follower (for example, jobs in exchange for votes or promotion in exchange for hard work). The end result is some kind of "payoff" for both the leader and the follower, with the leader giving no thought to the follower's needs or goals.

2. *Transforming:* In contrast to transactional leadership, transforming leadership occurs when the leader and followers engage more fully with one another so that the leader becomes concerned with the follower's needs and goals; the leader makes a conscious effort to assess these needs and goals and to induce the follower to develop them so that they fuse with the leader's own. The outcome is positive for both in that they raise each other's motivation and morality to higher levels than either would otherwise have achieved. It has, therefore, psychological "payoffs" that transcend material rewards.

Not surprisingly, Burns believes that great leaders are those who are more transforming than transactional in their relationships with their followers. This is because such leaders recognize and develop the potential in themselves and their followers, and thus cause both to become greater than either would be without the other.

Quite recently two other authors have written about characteristics that are hallmarks of leadership; both seem to fit in well with the transforming approach. The first characteristic is identified by Jean Auel in her phenomenal book, *The Clan of the Cave Bear,* in which she demonstrates that true leadership can only take place when leaders are able and willing to subordinate their own good to the good of the group. There is a certain quality of selflessness in true leaders that Auel captures when she describes the change that takes place, and the negative consequences that ensue, when an exemplary chief of the clan steps down and is succeeded by his son, who is primarily concerned with himself and his own needs.[3]

The second leadership characteristic is spelled out by Margaret Mahoney in an article she wrote for an annual report of the Commonwealth Fund. She describes leaders as people who are able to view things in their totality:

> Leaders like [General George] Marshall share common characteristics—above all, the ability to see the picture whole. And in each case, this ability is accompanied by the ability to inspire—to create momentum, as Martin Luther King did for the Civil Rights Movement; to engender confidence, as John F. Kennedy did in the fragile 1960's. Such leaders win public trust in part because their breadth of mission brings communities together around a common purpose.[4]

Without question, Mahoney could easily have included Florence Nightingale in this paragraph; her ability to understand and influence the world beyond Scutari was fundamental to her legendary success.

NURSE EXECUTIVES AS TRANSFORMING LEADERS

Given the notion of transforming leadership, with the accompanying characteristics of putting the good of the group ahead of the good of self and the ability to see the big picture, how can nurse executives apply these concepts to their practice and thereby improve their leadership? Here it may be helpful to explore some specific examples, one from each role subset (i.e., nursing and administration).

Looking first at the nursing realm, the factor that is probably the prime cause of most successes and most failures is communication. This idea has been expressed so often that it has probably become trite. Yet if one attempts to apply the concept of common goals and needs between the leaders and the led, especially in the larger context, one must conclude that fine leadership cannot be accomplished without ongoing personal communication. This lesson is contained in the data that were collected for the *Magnet Hospitals* study. Strong nurse executives who are functioning as true leaders have, and use, the opportunity to share their overall view of the organization with their subordinates and, in so doing, help them to endorse their goals for the department and for the institution. In turn, members of the staff have the opportunity to participate in shaping or reshaping those goals.[5]

Each nurse executive has a set of goals for her or his department, and these require exerting leadership with our staff. For goals to be accomplished in a transforming, rather than transactional, style nurse executives need to establish an ongoing dialogue, not only with their management staff but also with everyone within the department. This is no easy task, especially in some of the very large settings.

It might be useful at this point to describe a communications mechanism that we have been developing for the past several years at NYU Medical Center. This institution is an 878-bed, highly specialized tertiary setting located in the middle of New York City. Our nursing administration team is many-layered, which complicates the process of two-way communication and efforts to implement a participative management philosophy.

Several years ago we held a two-day retreat for the upper-level nursing administrators (clinical assistant directors and above) at a conference location away from the hospital. We spent the time discussing general managerial concepts from the recent literature, especially as they applied to the problems with which we were confronted; future goals and plans involving the larger medical center; our own accomplishments in nursing during the previous year; and departmental goals for the following year.

This experience proved to be most beneficial because it created an environment in which there could be an open, constructive exchange of ideas and knowledge. It also served as an arena in which the participants could learn from each other and, as a result, be stimulated to set new levels of professional expectations for themselves. More importantly, it provided an opportunity to focus the planning activities for the department in the context of the larger systems within which all of us must work. Thus, the Medical Center as a whole, as well as the state and national environments, were taken into account in all of our discussions.

Because we found the retreat such a useful and productive vehicle, we have continued to hold one each year. In fact we developed the idea further by beginning similar retreats for each of the clinical areas. All assistant directors now hold annual management retreats for their respective services. These are attended by their management staff (head nurses and assistant head nurses) and follow much the same format as described above, with one important variation: My associate and I are invited to attend a summation at which the group presents a

> *In the administrative as in the clinical realm, effective communication is also the key to success.*

synopsis of their discussion, including their goals for the coming year.

To date we have found the retreat approach highly successful, and we are also aware that to some extent practice makes perfect in this, as in most endeavors. Each year we become more comfortable, more confident, and more productive in working together. Management retreats are certainly not a novel idea. They are presented here, however, as an example of the kind of deliberate structure that must be devised in order to support the process of transforming leadership. Good will and good intentions are simply not enough.

In the administrative as in the clinical realm, effective communication is also the key to success. As a member of executive management, the nursing director is in a position to influence the important budgetary decisions that must inevitably be made in this cost-cutting era. Because of the knowledge gleaned through a number of years as an integrator, the nurse executive can be especially helpful in making these decisions as informed as possible and in keeping the goal of safe, competent care uppermost in the minds of those who share responsibility for the organization.

NURSING AND PROSPECTIVE PAYMENT

In addition, the introduction of the prospective payment system in the United States has served to highlight the importance of nursing in general and the nurse executive in particular for the health care system. This has done a great deal to facilitate the nurse executive's ability to tie her or his goals closely to the goals of peers on the executive management team. Administrators who are knowledgeable have come to understand that the nurse has a powerful influence on the length of time that patients must stay in the hospital. Both the caregiver and the integrator roles have an important impact on the discharge timing for many patients, especially in situations where primary nursing is the model for care delivery. One of the primary nurse's major advocacy roles is to expedite patients' movement through the system and to assist them in returning to the most independent and highest-quality life possible. Because of that role, primary nursing and a prospective payment system probably represent a marriage made in heaven. Unfortunately, the potential benefits of such wedded bliss are unrecognized in many settings. Without question, the burden of responsibility for making this connection and emphasizing it to other administrators rests with the nurse executive. Clarifying the relationship between nursing care outcomes and the larger reimbursement system is a leadership task.

Beyond the institutional walls, nurse executives also have a critical role to play, and it is this arena in which we have been least visible and, quite candidly, have made the least impact. For example, as the prospective payment system has been instituted in the United States many legislators and other interested parties have voiced concerns that patients will suffer untoward consequences from having been discharged too quickly from acute care hospitals (the "sicker-quicker" syndrome). Many policy makers were calling for documentation regarding patient problems when the program was first introduced.

Many nurse executives now know that the negative pressures resulting from the sicker-quicker phenomenon are being felt as much by nurses as by patients and may, interestingly enough, be one of several critical variables accounting for our national nurse shortage. The stresses involved in caring for patients in a system characterized by significant increases in the acuity of patient illness, by pressure to compress the elements of care into a shorter time frame, and by little or no increase in the productivity of support departments have been well documented. What is of concern is the effect they have had on nursing students and on potential nursing students. Today, as at no other time in our history, we have documented evidence of professional nurses advising students already enrolled in programs to change their area of study, indicating that almost any alternative would be preferable to nursing.

THE POLITICAL CHALLENGE

We must be articulate in helping policy makers to understand that in hospital care, ultimate responsibility rests with nursing. To put pressure on hospitals is to put pressure on nurses. Thus, the real negative effects of the sicker-quicker syndrome probably appear first within this group of practitioners and perhaps only later among large numbers of patients. Again, nurse administrators are faced with a leadership challenge: in essence, to assist policy makers to see the larger picture, especially as it relates to the changes that they have imposed on the health care system. It may well be possible to align the needs and goals of the nation's influential with those of nursing, but this will require great political expertise—transforming leadership at its finest. To be sure, we must gather and present objective evidence that will support our solutions to health care problems. We must, however, be prepared to take that process one step further and exercise leadership in the political arena, if we are to succeed.

LEADERSHIP AND THE SELF

One quality of transforming leadership that was mentioned above, the ability of the leader to place the good of the group above the good of self, has thus far been neglected. Nurses executives have excelled in this area, perhaps as a result of having learned this lesson well from many of our early leaders, Florence Nightingale in particular. To dwell on this would be tantamount to "preaching to the choir."

However, one word about selflessness may be in order. Health care settings today require a great deal of time, energy, and commitment from every practicing nurse executive. Oddly enough, putting the good of

the group ahead of the good of self may require learning various strategies for self-care. For each of us the specifics may vary, but in every case sufficient time must be taken away from day-to-day operations to enable us to keep the challenges we face in perspective and to generate the energies required for transforming leadership.

•   •   •

Without question the nurse executive role offers leadership opportunities offered by few other roles: opportunities to influence nurses and nursing practice; opportunities to influence other disciplines; opportunities to influence the delivery system; opportunities to make a difference for patients, both today and for the future. Who could ask for more?

REFERENCES

1. Lawrence, P.P., and J.W. Lorsch. *Organization and Environment* (Homewood, Ill.: Richard D. Irwin, 1969.)
2. Burns, J.M. *Leadership* (New York: Harper and Row, 1978.)
3. Auel, J.M. *The Clan of the Cave Bear* (New York: Crown Publishers, 1979.)
4. Mahoney, M.E. Leaders. In *The Commonwealth Fund Annual Report.* New York: Commonwealth Fund, (1984), pp. 12–13.
5. McClure, M.L., et al. *Magnet Hospitals: Attraction and Retention of Professional Nurses* (Kansas City, Mo.: American Nurses' Association, 1983.)

Part V
Study and discussion questions

1. What specific realignment and readjustment of nurse-physician roles is necessary to successfully implement collaborative practice?

   Suggested Topics Include: Understanding of each other's work; sensitivity to educational preparation and experience; power, authority, and control issues; inter-sender role conflict around ideology.

2. In designing and implementing collaborative practice, what organizational and managerial factors need to be addressed by management?

   Suggested Topics Include: Total quality management and quality assurance; revision of hospital policies and protocols; evaluation of patient care plans; group methods of work organization such as team meetings, rounds, conferences, inclusion of residents and students.

3. Evaluative data to demonstrate the cost/benefit of collaborative practice are crucial when comparing this system of care delivery to others such as case management. Prioritize the most important variables from your institution's perspective. How does this listing interface with the philosophy statement, values clarification, and nursing model currently used by the Department of Nursing?

   Suggested Topics Include, in Order of Priority: Quality Patient Care; cost of implementing the system; cost reductions due to greater system efficiency; professionalism of nursing care and ramifications regarding employee job satisfaction, attendance, turnover, etc.; institutional risk management and patient safety issues.

4. What is the role of hospital administration (other than nursing management) in facilitating the implementation of collaborative practice? What is the process you would select to involve hospital managers in this change?

   Suggested Topics Include: Targeted locations for change; communication to key groups as medical staff, board members, etc.; media visibility within the local community; systems issues that need change to facilitate collaborative practice; shifting of resources to promote and maintain change.

5. What are the legal ramifications/risks of permitting nurses to practice more autonomously and independently within the scope of practice in your state?

Suggested Topics Include: Identify the scope of practice statement and any other relevant declaratory rulings around RN scope of practice, advanced practice, and prescriptive authority. Discuss the legal liability around errors of omission, as well as acts of negligence.

Index